Invisible China

INVISIBLE CHINA

HOW THE URBAN-RURAL DIVIDE
THREATENS CHINA'S RISE

Scott Rozelle and Natalie Hell

The University of Chicago Press
Chicago and London

The University of Chicago Press, Chicago 60637
The University of Chicago Press, Ltd., London
© 2020 by Scott Rozelle and Natalie Hell
Published 2020
Paperback edition 2022
Printed in the United States of America

31 30 29 28 27 26 25 24 23 22   1 2 3 4 5

ISBN-13: 978-0-226-73952-6 (cloth)
ISBN-13: 978-0-226-82401-7 (paper)
ISBN-13: 978-0-226-740515 (e-book)
DOI: https://doi.org/10.7208/chicago/9780226740515.001.0001

Library of Congress Cataloging-in-Publication Data
Names: Rozelle, Scott, author. | Hell, Natalie, 1991– author.
Title: Invisible China : how the urban-rural divide threatens China's rise / Scott Rozelle and Natalie Hell.
Description: Chicago ; London : The University of Chicago Press, 2020. | Includes bibliographical references and index.
Identifiers: LCCN 2020013172 | ISBN 9780226739526 (cloth) | ISBN 9780226740515 (ebook)
Subjects: LCSH: Economic development—China. | Rural-urban relations—China. | Rural poor—China. | Equality—China. | Education—China—Regional disparities. | Rural poor—Health—China. | China—Economic conditions—Regional disparities.
Classification: LCC HC427.95 R72 2020 | DDC 330.951—dc23
LC record available at https://lccn.loc.gov/2020013172

Contents

Author's Note

This book is different from most books about China intended for a Western audience. It is not another sensationalist account that criticizes everything about China. It is not written by a journalist or a businessman with a big idea but limited direct knowledge of the country. Instead, it is the product of decades of firsthand research. Not only that, it is written in the spirit of hope—hope that China will find solutions to its current problems. I hope I can convince you, the reader, that it is in everyone's interest for China to do so.

China's rise is one of the most dramatic stories of the twentieth century. Most Western observers see a rising China as an inevitable threat to Western dominance. But China's continuing rise is far from inevitable. There are still some very important steps that must be taken and high hurdles that must be cleared if China is to finish the arc of its stunning growth. And in our interconnected world, it is in the interests of us all that China stay the course. The health of the global economy, and the global political system, likely depends on it.

The path that brought me here has been a long but rich one. When I first traveled to China in 1983, I fell in love with the country, especially with its rural people. Since that first visit, I have conducted thousands of interviews with rural people from all walks of life—farmers, entrepreneurs, migrant workers, doctors, teachers, and the elderly. My collaborators and I have visited thousands of schools and collected survey data from millions of students across China. And after decades of careful research, I have uncovered a challenge that, if not addressed, threatens to derail the Chinese dream.

It's not too late for China to take action. In fact, over the past few decades, the Chinese government has had a remarkable record of addressing big economic challenges, even problems that most observers thought were insoluble. However, the challenges I highlight in this book have remained invisible for far too long, not only to the outside world but also to many Chinese. One of the keys to taking action is to know there is a problem. Clarifying those challenges, I hope, will be one of this book's primary contributions. And I hope that China's government will act decisively in addressing the challenges—as it has addressed so many others.

Today China and the world are facing a new challenge in the form of the 2020 coronavirus pandemic. This problem did not exist when I wrote this book. If anything, I fear this book's message may be even more urgent in light of this new global crisis. While no one can predict what is going to happen in the coming months and years, there are unparalleled stresses on China's economy today. For the first time in forty years, China experienced negative growth rates and high formal unemployment rates in the first quarter of 2020. In the rural economy, several months after the pandemic stay-home orders were relaxed, survey results show less than half of China's rural labor force is back to work. Meanwhile, there is widespread talk within China of the need to "deglobalize." Internationally, economic downturns in China's major trading partners, in addition to the potential political turn against global interconnection, may further accelerate China's looming labor transition. Some are hoping China will be the bulwark that can right the global economy and prevent further disaster. Instead, I fear there is a real chance that COVID-19 could be the trip wire that exposes the underlying human capital crisis I lay out in this book and sets in motion forces that divert China from its current economic path, with potentially grave effects for China's trading and diplomatic partners around the globe.

The course of the next several decades—for all of us—depends on what happens in China today.

Two final points: First, a note on naming. We adhere to Chinese naming conventions (surname followed by first name) throughout. Some names in individual stories have been changed to protect the anonymity of our sources. Second, this book is the result of a collaboration between two coauthors, but for the sake of simplicity it is written in my voice.

Scott Rozelle

May 24, 2020

Introduction

Whenever I bring students, colleagues, or prospective donors to rural China for the first time, I ask the same question. I pull a hundred-yuan bill from my pocket and hold it up. "You see this?" I say, looking around theatrically. "Whoever can find a working-age man in this village gets one hundred yuan. He has to be between eighteen and forty, and he has to be healthy." Everyone laughs, thinking one of them is about to make some easy money. But every time, as we go around the village, no young men appear. By day's end, I always win my bet.

This little game illustrates a broader point. China's rapid economic rise was brought about by an enormous expansion of jobs in the cities. Given that the majority of China's population is from rural villages, this has meant a massive rural-to-urban migration over the past several decades. Numbering at least 350 million people, this may be the largest peacetime migration in history.

Viewed from a poor rural village, then, China's economic fortune can most easily be read by observing who is not there. When times are good, as they've been for the past several decades, the young and able-bodied are off working in the cities and sending their paychecks home to support their families. It's this work (in factories, on construction sites, or in the growing service sector) that allowed hundreds of millions of people who were once restricted to subsistence farming, threatened with starvation every bad-weather season, to escape poverty and live newly stable lives. This trend—the out-migration of every able-bodied young man, as well as most young women—was so persistent that for years and years I never lost my bet.

That's the way it was until spring 2016. That April, I was in a rural village with a new colleague. I held up that same old hundred-yuan bill and made the same old joke, asking my guest to try to find a working-age man. To my surprise, we discovered young men almost everywhere. They were not only in that village but in others too.

In one village, three of the five families on one stretch of road had young men at home. Down another side road, I could see a group of men sitting outside and talking. One man was sitting astride a motorcycle parked in front of a small house, smoking a cigarette. He looked to be in his early twenties. I greeted him and asked what he was doing in the village. He took a long drag before answering. "Well, I've been working construction in Zhengzhou for a few years, but they shut down my site—just stopped construction in the middle of the building. At first I thought it was no big deal, sometimes a site does just close. I'll find another job, I thought. But I looked everywhere for weeks. No one's hiring. What could I do but come home?"

His wife came out of the house and joined us. She looked about seven months pregnant and was balancing a toddler on her hip. "We just don't know what to do," she said. "None of us ever imagined there would be no jobs. A bunch of our friends are stuck back in the village too, for the first time any of us can remember."

Just making light conversation, I asked, "So what are you going to do? Go back to farming?" The man snorted with laughter, glancing behind him at their tiny plot of steep, dry land. He didn't mince words. "We're sure as hell not going to stay here and farm in this backwater," he said, stubbing out his cigarette. "Actually, I've never farmed in my life, and I've got no intention of starting now. If no one's hiring . . . then maybe we'll have to take matters into our own hands."

"*Ai-ya*," his wife said. "Don't say things like that." She turned back to me. "We're going to head to Shanghai and try our luck as soon as the baby is born. We have a friend there. He says it's getting harder to find jobs there too, but we'll try. There must be something."

She looked at her husband, who kept his eyes down, lighting another cigarette. She looked at her pregnant belly, then she looked at me. "It will be fine, right? It has to be."

Rise or Fall

Right now, as you read this, a massive drama is unfolding in China. This isn't a story you've heard elsewhere. Indeed, almost no one inside or outside China is aware of it.

This drama is not the incredible economic growth that China has experienced over the past three decades. That story is familiar to most. China, once a place of rampant deep, stark poverty, has transformed itself with astonishing speed into an economic powerhouse. Average incomes have increased ten- to twentyfold in a single lifetime—a scale of progress that is hard to imagine. Most observers assume this progress will continue: headlines like "China's Rise, America's Fall" and "The Inevitable Superpower" suggest that China's destiny is written in the stars.

But there is a profound weakness behind China's rapid rise, only beginning to become apparent. And contrary to the rhetoric that pits China against the United States, it's in all of our best interests for China to maintain its economic stability. The risks to the global economic system of a flailing China would be far worse.

China's growth was brought about in no small part through a tried-and-true development strategy: opening up to foreign direct investment and welcoming investment in low-skilled, labor-intensive industries on a massive scale. This initial policy was followed by the steady removal of restrictions on domestic investors in new industries and the creation of new incentives to accelerate investments. In the 1980s, lured by China's massive population and low wage rates, factories popped up across the country, and the entire economy reaped the benefits. Workers left farms in droves to start work in the factories and in the construction and mining industries that were growing to fill their needs. Rising incomes created positive ripple effects throughout the economy, driving up demand for home building, for services, and for manufactured goods. The combined power of all of these reforms set off a virtuous cycle that boosted the economy year after year. Critically, the foundation of all this growth was the sheer number of China's unskilled workers. Most of the workers in the factories, construction sites, and mines were from poor rural villages and had no more than an elementary or middle school education.

Although this national economic strategy was hugely effective for three decades, now the engine of growth is beginning to run out of gas. Today China's unskilled wage rate is rising rapidly. Although higher wages are good for workers in the short run, in the long run this climbing wage rate is going to bring an end to China's comparative advantage in low-skilled, labor-intensive production. In a globalized world when wages rise, companies simply find cheaper labor elsewhere or (increasingly) find a way to automate.

That's what's happening in China today. Every month, tens of thousands of workers are being laid off in China's key industries. Construction is slowing precipitously. Samsung has moved hundreds of thousands of jobs from China to Vietnam. Nike is now making most of its tennis shoes outside China. This exodus is occurring across the board—in textiles and toys and tools and Christmas decorations. Ten years ago, almost every product for sale in an American Walmart was made in China. Today that is no longer the case. Meanwhile, the spread of new robotics and automation technology is further driving down demand for the Chinese factory worker. And China doesn't have a good backup plan.

If China wants to continue to grow, to become a stable and prosperous high-income country, it will need a new economic strategy. There are historical examples: many now highly successful countries and territories also got their start by relying on unskilled labor. South Korea, Taiwan, and Ireland, for example, developed strong manufacturing sectors and quickly grew from countries rife with poverty to stable economies that provide their citizens with high living standards and strong institutions. Can't China do the same?

I hope so, but I fear it may not be possible. For all the wise decisions the Chinese government has made in recent decades to bring about China's rapid rise—decollectivizing, building roads and public transportation, investing in labor-intensive industries, and opening the nation to foreign investment—it has failed to invest enough in its single most important asset: its people. Today China may be the second largest economy in the world, but it has one of the lowest levels of education of any nation. Data from the 2015 national microcensus reveal that only 12.5 percent of China's labor force has a college education. This is lower than any country at China's level of development, and even lower than many poorer countries. China is dead last in college attainment (fig. 1A). China is just as far behind when it comes to high school. According to the 2015 microcensus, about 30 percent of China's current labor force has a high school education or more (fig. 1B). These figures put China behind all other middle-income countries, including Mexico, Thailand, Turkey, and even South Africa.[1]

This is an almost unbelievable oversight by China's past leaders (as we will see in chapter 4, it appears that the current leadership has started to make positive changes). Yes, China's elites are excelling, attending the world's best universities and outscoring all other countries on international scholastic tests. But educational resources have been allocated in a fundamentally unequal way, and the vast majority of the Chinese population—the overlooked rural people—have been left far behind.

Education is critical for a number of reasons. As I said, for the past several decades, China's economic growth strategy has relied almost exclusively on low-wage, low-skilled workers. The most rudimentary education sufficed for the jobs that powered China's rise: hauling bricks on a construction site or soldering the same two widgets together over and over on a mobile phone assembly line. But now those low-skilled jobs are leaving for other countries or being replaced by automated processes. If China wants to transform itself into a stable high-wage, high-income country, it will need a labor force that can handle more complex, constantly changing, nonroutine jobs. New employers—domestic or foreign—will require workers who can read critically, do basic math, make careful logical choices, use computers, and speak English. Potential employers are not going to set up shop in China—at its new, higher wage rate—if

A. Proportion of the Labor Force With College Education in 2015

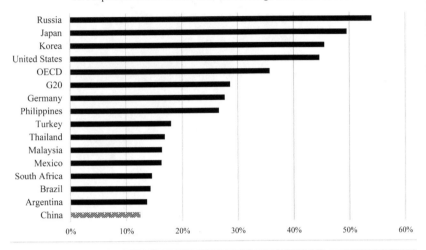

B. Proportion of the Labor Force With High School Education in 2015

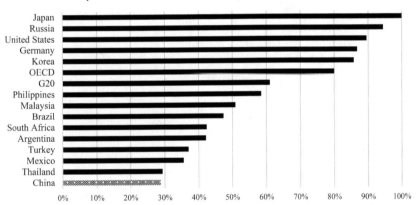

Figure 1. Educational attainment by country (full labor force). *Source:* Hongbin Li et al., "Human Capital and China's Future Growth," *Journal of Economic Perspectives* 31, no. 1 (2017): 25–48.

so few of the available workers have even these basic skills. Thus education will matter more than ever before.

Witness South Korea and Taiwan. As these "Asian Tigers" were beginning to transition from a reliance on unskilled manufacturing, they could count on the fact that nearly three-quarters of their labor forces had graduated from high school. In 1990, the rate of university education in the Taiwanese and South Korean labor forces was

45 percent and 37 percent, respectively. Early investment in human capital (even when the countries/territories were lower-middle income) then played an important role in their ability to transition to a high-wage, high-productivity, and innovation-based economy as their manufacturing sectors dried up. With a broadly uneducated labor force, China is in a very different position. That may mean the difference between continued growth and stagnation—or even catastrophe.[2]

The Invisible China

This book is an account of an impending challenge and the mechanisms that have allowed it to develop. It may seem hard to believe that such a big story, with such far-reaching implications, could be so little known. But the explanation is simple: the problem is brewing in a place where not many people have thought to look.

I have been working exclusively on China for the past forty years. While most reporters hoping to understand China's future have surveyed the massive changes occurring in China's megacities, my work has focused on a part of China that far too few people seem to be aware of: the poor, rural interior. The Invisible China, as I call it, is almost completely absent from the headlines, yet it is in rural villages that China's future may well be decided.

I use "the Invisible China," or "the Other China," as a reference to Michael Harrington's 1962 best seller *The Other America*. This impassioned work of nonfiction described many of the "invisible" problems in the most vulnerable communities of the United States. Harrington's book stirred the conscience of the nation and went on to become one of the main inspirations for Presidents John F. Kennedy and Lyndon Johnson in undertaking the so-called War on Poverty, a broad-based program that included a massive effort to improve the quality of education, nutrition, and health for America's poorest children. Today China is in its own historical moment, in some ways similar to the America of the early 1960s. While the dominant narrative of China in recent decades has been of unstoppable growth and ever-climbing incomes, the Invisible China—a place of rampant poverty, undereducation, undernutrition, and undertreated health issues—remains vast and intransigent and almost completely unacknowledged.

Why must we look to China's countryside today? For two reasons, primarily. First, the divide between China's cities and its rural villages is stark. The average citizen in urban Shanghai makes twelve times the income of someone living in rural Gansu. In the United States, by contrast, the average income differential between Manhattan and West Virginia is less than a factor of four. This is not just an income gap. In fact, in China the distinction between "rural" and "urban" is codified by law. Under the *hukou* (household registration) system, at birth all Chinese citizens are divided into two categories: rural or urban. This status is stamped on their identity cards and affects their life chances in ways I will explore in great detail in this book. Suffice it to say that in China, urban and rural sit on opposite sides of a wide and largely unbridgeable chasm.

Rural and urban China are divided not only in identity and income, but also in human capital. The urban labor force (everyone from twenty-five to sixty-four years of age) is far more educated than the rural labor force. At the time of the 2010 census, 44 percent of the labor force in China's cities had at least a high school education, four times the rate among working-age individuals in rural areas (only 11 percent). Today, fully 93 percent of urban youth attend high school (a rate higher even than that in the United States and Germany overall), while many rural children barely make it to the end of junior high. The gap is not only in attendance; urban children also consistently perform far better on academic tests. China's human capital crisis is a rural problem.[3]

This brings us to the second reason we must look to the countryside. Thanks to simple demographics, most of China's future labor force is growing up in the countryside. In particular, according to hukou status, only about 36 percent of China's overall population is urban and fully 64 percent is rural (some 800 to 900 million people). Owing to uneven birthrates between the cities and the countryside (until recently urban families could have only one child, while rural families often had two or three), China's *children* are even more concentrated in rural areas. More than 70 percent of China's children have rural hukou status today. This means that China's future workforce is predominantly growing up in rural villages, where educational outcomes are still lagging far behind. Thus the ability of China's future labor force to be successful and contribute to the national economy will depend primarily on what is happening today among overlooked rural children. In other words, rural human capital is going to disproportionately shape China's future human capital overall.

The failure of rural education is only the tip of the iceberg. China's urban-rural divide is evident from earliest childhood and is as much a health crisis as an educational one. As we will see, one of the central reasons rural children are falling behind in education is that they lack other basic necessities. My research team has found that over half of rural babies are undernourished, and more than half of toddlers are so developmentally delayed that their IQs may never exceed 90. Our studies have shown that 40 percent of schoolchildren in many rural communities in southern China attend school every day with intestinal worms quietly sapping their energy. More than 30 percent of rural students (in grades four to eight) have vision problems but do not have glasses. These early barriers to health and learning have lasting consequences. In fact, a large share of rural junior high school students are also cognitively delayed relative to international averages. Is it any wonder so many poor rural students never make it to high school?

These are issues with lifelong consequences. Millions of rural children are growing to adulthood without the basic resources they need. With so little education, they are going to struggle to find work in China's future higher-value-added economy. If things get bad enough, some of them may be left out of China's future economy entirely, forced to scratch out an existence on the margins.

The costs will not be borne by these children alone. The human capital of China's labor force will, in part, decide the future course of the entire country. Because the people of the Invisible China make up half of China's population and a vast majority of China's children, poor health and lack of education in the countryside may mean the difference between success and failure for all of China.

My goal is not to be critical of China. Indeed, I want China to succeed. There are many positive achievements that can be attributed to the current government and top education officials. I believe there is still a chance to avoid the worst consequences of the current human capital challenge. Rather than criticizing, I am writing this book to present the challenges and point a way forward, including concrete actions that China can take now to reduce the risks. The sooner action is taken, the lower the probability of a meltdown.

Too Big to Fail

Some readers, particularly those from the West, may be wondering why the subject of this book should matter to them. Yes, rural poverty is a problem the Chinese should address, but is this book purely about a humanitarian crisis in a foreign country? Or are there larger implications?

First, let me say that if you do care about humanitarian issues, China should be a top priority. China is home to 1.3 billion men, women, and children, each just as deserving of a life of dignity and peace as anyone else. The barriers to health and education they face represent one of the best opportunities in the world for reducing human suffering on a massive scale. A sense of moral responsibility has always motivated my decision to work on China, and I believe this thinking resonates with many people.[4]

But even if you are unmoved by the plight of poor rural children on the other side of the globe, I will try to convince you that this issue, for all its humanitarian value, also has enormous political and economic significance for China's future development, for regional stability, and ultimately for the world.

I believe it is in all of our best interests for China to keep growing and thriving. This may seem like a surprising argument. In the West, much of the popular debate takes it for granted that any gains in China's power will come at the expense of American dominance or will pose grave risks to world stability. Many people believe it is not in the world's best interests for China, a country ruled by a single-party government, with a large standing army, to continue its economic and political rise. I believe this argument is misguided. For all the risks of a rising China, the risks of a floundering China are far greater.

Of course it's not certain that China is headed for economic decline. As an economist I know how difficult it is to predict macroeconomic outcomes of any kind over the long run. As a longtime student of China's economy, I have seen China pull off one economic policy miracle after another for the past forty years. As the world watched in disbelief, China's top leaders successfully decollectivized and marketized a moribund rural economy in the 1980s and made it China's first engine of growth. In the 1990s, China pulled off an "impossible" reform of its state-owned enterprise sector. A hermit nation in 1979, in 2001 China joined the World Trade Organization with relatively little trade protection and still thrived. But I believe China's poorly educated population presents a grave risk to its future—one that needs to be taken seriously.

Any stagnation or serious fall in China's growth and stability would have serious ramifications far beyond its borders. For one thing, China has come to occupy a vital position in the global economy. In the past several decades, China has become one of the world's main growth engines, its massive labor power pushing the world economy forward. If something makes that engine stall out, we will all almost certainly suffer.

Let's consider a few examples of ways that economic decline in China would hurt the rest of the world. China is involved in as much as 30 percent of all world trade and is the biggest trading partner of countless countries around the world (more than the United States). Any fall in China's demand for imports would therefore hurt the economies of all those countries in serious ways. China is also crucial because of its role in manufacturing. Today 95 percent of the world's major companies have some part of their supply chains in China. Almost all those companies would be adversely affected by a steep and permanent decline within China and a set of broken supply chains. This outcome would also likely drive up prices around the world. When the prices of everyday goods rise, people are left with less money to meet their essential needs. In simple terms, standards of living would decrease sharply and suddenly for ordinary people around the world.

More recently, China's immense market of newly prosperous consumers (living in China's cities) has become a critical export market for industries around the world. If Chinese consumers suddenly had less money to spare (for instance, because they had lost their jobs or seen their savings decline because of a rapid economic downturn), all those industries would suddenly have a lot fewer customers. The list is long and contains the products of many of the world's top companies: Apple, Rolex, BMW, Boeing, Starbucks, Louis Vuitton, Sunglass Hut, and more. All those companies—based in the United States, Europe, South America, or Southeast Asia—would be hard hit by a fall in Chinese demand. The world is discovering just how intertwined we are—with critical segments deeply embedded in China.

For Americans in particular, China's economy is key. For all the talk of competition between the United States and China, today the American economy is more dependent on China's continued economic health than ever before. Tens of thousands of American companies rely on China for manufacturing. American foreign direct investment in China was US$92 billion in 2016. China's increasingly powerful consumer market is a destination for many American products. China may once have been in competition with the United States for manufacturing jobs, but today China is the fastest-growing market for products that are made in America. With any economic crisis in China, all those businesses—and the individual Americans who depend on them—would be hard hit.[5]

Because of all these factors, today China's economy is the largest individual contributor to the growth of world GDP. In the effort to maintain global economic stability, China may well have become "too big to fail." If China were to stumble, global markets could go into free fall. Indeed, economists estimate that even if China was to keep growing but its growth rate was cut merely in half, that would be enough to reduce global growth by a full percentage point, making global recession all but inevitable. Global recession would, of course, be devastating for nations all over the world. The 2009 recession created hardships across the United States and around the globe, and a substantial fall in China's growth would be just as bad, if not worse. I'm talking about millions of Americans losing their jobs. The stock market would be hard hit, leading to falling 401(k) investments for ordinary Americans and decreased financial stability for all kinds of corporations. A failing China could single-handedly shift the course of the economic future for us all—leaving our children less likely to succeed in the decades to come.[6]

This is the economic side of the picture, but it does not stop there. If China does fall into economic decline, there may also be social and political costs resulting from the crisis. It is hard to predict with certainty, but I imagine this could play out as follows. If investment lags, China's already slowing growth rates will slow further, and its already sky-high inequality (it has one of the most unequal income distributions in the world today) will increase. This is bad news for the Chinese worker. As China's wages rise and low-skilled jobs disappear, it is possible that China will experience a massive polarization of the workforce. At worst, this human capital crisis could leave 200 to 300 million or more unemployable in the formal workforce. Unskilled manufacturing jobs and construction jobs will have disappeared, and they will not have the skills to qualify for anything else.

The expelled workers will have a hard choice to make. Very few are likely to go back to the farm. Farms in China are tiny (the legacy of land redistribution), the average plot barely large enough to support the caloric intake of a family of four. Many out-of-work Chinese will have no choice but to join the informal labor force, selling fried noodles or washing windshields at intersections, or working as waiters. But the economy can employ only so many of these informal workers, and with millions of laid-off workers looking for something to do, wage rates will fall further. Such jobs offer no benefits, little prospect of upward mobility, and no stability or security. Many will likely be gravely disappointed.

Perhaps most seriously, such a dynamic has the potential to undermine the tenuous social contract that has been holding Chinese society together throughout its recent reform period. Over the past two to three decades, the research of Marty White, a sociologist at Harvard University, has shown that despite high and rising levels of inequality in China, there has been little resentment or anger from those in the lower economic classes. White's research has repeatedly found that those in the lower echelons of the economy are not unhappy or disaffected. Instead there is optimism because most people know they are better off today than ten to twenty years ago. Moreover, most people—even the poor—believe things will continue to get better not just for them but also for their children. These beliefs have helped to maintain peace and stability, giving hundreds of millions of people the incentive to work hard, contribute to society, and pay taxes. If China is thrown into economic crisis or these workers are thrown out on the street, this optimism and social trust may come to an abrupt end. If many Chinese suddenly no longer have reason to believe in a better future, resentment may begin to rise.

I fear that some workers could be so disappointed and dissatisfied that they could be pushed outside the system entirely. In particular, if the economic crisis is large and severe enough, this dissatisfaction might cause some of the newly unemployed to turn to crime. It may be hard to believe this could happen in China. But if young hardworking men and women suddenly find the rug pulled out from under them, they may be left angry at the system. If their dreams and their belief that life will get better start to fade, some may take this more radical route. The example of other stagnant middle-income countries suggests that a sharp rise in organized crime could be the ultimate outlet for this disaffection.

We should also consider another factor that could transform a crisis into a catastrophe: about forty million extra men. For several decades (under the One Child Policy), China has had a widely skewed birthrate. Today China has the highest male-female sex imbalance the world has ever seen. Several cohorts of these children have already come of age, and many more will soon reach adulthood. Thanks to the numbers alone, many men will be unable to marry. If the economy stagnates, pushing millions of people out of the workforce, what will droves of unmarried, unconnected, unemployed young men do? Already you can find a few young men drifting back to their villages and hanging out in towns. Like the young man I found suddenly back home in his village, they are worried about the future and increasingly frustrated that the promise of a better life seems to be disappearing. We need only look to the cartels that have torn apart Mexico and the favelas of Brazil to understand the most catastrophic potential consequences.

If the crisis really does reach this point, with a stagnant formal economy that leaves out millions of people, and rising crime and gang activity, the political ramifications will be serious—and are unlikely to remain isolated within China's borders. Keep in mind that China is governed by an authoritarian ruling party and armed with the largest military in the world. For the past few decades, the Chinese Communist Party (CCP) has maintained legitimacy over a vast population based on the promise of steady economic growth. How will the CCP react if economic growth begins to slow or shudders to a halt? How will the government maintain legitimacy if half the labor force is left structurally unemployable? As an economist, I hesitate to make strong predictions. But from reading the literature, I fear that the CCP could pivot from its current emphasis on economic growth to the fallback plan of many desperate leaders around the world and throughout history: an appeal to nationalism, or worse. The resulting political turmoil could have serious ramifications on the world stage.[7]

For all these reasons, I believe that if anything happens to China, we will all suffer. It's true that poverty and educational deficits exist in other parts of the world as well, but when a country like Venezuela or Thailand falters, the world doesn't shudder. Simply put, none of us can afford for China to stumble. The plight of rural Chinese children may sound like a distant problem, but this crisis has the potential to shake the world's foundations.

China's Invisible Challenge

As a professor, I give a lot of presentations. Month after month I travel around the world, including China, presenting my research to fellow academics, students, government officials, and business-people. No matter the audience, these presentations are met with disbelief. How can the China we hear so much about, the "inevitable superpower," still be struggling with these basic barriers to human health, education, and dignity?[8]

Part of the problem is that some of these issues are invisible—literally. Anemia, for example, can gravely inhibit a child's ability to grow and to learn, but it's not visible to the naked eye. Intestinal worms are hidden in the bowels. Babies' cognition mystifies parents in developed countries with access to all the best resources, let alone poor rural peasants with no one to turn to for good information.

The other problem is that rural China itself has become invisible to the rest of the world. It certainly seems like the world is full of pros-perous Chinese: they can be seen shopping for luxury goods in Paris, traipsing through Disneyland and Times Square, flocking to Ameri-can universities, and gracing the cover of *Time*. But these highly vis-ible emissaries of the Middle Kingdom are members of the urban elite, and China's cities are small islands of prosperity in a massive country where more than half the citizens still struggle just to get by.

So great is the urban-rural divide in China that the Invisible China has become invisible even to many Chinese. China's inequality is wide, and it's also geographical. The prosperous cities of China's eastern coast are full of the wealthy and the newly middle class, whereas the vast droves of poor Chinese are still mostly restricted to remote villages in the country's western and southern interior. Urban Chinese used to take a bus or a slow train for cross-country business trips or visits home, with the Invisible China observable through the open windows and at the stops along each route. Today city people hurtle past poor rural areas at almost two hundred miles an hour on high-speed trains or hop over them on cheap flights in Boeing jets, never laying eyes on the Invisible China.

The Invisible China has become difficult to see for all but the most dedicated. Since the 1980s, my partners and colleagues in China (now known as the Rural Education Action Program, or REAP) have been working to systematically understand and describe rural China. A mix of economists, education specialists, and public health researchers from top universities in the United States and China, REAP has run more than one hundred large-scale efforts at data collection in the field and has gathered data from more than 500,000 people from twenty-six of China's thirty-three provinces. In a country where official statistics can be insufficient and rural areas have become so invisible, it is only through this kind of commitment, patience, and specialized expertise that it is possible to understand rural life and thus to see the problem that is coming.

So how is it that rural China has fallen so far behind? Why has the government failed to invest sufficiently in education and health? And what can be done to minimize the dangers China faces today? These are several of the big questions this book addresses. The stakes are too high for this problem to remain invisible for much longer.

1: The Middle-Income Trap

To much of the world, China's future seems certain. Journalists have christened the twenty-first century the "Chinese century." In my local school district, there is an annual lottery to get one's child into the Mandarin-immersion program; every year for the past ten years, it has been oversubscribed by three to one or more. People around the world are enrolling their preschoolers in Chinese class and imagining what the world will be like when China calls the shots.

But that bright future as an economic powerhouse and global superpower depends on China's ability to keep growing. It has had persistent success over the past few decades, but the fact that China has grown so successfully to this point does not necessarily mean its growth will continue.

Imagine all the countries of the world scattered along the route of a hypothetical board game. This is the game of economic development, and the goal is simple: raise average incomes in your country as quickly as possible, and don't go backward. All countries start at the bottom—in poverty. With luck, hard work, and some strategic choices, they can begin to grow. Over the past few centuries, most of the world's countries have seen growth. Indeed, on average there has been movement up the board.

But development is not a linear process where equal inputs of hard work and investment lead to equal outputs. As economist Paul Collier observed, development is like a game of Chutes and Ladders. If a country is lucky enough to land on a "ladder," it gets whisked to a higher level on the board. Landing on a "chute," on the other hand, means moving just as quickly to a lower point in the game and having to retrace one's steps. Certain rolls of the dice yield really big returns surprisingly quickly; other rolls of the dice (and sections of the board) are riddled with big challenges.[1]

For the past several decades, China has been riding one of the most reliable ladders on the board: a ladder that rewards countries for specializing in low-wage manufacturing. But now wages are rising and are unlikely to come back down, so China can't ride that ladder any further. Instead, it needs to roll the dice once more and try to thread its way up a new section of the board.

The problem is that China's rapid growth has led the country to one of the most dangerous parts of the game. As it searches for the way forward, China is teetering on the edge of one of the longest chutes of all.

This chute is known as the middle-income trap. It is so perilous that most countries that have made it to China's place on the game board have fallen victim. There's reason to fear that China may be particularly susceptible.

The Middle-Income Trap

Contrary to what news stories about China's luxury consumer markets and increasing global political power might make you think, China today is not a rich country. It may be nearly the world's largest national economy, but its per capita income remains strictly middle of the pack. According to the World Bank, in 2016 China ranked 75th in per capita income. According to the CIA *World Factbook*, it ranks 106th out of 228 countries. This puts China on the level of countries like Algeria, Costa Rica, and Thailand.[2]

One of the fundamental facts of the development board game is that countries at different income levels face different opportunities and different challenges. To put it another way, at each income level a country must cross sections of the board with different ladders and different chutes.

China started the post–World War II period as a poor country— close to the bottom of the game board. That stretch of the board does have its share of chutes, but China was lucky enough to avoid them. It didn't get stuck in a cycle of violence (like Rwanda or El Salvador) or hobbled by elites fighting over scarce natural resources (like Venezuela or Papua New Guinea). These are some of the most common hurdles blocking a poor country's development.[3]

Instead, back when China was still poor, it managed to hit on a major ladder out of poverty. Starting in the late 1970s and early 1980s, climbing the ladder of low-wage manufacturing, China grew from a per capita income of less than US$1,000 in 1980 to a per capita income of more than US$15,000 in 2016, a stunning feat in so short a time. There are a number of other middle-income countries that used this ladder to rise out of poverty: Ireland, Turkey, and Thailand, for instance. Other poor countries are beginning to demonstrate success with a similar economic strategy: Vietnam, Bangladesh, and Peru.[4]

But now, after so much successful growth, China has become a middle-income country and so has entered a part of the game board where the ways to grow (the ladders) and the ways to stagnate or decline (the chutes) are different. Unfortunately, the middle-income stretch of the board is littered with chutes that have tripped up more countries than have made it through.

In a 2004 article in *Foreign Affairs*, political scientist Geoffrey Garrett shared a startling observation. He looked at the history of recent economic development and noticed that while rich countries were continuing to do well and many poor countries were achieving strong growth rates, the countries in the middle of the global income spectrum were growing more slowly and less successfully than anyone else.[5]

In a report that made ripples throughout the development world, economists at the World Bank demonstrated the full extent of the problem. The report showed that out of 101 countries that were middle income in 1960, only thirteen had made it to high-income status by 2008. The rest remained stuck or even ended the fifty years poorer than before.[6]

The figure compiled by that team has become quite well known and is reproduced here (see fig. 2). It shows the economic history of the past half-century, with countries arrayed by their per person in-

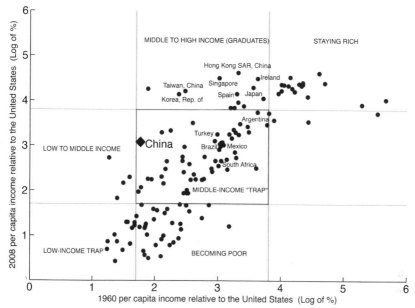

Figure 2. The middle-income trap. *Source:* World Bank, Development Research Center of the State Council, the People's Republic of China, *China 2030: Building a Modern, Harmonious, and Creative Society* (Washington, DC: World Bank, 2013). © World Bank, https://openknowledge.worldbank.org/handle/10986/12925 License: CC BY 3.0 IGO.

come (relative to the United States) in 1960 compared with 2008. As you can see, most of the countries that started the 1960s as middle income (the center third of the figure) have remained stuck in place or have even lost ground. Only a tiny fraction of these countries (among them recent stragglers like Greece) have been able to catch up with the world's small club of rich countries.

This is the middle-income trap, and it is something to be feared. While a few countries have escaped it, the vast majority have gotten stuck here. For nearly sixty years (at least), they have been unable to progress along the game board. These are countries like Mexico, Brazil, Thailand, and South Africa. Their dreams of further growth have been elusive.

That is not to say these countries have been stagnant or unmoving. Many have traveled a more tortuous path. They grow, grow, and grow only to collapse. Or they grow, grow, and grow only to stagnate.

During each collapse or period of stagnation, a lot of people get hurt. Each time, the common people lose jobs, lose money, and lose their sense of security, and they must start all over again.

Mexico has experience with this pattern. In the late 1970s and early 1980s, low wages and a brand-new trade deal with the United States and Canada made Mexico the go-to destination for the assembly of manufactured goods. International companies opened new factories across the country, and Mexican workers flocked to fill them. Growth soared, and people around the world spoke of Mexico's "economic miracle." Mexico was admitted to the Organisation for Economic Co-operation and Development (OECD) and was widely expected to soon join the ranks of the world's rich countries. But by the mid-2000s, that dream was dead. Mexico's growth stalled, and all that promise was replaced by economic stagnation and large-scale social upheaval. The costs for the people of Mexico have been huge, and Mexico remains far from achieving high-income status.

Brazil, too, has been on the brink of becoming high income several times but never made it over the last hurdle. No fewer than six times since the 1960s has Brazil suffered economic downturns that reversed the nation's previous efforts at growth. Ordinary Brazilians have suffered in each of those downturns, losing jobs, plans for the future, and their life savings. And still Brazil remains middle income.

These economic downturns also have grave political and social costs. Crises in the economic realm make people more likely to turn to the informal sector or even to crime. Economic distress also increases the odds of social or political unrest. All too often the middle-income trap has left countries struggling under renewed poverty, crime, and even large-scale violence. For the people in these countries—and the international trading or diplomatic partners who depend on their stability—the middle-income trap is devastating.

This is the danger China faces today. It has grown successfully from a poor to a middle-income country. That is a wonderful thing. This growth has lifted millions of people out of poverty and set China on a course for the potential of much greater stability and prosperity. But the journey is far from over. Now that China is a middle-income country, the rules have changed. If China wants to avoid looking like the next Mexico (and to follow the course of South Korea instead), it had better pivot quickly.

The Graduates versus the Trapped

So what's the difference? Why do some countries make it through middle income without slowdowns while others get stuck in the trap? Let's start by looking at the exceptions: the small number of countries that have managed to beat the odds and avoid the trap. I like to call this small group of countries the graduates.

Some of the graduates have followed paths that China cannot hope to replicate. Spain, Portugal, and Greece, for instance, made the jump only after they were incorporated into the European Union. With EU membership came a number of benefits, including new trading partnerships, support for social programs, and the ability to share a currency with some of the world's richest countries. As a result, these countries were able to ride the EU's coattails all the way to high-income status (though their recent struggles suggest that even that path may not be foolproof in the long run). This option, obviously, is not available to China today.

Likewise, some of the countries of the former Soviet bloc have been held up as success stories. Poland, Hungary, and the Czech Republic, for instance, have also nominally moved from middle to high income in recent decades. But this is misleading. These countries were already rich before the Iron Curtain fell across Europe. What has happened since is more a return to their earlier prosperity than a case of successful development from scratch. Here, too, it seems unlikely that China can hope to follow this path.[7]

But a few of the graduates appear to have enough in common with China that they might serve as models. The Asian Tigers (Taiwan, South Korea, Singapore, and Hong Kong) all grew steadily from poverty through to their present place at the top, passing through the middle-income phase with hardly a hiccup. Ireland and Israel have followed a similar path. These countries/territories had neither the benefits of membership in formal unions with rich countries nor histories of high GDP. So how did they do it? What separates places like Taiwan, Israel, and South Korea, which have been able to beat the odds and graduate from middle- to high-income status, from places like South Africa or Mexico that have gotten stuck in the trap?

I believe there is one crucial difference between the graduates and the trapped countries: human capital. To economists, "human capital" is like financial capital, but instead of money, it refers to all the traits that enable people to contribute to the economy as workers—and to make a better life for themselves and their families. Health, nutrition, and education are examples: they enable the people of a country to be better workers and better citizens. In their efforts to avoid the middle-income trap, countries need human capital; it is one of the most crucial components of success. To explain why human capital is so critical, let's first look at one simple indicator of human capital—the share of the adult population with at least a high school education.[8]

At first glance, it's already clear that human capital and development tend to go hand in hand. In poor countries—those that have long been stuck at the very beginning of the game board—the rate of education typically is very low. In Bangladesh, Haiti, and Ethiopia, for example, the share of the labor force that has been to high school is below 15 percent. Likewise, countries in the middle of the game board generally have middling levels of high school education. As of 2015, for example, 47 percent of Brazil's labor force had attained a high school education; for Mexico the figure was 35 percent, and for Turkey, 37 percent. The countries that are farthest along the path of the game board—those that have been rich and prosperous for several generations—have uniformly high human capital. In the United States, 90 percent of working-age people have at least a high school education, for example, and in Germany it's 87 percent. In Japan the figure is higher than 99 percent. The trend for these nations is clear: on average, high school attainment among countries that are members of the OECD—the club of the world's richest countries—is 78 percent.[9]

But with a bit of historical data, another trend emerges that is far more relevant to the question at hand: the very small number of countries that have made it out of middle-income status in recent decades—the graduates—all have very high levels of high school education. Even more surprising, they've had those high levels for decades. In particular, back when they were still middle income, the graduates (places like South Korea, Taiwan, and Ireland) all had high school attainment rates comparable to those of the rich countries.

Table 1 shows this trend. All the countries that remain at the middle-income level today—most of which have been trapped there for decades—have levels of high school attainment between 30 and 50 percent. On average, the rate in these trapped countries is only 36 percent. The graduates, by contrast, had an average high school attainment of 72 percent back in the 1980s when they were still in the middle-income bracket. That was almost identical to the average attainment in the rich countries.

In this book I will argue that the upfront investment in human capital was critical in preparing those countries to grow and thrive and keep moving up the game board. A highly educated population became the last ladder these countries needed to make it all the way to high-income status. China does exhibit some of the traits of the graduates before their final rise, but unless it develops its base of human capital, it may not be able to follow in their footsteps. Human capital is simply too important to ignore.

The Importance of Human Capital

In many of the world's poorest countries, most of the labor force has exactly the same job: farmer. But when countries start moving up the development game board, that begins to change.

Countries at different levels of the development pathway tend to specialize in different types of jobs. This is built into the very nature of development. In a low-income country, the average worker has a low-income job. In a middle-income country, the average worker has a middle-income job. Of course.

Table 1. Share of the labor force with at least a high school education

Country	High school attainment
Low-income countries (2015)	
Low-income average (2015)	< 20
Middle-income countries (2015)	
Turkey	37
Brazil	47
Argentina	42
Mexico	35
South Africa	42
China[1]	30
Middle-income average (2015)[2]	36
High-income countries (2015)	
United States	90
Germany	87
Japan	100
High-income average (2015)[3]	78
The graduates—pre-transition (1980)	
The graduates average (1980)[4]	≈72

Source: Hongbin Li, Prashant Loyalka, Scott Rozelle, and Binzhen Wu, "Human Capital and China's Future Growth," *Journal of Economic Perspectives* 31, no. 1 (2017): 25–48; *Education at a Glance 2015: OECD Indicators* (Paris: OECD, 2015), www.oecd.org/education/education-at-a-glance-2015.htm.

[1] Attainment in China is calculated based on data from the 2015 One-Percent National Sample Census (2015 microcensus). For more information, see Lei Wang, Mengjie Li, Cody Abbey, and Scott Rozelle, "Human Capital and the Middle Income Trap: How Many of China's Youth Are Going to High School?" *Developing Economies* 56, no. 2 (2018): 82–103.

[2] This is the average for all countries that are middle income by OECD definition in 2015.

[3] This is the average for OECD member countries in 2015.

[4] This is calculated by averaging the 1980 levels for South Korea, Taiwan, Israel, and Ireland.

The reason this matters for our story is that jobs that are paid different amounts tend to require different educational backgrounds. It doesn't take much formal education to be a good farmer—the kind of job that abounds in a poor country. It also doesn't take much formal education to be a good worker on a construction site or even an assembly line—the kinds of jobs that predominate in middle-income countries. It does, however, require a good education to be successful as an office worker, a technician in a high-tech factory, or even a manager or specialist in a high-wage service job—the kind of jobs that power a high-income economy.

The point is this: a country cannot maintain high incomes without a workforce that has the education (and the health and nutrition) to be successful in high-income jobs. Given that technological change is now increasingly biased in favor of those with skills, it has become even more important for rich countries to have a highly educated workforce. In the United States or Great Britain or Japan, there are few jobs—and even fewer *desirable* jobs—available for those without a high school education or higher. If China wants to function like a high-income country, it needs a labor force that can handle high-income jobs.

But there's a catch. In our globalized world, countries can now develop very quickly. Like China, they can shoot from the bottom of the game board to the middle level in mere decades. In most of the world's rich countries, that same progress took centuries. That speed of development is a problem, however, because the human capital that a rich country needs must be accumulated far in advance. It takes twelve years to give a single cohort of children a basic twenty-first-century education. To upgrade the education of the entire labor force—full of older people who came of age before education mattered so much—takes far longer. All told, it takes about forty-five years. Thus a country cannot wait until it reaches high-income status to begin producing the human capital it needs to support growth.

The result is that many middle-income countries do not accumulate the human capital they need while they are still middle income. So long as they are in that stage, lower levels of education work just fine. Then, if they are lucky and their growth pushes wages high enough that they might soon count as a high-income country, the lack of human capital in the labor force undermines this progress, leaving them stuck in a deadly trap. With concerted efforts to make human capital a priority, countries can avoid this trap—as the history of graduates like South Korea and Ireland clearly shows. But it's a difficult balance to strike.

This is the challenge China faces. Based on its stock of human capital, China looks a lot more like 1980s Mexico or Turkey than 1980s Taiwan or South Korea. No country has ever made it to high-income status with high school attainment rates below 50 percent. With China's present high school attainment rate of 30 percent, the country could be in grave trouble.[10]

During a recent National Party Congress, China's top leader, Xi Jinping, proclaimed that China had entered a "new era of modern economic development." National research institutes, central government think tanks, and officially sanctioned academic journals were all put on notice that henceforth they were to refrain from using the term "middle-income trap." Clearly, according to China's top leaders, the middle-income trap no longer looms: the threat is over and there is nothing to fear. The "new era" has already begun. Unfortunately, this may have been wishful thinking.

2: China's Looming Transition

All across China you can hear the sound of factories closing their doors. Workers are being laid off and told to seek opportunities elsewhere. What started as a trickle has become a steady flow.

In 2015 electronics manufacturer Samsung announced that it would be moving its production base from China to Vietnam, taking hundreds of thousands of jobs with it (directly and indirectly). Indeed, Samsung has already created so many well-paid jobs in northern Vietnam that it is being touted as the new cornerstone of the country's national economy. The shoe industry, long dominated by Chinese suppliers, is relocating its factories in increasing numbers to countries such as Ethiopia, where shoe exports increased fivefold in the past five years. The tariffs imposed during the height of the US-China Trade War seems to have accelerated the exodus of China's manufacturers, but this is just a continuation of the existing trend. As one veteran of China's manufacturing sector put it in early 2020, "Even if the tariffs went away tomorrow, most people are not coming back." Companies are facing rising labor costs, and many are choosing to cut costs by moving their operations elsewhere—both big-name companies and the many small companies that supply them. All these changing industries add up to big losses: every year forty thousand factories are shutting down across China, eliminating jobs in droves.[1]

It's true that some industries will be tougher to move out of China: some of the high-end electronics, automobile parts, and sophisticated tools, for example. The current thinking is that the supply chains in these industries are so complicated and entrenched that it will be difficult (and prohibitively expensive) to coordinate the move of so many factories and their suppliers out of China. But not even these jobs are safe. When labor costs rise and offshoring isn't an option, there's another time-honored way to cut costs: automation.

Over the past decade China's factory owners have begun to automate on a large scale. The mechanization is happening fastest in the manufacturing of automobiles, electronics, and metals. China is currently adopting robotics faster than any other country. As of 2016, China had become the world's largest customer for industrial robots, accounting for 30 percent of global sales. While it is hard to predict when and where, the revolution in automation and robotics has begun and will only accelerate. In fact, automation is likely to threaten more jobs in China in the coming decades than globalization took away from the United States over the past thirty to forty years. Whether the Chinese workers are replaced by Vietnamese workers or by machines, these jobs are not going to be available anymore.[2]

This is a monumental shift. During the late 1990s and early 2000s, whenever Chinese colleagues came to visit me in the United States, I always took them on an excursion to the nearest Walmart. We'd go down each aisle, and I'd ask them to choose a random number to determine how many steps we'd take, then another random number to decide which shelf to reach for. We'd pick the randomly selected item off the shelf and turn it over to see where it was made. Back then the fun of the game was this: absolutely everything was made in China. It didn't matter if you were in the toy section, the electronics section, or the clothing section, the words "Made in China" were everywhere. This simple game was a quick way to demonstrate just how completely China had dominated global manufacturing.

Recently I decided to see how much things have changed, so I made the same trek. I drove to the nearest Walmart and picked random numbers. The first item I pulled from the shelf, a T-shirt, was made in Bangladesh. The next item, a pair of shoes, was made in India. A toy I pulled off the shelf was made in China, but in the next aisle the plastic calculator was made in Mexico. There are still plenty of items coming from China, but "Made in China" no longer rules the shelves. The market has begun to move on.

As the factories leave or automate, many other industries in China are taking big hits too. For decades China's construction industry has employed huge numbers of ordinary people, raising buildings and building roads on a massive scale. That building boom made its way across the country, starting with the megacities of Shanghai and Beijing, then moving steadily inland—to Zhengzhou, then Xi'an, then Yinchuan, erecting skyscrapers, building factories, and raising mass housing units in dense rows. Now the only city that's still building at any scale is Guiyang—the poorest provincial capital in the country. I visited Guiyang in fall 2017 and saw the effort going on in the city. The rate of building in Guiyang is so fast that it too will soon be finished.

The progression of road building has been much the same: a network of public highways and roads (almost three million miles worth) now stretches all the way into the remote parts of China. In the 1950s there were literally no expressways in China. Zero. The roadways were still dramatically underdeveloped in the early 1990s. The next twenty years were different. By 2011 China's expressway system had surpassed that of the United States as the world's largest. By the end of 2017, the total length of China's expressway system was more than 80,000 miles. It's now the world's longest expressway system by a wide margin. But today the expressway-building craze is nearly over.[3]

No matter how desperately the government might want to continue this job-creating boom, after all these years there's almost nothing left to build. Thus the behemoth construction industry has also begun what is likely to be a steady decline. Hundreds of thousands of good jobs for common people are being lost. This loss of momentum is rippling out into the many industries that depend on construction, too: as of 2016, the state-sponsored coal and steel industries began the work of eliminating 1.8 million jobs. The metals-mining industry has also begun shedding jobs.[4]

In response, of course, China is trying to take action to offset the job losses and the fall in manufacturing, construction, and other economic activities at home. One of the most high-profile efforts is China's Belt and Road Initiative (BRI). Launched in 2013 by Xi Jinping, this has been touted as the world's largest infrastructure project. A big part of the plan involves China's lending money to developing countries to finance infrastructure projects using some amount of both construction materials and labor from China. In a few BRI projects, Chinese workers have built roads, railroads, and wind farms throughout Central Asia, Southeast Asia, and Africa. According to China's own data, over the past five years China invested over US$90 billion under the banner of the BRI and signed cooperation agreements of some kind or another with 125 countries.[5]

The hope is that the BRI will provide a way for China to achieve greater economic and cultural power overseas while also boosting international economic growth. And it could, in theory, also resolve some part of the problem I've laid out here. Even if China has already built all the skyscrapers, roads, and bridges it needs and is running out of projects for its formidable construction industry at home, there are many countries around the world that could use better infrastructure. Why not send Chinese workers and materials to those places, thereby maintaining the same feverish demand in the domestic industrial sector and keeping China's many unskilled workers fully employed?

While this effort has managed a large scope in the past several years and received a lot of attention, I find it hard to believe that the Belt and Road Initiative will do much to avert China's problem. In spite of the fanfare at the program's announcement, it has already fallen far short of the intended scale—especially in using Chinese labor outside China's boundaries. In some projects Chinese workers have been used, but in many others the partner country has insisted on using local labor. In addition, there has already been pushback against this program in many BRI recipient countries. Recently, even greater challenges have arisen. At least seven countries have canceled or substantially downsized proposed projects. There has been heavy criticism from the West that corruption is rampant in these projects. A 2019 official forum in Beijing took a much more subdued tone on the expectations for the future of the initiative.[6]

In general, then, there are reasons to doubt that the initiative can replace the lost demand for Chinese workers. The BRI has been welcomed in some countries. This will likely continue, providing an outlet for a small share of China's extra workers. But not many countries are going to be willing to borrow large amounts of money to finance these efforts, and even fewer will allow massive numbers of Chinese laborers into their countries. I therefore do not see this program as a solution to the problem I've laid out. China is still going to be left with too little economic growth and too many left-out unskilled workers.

For now, most observers remain calm. China's growth rates may have fallen, but they were astonishingly high before, so they had to come down eventually. That's what always happens in this part of the development pathway anyway. For now it seems that most Chinese workers are still doing fine. The unemployment rate remains low, and most people still report that they can find new jobs. The young men I meet in the remote villages say that although it's getting more difficult and they have to travel a lot farther, if they're willing to go the distance, there are still jobs to be found. But the wheels of change are turning, and the current equilibrium will not last forever. I think it is clear that before long there will simply not be enough jobs to go around; certainly not for those who are poorly trained and don't have the ability to learn new skills and adjust to new environments.

This is not a blip. This is the beginning of a new era for China. I'm not sure most people in China—from the highest leadership to the assembly lines—see it coming, but the signs are clear.

A Ladder Out of Poverty, but No Further

The modern world is globalized. Rather than operating only within the borders of a single country, companies can now stretch their operations across the globe. They can make their goods wherever it's cheapest, sell them wherever they can earn the highest return, and keep their money wherever it's taxed the least. This flattening of our world has brought many consequences, intended and unintended.

One of the best results is that it has created a magnificent ladder out of poverty.[7]

The strategy is relatively simple: open your borders and attract the factories that produce the world's labor-intensive goods using low-wage labor. What are these goods? Well, many are the things for sale at Walmart: cheap plastic toys, five-dollar T-shirts, a tool to fix the kitchen sink, and your Christmas decorations. Some of these factories produce components of final consumer products—the metal clips that hold a bra strap together, the button of your jeans, the zippers for high-end backpacks. Still other technologically advanced goods are assembled by low-skilled workers on assembly lines: smartphones, computer monitors, drill motors, and motorcycles.

The key is that these jobs are routine. An assembly line job takes discipline and determination, but it doesn't require any of the other things a human resource manager might look for in a different industry: educational background, experience, or language skills. Pretty much anyone can work on an assembly line and do well with minimal training. I've done interviews in mobile phone factories. It takes twelve to fifteen minutes to teach someone that kind of job, and they're up to their maximum output after only three days. A hiring manager proudly informed me that anyone with two hands could do this job. So in our globalized world, profit-maximizing companies making these goods naturally set up their factories in whatever country the workers will work for the lowest wage.

This strategy works out pretty well for really poor countries—at least in the short run. It's a good way to move from the bottom of the Chutes and Ladders board to the middle level. It works something like this. If you're a poor country, then by definition you have a lot of citizens who don't make much money. Thus it doesn't take a very high wage to make it worth their while to stop what they're doing (generally farming) and sign up for a new low-wage job. To be sure, you and I wouldn't think a sweatshop is a great place to work. But in fact it pays a lot more than subsistence farming. So lots of people jump at the chance to take these jobs, and their incomes rise quickly.

The miracle goes beyond the transformation of the life of the individual former farmer, now worker. It lies in what these factories do for the local economy. The factories kick off a system that generates jobs—lots of them—for the poorest members of society and serves as the engine propelling an entire developing economy.

Factories themselves hire lots of workers, including poor people, raising local income levels. Rising incomes drive up demand for home building, for the budding service sector, and for manufactured goods, all of which send ripples into the rest of the local economy. Factories need a lot of buildings and raw materials, so they spur the growth of construction, mining, and other supply sectors. This provides another source of jobs (and income) that can be filled even by the poor and uneducated—as with factories, in a developing country it doesn't take much formal education to excel on a construction site or in a mine. With all the new business, the government can tax its way to higher revenues, which in turn promotes the development of the roads and other infrastructure that support yet further development—as well as the jobs that come with new public services.

This virtuous cycle is powerful, and at least since World War II it has been the world's most successful ladder up the first stretch of the Chutes and Ladders board. This strategy—producing a ton of the products a Walmart sells—has fed the growth of all the most successful previously poor countries in the past half-century. Countries as different as South Korea, Brazil, Turkey, Thailand, and Ireland have followed this path, harnessing the labor of poor workers to rise quickly out of the deepest poverty and into new levels of middle-income prosperity.

It's this strategy that's responsible for the Chinese miracle. It was the massive buildup of manufacturing capacity—the complete dominance of the aisles of my local Walmart—that gave China its double-digit growth rate. With the manufacturing came the suppliers, services, infrastructure building, housing, and on and on. This cycle allowed 400 to 500 million people to emerge from poverty, improved living standards across the entire population, and gave rise to the world's second largest economy. This has rightly been held up as a victory for the poor. For all the unintended consequences, the globalization of manufacturing (and its spillovers) has done more to reduce global poverty than any policy ever undertaken.

But for all the benefits, for any country on the rise this strategy can work only so long. Remember, the cardinal rule of the globalized world is this: labor-intensive manufacturing will go to whatever place has the lowest wages. If wages rise too high in one place, the factories pull up stakes and go elsewhere. Or they automate. And all the capacity to drive national economic growth and reduce poverty goes with them. This is exactly what's happening in China today.

From 1990 to 2005—the era of China's complete dominance of the Walmart aisles—there was almost no change in China's unskilled wage rate, which remained steadily low enough to keep the factories coming. The wage was just high enough to pull young men and women off the farm. If the number of factories hiring rose too fast and drove up wages, thanks to China's massive population, there was always a new batch of young men and women ready to leave the farm and take their place on an assembly line or behind a wheelbarrow hauling bricks over to the scaffolding, thus pushing the wage rate back down. More jobs, more migrants. Yet more jobs, even more migrants. As first it seemed the number was infinite. That consistent flow kept China's wage rate stable for fifteen years.[8]

Since 2005, however, things have begun to change. In particular, China's wage rate has begun to rise. In fact, it has risen about 10 percent a year ever since. So of course companies are looking around to find the new place that will give them a lower wage rate, and many factories are headed out of China. As China's unskilled wage rate continues to rise, more and more factories will leave, moving to greener (cheaper) pastures. Now, perhaps, it's Vietnam's turn to ride this ladder out of poverty.[9]

Why are China's wages rising? For two reasons. First, demand is still growing. China's growth rate may have fallen from its peak of 10 percent a year, but it's still high (about 6.9 percent in 2017), which means there's still increasing demand for the products created in Chinese factories. Rising demand naturally pushes up wages. That's Econ 101 stuff.

But that's not the only reason for the increase. The other important factor is that the dynamic keeping Chinese wages low for so long has finally come to an end. During the early period of China's growth (the 1980s, 1990s, and early 2000s), wages stayed low because anytime wages rose, more people would stream off the farms. China's rural population was so big that this took a long time. But even China has a finite population, and as of the mid-2000s there was simply no one left. As a result, although GDP continued to rise in that period, wages rose even faster without being pushed down by new migrants. Until 2016 it was rare to see an able-bodied young man (or woman) in a rural village. After that, the supply of surplus labor (which once seemed infinite) had finally been used up.[10]

For another thing, China has entered a new phase in the demographics of its labor force. What used to be a growing population has now begun to shrink—China's workforce reached its peak size in 2010. Falling fertility rates (and the One Child Policy) are to blame, but the economic effects are clear. Now each year more people are retiring than are entering the labor market. With fewer people available to take existing jobs—and all the surplus labor already incorporated into the industrial economy—rising wages are no longer pushed down by the entry of new workers.

This means that rising wages are here to stay. Even if the growth rate of China's economy were zero and there were no additional demand for labor, China's shrinking population would keep driving wages upward—for a long time.

Thus the truth is that China has already ridden the low-wage manufacturing ladder as far as is possible. It was useful—it got China to middle-income status. But that strategy won't work any longer. Wages are not coming down anytime soon—certainly not far enough to bring back the factories that are moving elsewhere. For those factories that will not or cannot move, rising wages are giving factory owners a strong incentive to search for ways to mechanize and to replace their workers. All of this means that China's future cannot be in low-skilled manufacturing. That window of opportunity has closed.

The Next Path to Prosperity

Why is this a problem? Can't China just move across the Chutes and Ladders board and find another ladder? After all, the exodus of the factories is a milestone in China's development, marking the elimination of most of the nation's poverty, the building of modern infrastructure on a large scale, and the rising living standard of everyone in the country. If China no longer has the kind of economy that supports a still-poor country, that makes sense: it's not so poor anymore.

But this turning point is also a challenge. For one thing, the departure of the factories and the slowing of construction, mining, and road building leaves a vacuum: over the next decade millions of workers will lose the jobs they have now. What will they do instead?

This turning point also means that China is entering a world in which the old rules no longer apply. The old engine of growth (low-wage manufacturing) is not coming back. To maintain the progress that has been made, China will need to adapt and to figure out a new strategy.

Luckily, history holds some important lessons. As we know, not many countries have done this—made it through the middle-income section of the game board and arrived at high income. But a few have done it. This is exactly what the other Asian Tigers (Taiwan and South Korea, for example) did. It's also the strategy that worked for Ireland, Israel, and New Zealand. In this chapter I focus on the recent economic history of Taiwan—a good choice given its similarity to Mainland China—to get a sense of what a successful push from middle income to high income might look like.

Just like China, not so long ago Taiwan was poor. At the end of World War II, Taiwan was a shambles. Also like China, Taiwan's first growth surge happened in unskilled manufacturing. Starting in the 1960s and 1970s, Taiwan started climbing the low-wage manufacturing ladder. Before "Made in China" ruled the world, many of the same products were "Made in Taiwan." Taiwanese (and South Korean) products filled the aisles of Sears then in the same way Chinese products filled the emerging Walmart in the 1990s. It worked: Taiwan quickly made it to middle income.

Then, of course, the turning point came—the same turning point China is at today. By the 1980s, after years of growth, virtually everyone in Taiwan had a job. The labor surplus had been all but used up. Taiwan in the early 1980s was where China was in 2010. The only way Taiwanese manufacturers could keep their workers was to offer higher wages. The rising wage rate quickly impinged on profits, so manufacturers of products made or assembled with low-skilled labor—toys and textiles and simple electronics—responded by moving their factories out of Taiwan and into countries with lower wages.

From 1986 to 1989, Taiwan lost about 300,000 manufacturing jobs. From 1990 to 1998, 80,000 Taiwanese businesses moved offshore, half of them relocating right across the strait to China. With workers in Mainland China willing to work for a small fraction of what Taiwanese workers commanded, it was an easy choice.[11]

But so what? If you visit Taiwan today, you'll find a bustling economy with good jobs, high living standards, and stability. It seems Taiwan did just fine. How did Taiwan navigate this turning point?

To deal with rising wages, Taiwan moved up the supply chain. Rather than distinguishing themselves in global competition by the low price of their workers, Taiwanese companies were able to start distinguishing themselves by the quality of their products, the novelty of their inventions, and the prestige of their brands. Led by pathbreaking companies like Acer, Morse Chain, and LCY, Taiwan's economy surged. By 1990 Taiwan made 30 percent of all the world's computer monitors. These monitors became clearer, bigger, and shinier every year. During the same years, the country became the leader in silicon chip design and manufacture. The list goes on. People began to equate Taiwan with good-quality, high-end electronics.[12]

The Taiwanese economy also greatly expanded its service sector. In the 1980s and 1990s, as the share of the population working in manufacturing fell, the share working in the high-end service sector rose dramatically, quickly reaching almost half of the national labor force. In the 1970s when I was a student in Taiwan, Taipei was known for its shabby restaurants, night markets, and street hawkers. Today people from all over the world go to Taiwan to eat some of the best Chinese food in the world in the most remarkable dining settings anywhere.[13]

This pivot was so successful that unemployment did not rise. In fact, in this surge from middle to high income, Taiwan's unemployment rate stayed as close to zero as possible. Everyone in the economy benefited: the entrepreneurs, the new investors from across the Strait and their management teams, *and* the workers—both higher- and lower-skilled. With wages rising and with new job opportunities for all, not only did per capita income rise, inequality fell.[14]

Thus, in just a few decades Taiwan made the jump across all three phases of the development pathway. Starting as a poor economy with most of the population working in agriculture, by the 1980s Taiwan had ridden the ladder of low-skilled manufacturing to middle income, then made the final climb to the top of the game board to become high income. By the late 1990s, Taiwan's miraculous transformation was complete. Today Taiwan has living standards comparable to the world's rich nations, strong institutions, and a thoroughly modern economy. According to the World Bank, the nation is now richer than its former colonizer, Japan. Against all odds, Taiwan won the game of Chutes and Ladders.

Almost exactly the same thing happened in South Korea. You could replace "Taiwan" with "South Korea" and with almost no additional editing this story would still be true. Like Taiwan, South Korea went from being one of the poorest countries in the world to having high per capita income in a matter of three decades. And its companies also made the final jump by moving up the supply chain and distinguishing themselves by their skills and innovations. Another lucky winner of the Chutes and Ladders game.

A similar story could be told for Ireland. Ireland was a fairly poor agricultural country in the post–World War II era. During the 1950s it experienced a decade-long recession and was truly in the ranks of poor (or lower-middle-income) countries. But starting in the 1960s,

Ireland began to climb out of poverty thanks to the same ladder of low-wage manufacturing and (in Ireland's case) export-oriented agriculture. As it shipped textiles and processed foods to richer countries, growth increased in the 1960s and 1970s. Joining the European Union in 1973 clearly boosted its fortunes in the late 1970s and 1980s, but Ireland did most of the climbing on its own. In the 1990s and 2000s, in textbook style, the nation's economy pivoted from a low-wage, low-skilled, farm-based economy to become one of Europe's booming high-tech centers. It's more than a free-trade zone: in 2013 it was named by *Forbes* as the best place in Europe to do business. Ireland occupies one of the highest rankings in the world on the United Nations' Human Development Index, taking eighth place among all nations. According to the World Bank, Ireland's per capita income is now much higher than that of the United States or any other European country except Luxembourg and Lichtenstein. It has been an unlikely winner at Chutes and Ladders, too.[15]

The Billion-Dollar Question

There is nothing China would rather do—admit it or not—than follow the development path of its renegade island province. But will China be able to repeat the Taiwan/South Korea/Ireland miracle?

I believe Taiwan's success (and the success of the other graduates) depended on two complementary sets of workforce skills. One, it needed a highly skilled group of elite business leaders and entrepreneurs to head the economic transition. It needed the engineers, the venture capitalists, the designers, and the people with the ideas and the drive to make new inventions, or create new brands, and lead the way. These are the people who headed all the top brands that have made Taiwan a buzzword for high-quality design and technology around the world.

On this metric—the quality of the country's most highly skilled businesspeople, technical workers, and entrepreneurs—few will disagree that China is well prepared. In China's high-tech sector, for example, innovation has already become a thriving pillar of the economy. Initially there were a lot of naysayers. Many outsiders were quick to downplay this progress, pointing out that some of these companies grew only by borrowing (or stealing) the ideas of foreign companies: Baidu copied Google, Ctrip copied TripAdvisor, and Youku copied YouTube.[16]

Although this may once have been true, today China's high-tech sector is far past the point of mimicry. Alibaba may have gotten its start as a sort of Chinese Amazon, but it is now developing on its own as well as changing China and the world. Today, Alibaba handles more business than eBay and Amazon combined. China's other Internet giant, Tencent, is also world class. Tencent's social media app, WeChat, has earned such a reputation for innovation that Western companies like Facebook, Snapchat, and WhatsApp now try to copy its features. On their own merits, Alibaba and Tencent have become companies to watch the world over, with growth rates in 2017 surpassing both Facebook and Google. As far as innovation goes, then, it seems that China can likely handle the challenge.[17]

Once the people at the top (the inventors, designers, and entrepreneurs) start new companies, they also need to find key technicians and managers. China also seems well situated when it comes to a crop of highly skilled workers for new and innovative companies. There are now more than eight million new college graduates in China each year. Crucially, a large contingent of these college graduates are being trained in STEM fields. Chinese universities graduate four to five million students with engineering majors every year. In addition, more than 500,000 students are being trained outside China in many of the world's top universities. Many of these expatriates may choose to stay abroad rather than return to China, but many will go home and put their skills to use in China's budding industries.[18]

However, while having this cadre of elite businesspeople, investors, programming geniuses, and engineering stars is necessary, it's not sufficient. That's a key argument of this book. It was not just these headliner companies that produced Taiwan's shift from a middle-income to a high-income country across the 1980s and 1990s. It takes more than a handful of firms, even if they are large and successful. It takes efforts by everyone in the economy to shift jobs, start up new and needed businesses, and shut down those that cannot be sustained. Workers need to learn new skills. Individual entrepreneurs need to cater to new needs and work in new environments.

Thus, to follow the path of Taiwan, South Korea, Ireland, or any of the other graduates, China will also need a broader set of human resources. It needs the country's general labor force to be able to move into those new creative and higher-value-added jobs too—not just the elites.

At the time of Taiwan's transition, most workers were still doing low- to medium-skilled work. To be successful through this transition, those same workers had to be able to leave the factory floor and move into accounting jobs, or go from twelve hours a day making the same pattern on a sewing machine to operating a precision chip design machine. They needed to move from the regimented life on a construction site into handling the dynamic, ever-changing demands of high-end service sector jobs. The economies of Taiwan and South Korea and Ireland could not collectively move up the supply chain unless their workers were prepared to do higher-value-added work.

In general, what's required to take on that more skilled work is pretty simple: high-quality education. The skills required in these new jobs—flexibility, complex thinking, and good judgment—are the skills a formal education prepares you for. A robust literature has shown that it is the importance of formal education for this exact set of workplace skills that is behind the recent phenomenon of skill-biased technical change.[19]

Whereas low-wage factory workers and construction workers in poor countries do work that is routine (much the same every day), workers in high-income economies must be prepared to be flexible. High-income, modern, high-skilled economies change rapidly. That's why it's so important for workers to know *how to learn*. Jobs change. Workers switch jobs. They get assigned new tasks. As technological change happens, employees are expected to master new technologies that can be incorporated into their jobs. They have to be ready for whatever comes down the pike.

This is a big difference. If workers in a mobile phone assembly factory switch jobs, it takes minutes to teach them their new jobs, and they are up to their maximum output after three days. This is not true of the jobs that power a modern, high-income economy. Let me use my son, who was raised in the United States, as an example. After graduating from a public university, he got his first job in something as basic as sales. However, this was not a static job that once learned was always known. Over the course of five years, my son switched jobs four times. He went from selling memberships in an upscale gym, to being an online customer relations manager, to working in sports, then back to the gym. Each of those job changes required flexibility, learning a new industry, acquiring a new set of skills, mastering a new product, and interacting with people in a completely different way. To do that my son needed math skills, computer skills, critical-thinking skills, and creativity. That's the kind of thing that workers in a rich country are expected to be able to handle, and that is difficult to manage without (at least) a high school education.

Taiwan and South Korea and Ireland were lucky—or they had a great deal of foresight. All those workers who initially had been in jobs that didn't require high levels of education—the factory workers, construction workers, and miners—almost all had a good education anyway.

Each of these countries had made the choice at the highest level of government to expand and encourage education for all their citizens. In the late 1970s and early 1980s when the low-skilled wage rate was still one to two dollars an hour, nearly everyone in Taiwan and South Korea was attending high school. When Ireland was still poor in the 1950s, the educational attainment of its labor force ranked among the lowest in the world. But as it started to look to the future in the 1960s, one of the country's best strategic moves was to invest huge amounts in public education—even when it was still relatively poor. By 1995, fully half of Ireland's labor force under thirty-five years old was graduating from college. In the 1980s and 1990s, almost every youth in Ireland was going to high school.[20]

Ireland (and the other graduates) invested so much in education that it moved from a country with a relatively low-skilled labor force to a high-skilled one by global standards. That is what prepared Ireland to become a hot spot of high-tech industry in the 1990s and 2000s. Although Ireland's leaders did many things to create this development success story, many still cite Ireland's radical push for educational reform in the 1960s—before joining the European Union and before becoming middle income—as a critical element. Like Taiwan and South Korea, a highly educated labor force gave the nation's economy the engine to drive itself up the last part of the game board.[21]

Why did leaders in these countries do this? Why did they send a large share of youth to high school when—at least initially—they didn't need these skills to be successful in the labor market? They were truly putting into action something that Eric Hanushek, my colleague at Stanford and one of the first economists to focus on the study of education, often says: "Officials should not be asking what impact my investment into education will have on the economy today. Education investments are for the economy twenty years from now."

The question that keeps me up at night is this: Will the common worker be able to find stable employment in China's new economy? If not, can China really afford to float its entire economy on the innovation and industry of such a tiny portion of its people?

3: The Worst-Case Scenario

In spring 2016 I got a close-up view of China's coming labor transition. It was an unexpected opportunity. I was in the city of Wuhan in central China for a series of meetings, and as the first day wrapped up, a fellow economist told me he was on his way to a local job fair. One of the major state conglomerates, Wuhan Iron and Steel, had just announced it would be laying off fifty thousand workers. The layoffs would mean big changes to the local economy. It seemed like a shadow of the impending labor transition we both knew China was headed for. The job fair had been set up for the laid-off employees, and he was curious to see how the rehiring was working out. He invited me to tag along.

We took a cab across the city to a convention center filled with hundreds of booths representing companies looking to hire. We fell into conversation with one man in particular. Mr. Wang was about thirty-five and had recently been laid off from his job of eighteen years as an electrician.

As we watched, Mr. Wang gamely sidled up to the first booth, which represented a bank. The man running the booth, a human resources staff member, shook his hand and asked him to read a short page of text and comment on what he understood. Mr. Wang stared hard at the piece of paper, trying to force the characters into an order he could understand. He knew all the words and could read them aloud, but many of the terms were over his head. He kept getting confused by the logic of the sentences. For several minutes he stared at it, trying to make sense of what he was seeing. At first the man running the booth was patient and seemed sympathetic, but gradually the bank representative lost interest, turned back to his desk, and started looking around for workers who might be a better bet. After a few more minutes, Mr. Wang lowered his head with a sigh: "I'm sorry, I just can't make sense of it."

Now with less spring in his step, Mr. Wang turned to the next booth in the long line. This booth was for an accounting firm. All he had to do, the representative told him, was to fill out a worksheet of simple calculations. Mr. Wang leaned over the desk, gripping the small pencil, and stared hard at the numbers. He filled in a few answers, but he wasn't sure they were accurate. After a few minutes he glanced around nervously, laid down the pencil, and quietly stepped away.

A few hours later we ran into Mr. Wang in another part of the fair. "How did it go?" I asked him. "Did you find any good prospects?"

Mr. Wang heaved a great sigh and shook his head slowly. "I just can't seem to handle any of the tasks they've set for me," he said. "I think it's been too long. I just don't know how to manage this kind of work."

"So what are you going to do?" I asked.

He frowned and shrugged. "I just don't know. I was just talking to one of my coworkers from the steel mill. He told me I should get a job as a delivery boy. That's what he's going to do. I know that would pay the bills and keep my family afloat. But I can't even imagine it, riding around eighty hours a week in the wind and the rain and the mud," he said, shifting his bag on his shoulder. "Am I supposed to just compete with all the other desperate migrants in this town? I mean, I used to work for one of the most prestigious steel mills in China. I was good at my job. I never thought it would come to this." With another sigh, he mumbled, "I really don't know what I'm going to do." With that, he trudged out of the fair.

Mr. Wang is facing the challenge that is soon going to affect many people across China. China has reached its turning point. Whether by offshoring or by automation, the country's low-skilled jobs are soon going to disappear by the millions. A massive vacuum will be left in their wake—one that may be very hard for China to fill.

As many observers are quick to point out, China does have the ability to create new jobs, a process that's already beginning. In the tech industry, the high-end manufacturing industry, and the service sector more generally, new white-collar jobs are appearing quickly. There are lots of people ready to snap them up, too. This process will likely continue for a while. In the short term, the main problem is not likely to be a supply-side constraint.

But just as in other high-income developed countries in the twenty-first century, in China the new jobs will call almost exclusively for high-skilled workers. Some low-skilled jobs will remain, of course. Even a rich country requires janitors and waiters and delivery people. But the numbers simply don't add up. A high-income, dynamic modern economy can employ only a relatively small share of its population in unskilled jobs. In China today there are far too many unskilled people.

The inconvenient truth is that most of China's population does not have the skills to move up the supply chain or to swap a blue collar for a white one. As we've seen, currently about 70 percent of the Chinese labor force is "unskilled"—with no more than a junior high school education. Many of those with a high school degree or better will likely be able to find work in China's rapidly growing high-tech sector or in the nascent modern services sector. Those who have the basics of a good high school education and are willing and able to learn a new skill in a new sector of the economy should be fine. But what of all the people without even a basic modern education? With such a limited education, their ability to learn how to learn will likely be limited; many may be difficult, if not impossible, to retrain. Like Mr. Wang, they are simply not up to the tasks that employers are going to ask of them. If my analysis is correct, then China is heading for a massive polarization of the economy in the coming decades. Based on the numbers, two or three hundred million people may be rendered structurally unemployable.[1]

The Dangers of Polarization

When I describe the potential catastrophe facing China owing to this human capital problem, many people—particularly in China—tell me there has to be something wrong with my prognosis.

I can understand why they push back. China's elites are doing so well, and are so much more visible than the rural masses, that it's hard to believe China could really be in trouble. As many people tell me, "China has more engineers than anyone. More than six million of our students are graduating from college every year. We have enough brains and entrepreneurs and computer programmers to pull China into the middle of the twenty-first century. Who cares if a few peasants aren't making so much money? We're going to be fine!"

If only that were the case. It may well be that China's elites—the 30 percent of the labor force with a high school education, or the 12.5 percent or more who have been to college—will continue to do well. They can innovate, they can move up the supply chain, and they can compete on the world stage. But that may not be enough to keep China moving up the Chutes and Ladders board.

The future is hard to predict. Macroeconomic predictions are famously difficult, and many factors could tip China one way or the other—factors we can't even see from today's vantage point. I still hope China will be able to figure out a new strategy and avoid unprecedented layoffs, with the economic and social turmoil those layoffs could cause. China certainly has pulled off unforeseen economic miracles in the past.

But the risks are very great. There's reason to believe that a polarized labor force poses a real threat to China's economy—no matter how good the prospects at the elite level.

Polarization is dangerous for several reasons. First, it's likely to inhibit growth. It is a well-proven fact that it's always harder for high-income countries to grow than it is for low- and middle-income countries. But if China's labor force ends up polarized, a large proportion of workers will be left out, and China will have two to three hundred million fewer people available to power its much-needed economic growth. If so many people are left unemployed, underemployed, or otherwise unable to provide for themselves, the crisis will drain public resources that could otherwise be spent on investments targeted to growing the economy.

Second, having a poorly educated labor force may reduce incentives to invest in China. In our globalized world, work tends to flow to the countries whose people are best able to handle it. China will be stuck in no-man's-land, with wages too high for low-wage work and skills too low for large-scale high-wage work. That may mean less investment and less willingness to start new companies in China. Investors will go somewhere else. That combination of forces could inhibit economic growth for decades to come.

Other dynamics associated with such large-scale polarization have the potential to further stall economic progress. To start to understand this issue, let's think about it from the perspective of the people who are soon to be laid off—the Mr. Wangs of the world or, more generally, the unskilled rural workers.

For the past several decades, China's unskilled rural workers, all in all, have had a pretty good deal. I don't mean life for the common Chinese worker has been easy. Working in the trenches of China's rise—in the factories, the mines, and the construction sites that have powered this behemoth—has required tenacity and sacrifice. Many families have been separated in the race to move up in the economic world.

But still, in spite of the hardships, this period has been deeply hopeful. China is rising, gaining more power and prestige in the world than it has had in centuries, and most ordinary Chinese families have been able to trust that they are rising too. For this entire period, it didn't matter how much education they had or where they came from; so long as they were willing to work hard, they could succeed. Most people in the country have seen economic progress within their own families, with sons outearning fathers and daughters outearning mothers.

But very soon, thanks to the inevitable upward movement in China's wage rate, that miracle may grind to a halt for a huge proportion of China's people. As wages continue to rise, rural workers will see the low-skilled jobs that have been their bread and butter disappear. Recall that the demographic effects will ensure that China's unskilled wage rate is not going to fall anytime soon. China's population is aging, and its surplus labor has been completely used up.

No matter what happens on the demand side, rising wages are here to stay. The factories are not coming back.

With higher wages, any new companies opening up are going to have much higher expectations of their workers. As Mr. Wang found at the job fair, these companies will expect their workers to be able to read briefs and Excel spreadsheets, to think on their feet, and to make creative decisions. They will expect them to handle computers and to speak English, to learn new jobs and be flexible and productive across a wide variety of tasks. And so, suddenly, after decades of opening their doors to any worker with two strong arms and a good work ethic, China's companies are going to start demanding qualities that most of China's labor force simply don't have (and can't easily acquire): high levels of human capital.

Certainly some of the currently unskilled may be able to go back and get a bit more education. Adult retraining programs will be available. But adult training programs in developing countries almost never succeed. China's leaders are being naive if they think they can wait until 2030 to launch a massive adult training initiative and upgrade the labor force's skill level and ability to learn. It won't happen. It's true that a small share of the uneducated likely are naturally gifted. Indeed, when these few complete their training, they should be able to move into those higher-skilled fields. But for most of the unskilled, that ship has sailed. They didn't have good-enough education, health, or nutrition when they were children to handle the demands of schooling today. Not having a degree is going to be a barrier they cannot cross.[2]

What options will they have, then?

China's economy will still need some low-skilled workers. As Mr. Wang's colleague was considering, they can move from a job in the steel mill to a job as a delivery boy, security guard, or nanny. Certainly some people will choose to do this.

But these are lower-status jobs, with less pay, no benefits, and less stability than anything these workers have experienced. Will they be satisfied with that change in status? It's just going to get worse. Once the millions of factory workers and construction workers are laid off, just about everyone in the country with education below the level of high school (which, as I said, is almost everyone) is going to be competing for these low-skill jobs. That will drive down wages and further lower the status of these jobs. Like Mr. Wang, these workers will feel that their hopes for the future have been dashed.

What other options are there? One thing most of these laid-off rural workers will *not* do is go back to the farm. Farms in China are very small (the legacy of land redistribution under the Communists), so even if they wanted to go back, they would struggle to scrape out a living. What's more, most of the rural people who came of age in the past few decades have never known farm life—they migrated to the cities to find employment in the factories as soon as they were old enough to work. Thus it seems inevitable that very few will be content to return to that life, having known higher incomes and urban comforts. In 2015 I did a survey in an electronics factory to try to understand the perspective of China's factory workers. In that survey my team asked over one thousand randomly selected factory workers where they wanted to be in ten to twenty years. Fewer than 1 percent said they would go back to the farm. Most of them laughed at this question.

One man in his sixties pulled me aside to ask why we even included that question on the survey. I asked why it seemed so ridiculous. He told me straightforwardly, "My children will never go back and farm. We only have one acre of land. Before I left the farm for this factory, even when I worked hard all year in the fields, I made less than my son makes in a month at his job in the city. Not only that, it's hard and dirty work. No one in our village wants their children to become farmers. Who knows what will become of our village when my generation gets too old to keep working."

So if they can't get low-skilled jobs in the formal sector and aren't willing to go back to the farm, what choice will they have? For many of the structurally unemployable, there will be only one real option: the informal sector.

The informal sector describes the part of the economy where workers do not have regular salaried jobs with benefits and set contracts. These are generally small businesses (or microfirms), often one person working alone. In some cases that person may employ a family member, a friend, or a neighbor or two. Think of a small food stand or tiny moving company or even the individuals in so many countries who stand at intersections and wash windshields for a few coins. These jobs are open to just about anyone, because they don't rely on credentials or job interviews. In that 2015 survey in an electronics factory, most of the workers responded that in ten to twenty years they wanted to be running their own business (or microfirm). Almost none of them wanted to still be working in a factory, and very few thought they had any chance of moving into white-collar work. It's likely that many people will choose the informal economy—selling fried noodles in alleys or working as trash collectors, recyclers, window washers, or gardeners.

Again, these workers will be stuck with stagnant wage rates and falling earnings. And when you work for yourself on the sidewalk, it will be a job without stability or benefits. For ninety-nine out of a hundred, there will likely be no prospect of upward mobility.

The rise of the informal sector could also be bad for China's economy in general. Its growth—if it gets big enough—may hurt the formal sector (all the ordinary jobs in the economy). The informal sector can undermine brands, undercut intellectual property, and (most important), because by definition informal sector jobs do not pay taxes, it can weaken the safety net for everyone—effectively penalizing people (and companies) for going into the formal economy. Because informal firms are themselves less productive, they push down the productivity of the economy overall. And since informal businesses are not taxed, the informal sector also cuts into government revenues that could otherwise be spent on mitigating social problems or investing in the future.

The costs of this polarization do not necessarily end there. We have yet to take into account the social costs of these choices. The three options I laid out above are all likely to be deeply unsatisfying for most of China's workers. For decades these workers have believed the future would be brighter. But none of these jobs are likely to lead to upward mobility. None are likely to yield much status or even basic respect. Like Mr. Wang, workers will find that all the expectations they have lived by can no longer be taken for granted. He was not expecting to need to switch jobs during his working life. He had no idea that after decades of feeling useful in a good and stable job, he was going to be told he no longer had a place in China's future. After decades of hope, this transition could unleash great despair and resentment.

What will happen if many people suddenly discover they can no longer count on things getting better? Human psychology is strange: losing out on something you expected often hurts more than simply never having it. When people are faced with disappointment and helplessness, they often get angry, and it's easy to see how they could turn against their neighbors, fighting over scraps rather than investing in an expanding pie for everyone. This may be the strongest single force behind the middle-income trap: the loss of hope.

It is simply dangerous to have such a large class of disempowered and economically underutilized citizens. Many individuals—in spite of their disappointments and uncertainties—will persevere and lead the lives of law-abiding citizens. But I think it's entirely possible that some workers will be so disappointed in the fall of this ideal, and so dissatisfied with their meager prospects on the farm or in the informal economy, that they could be pushed outside the system entirely. I worry that this dissatisfaction may lead some to turn to crime or even to form organized gangs. It may be hard to believe that this could happen in China. But if their dreams and their belief that life will get better start to fade, some may take this more radical route. If they want to feel respected, to feel powerful, and to make good money again, they may decide their only choice is to take matters into their own hands.

This is not as far-fetched as it sounds. It has long been understood by crime researchers that crime trends closely follow jobless rates. At the individual level, this choice makes sense. If you can't find a job in the formal sector and are stuck competing with other small vendors to make chump change, who wouldn't look for an easier way?

If this does come to pass, it will set off a vicious downward spiral. The rise of crime will further reduce the economy's ability to grow.

Rising crime tends to make outside companies even less willing to invest. Who wants to set up shop in a place where all the cars need bulletproof glass and your workers may be held up on the way to the office? Small businesses spend time and resources dealing with the risk of being caught up in webs of extortion and blackmail. Crime reduces consumption in the service sector as people become afraid to go out at night or to visit different parts of the country. All this would likely reduce government revenue (it's difficult to tax the informal sector and impossible to tax the gangs) and increases costs for policing crime and for repairing damage from the violence. Because of this, the government would be financially less and less able to cope with formal unemployment and the other consequences of closing factories and construction sites.

Thus China's coming polarization may lead to an inescapable trap. If the nation finds itself with large segments of its population unemployed, underemployed, tied up in the informal sector, or even turning to crime, it may not be able to bring back the economic growth it needs to get out of this mess. The social and economic costs could be incredible.

The Case of Mexico

Although I am certainly not arguing that large-scale polarization and its potentially catastrophic consequences are a done deal for China (which, again, has showed an amazing ability to avoid catastrophes in its economic development path over the past forty years), this scenario is not just hypothetical. If China falls into a downward economic spiral as a result of low human capital and wide job polarization, it will be following in the footsteps of other middle-income countries that have fallen down this exact chute.

Let's talk about one country that has been where China is today and ended up in a very different place than the graduates we looked at in the previous chapter: Mexico.

Just like China, and Taiwan and South Korea before it, Mexico chose to ride our old favorite ladder out of poverty, growing through the expansion of low-wage, labor-intensive manufacturing (and a lot of associated construction). In the late 1970s and early 1980s, wages of about one dollar an hour attracted growing numbers of international companies to assemble their goods in Mexico's proliferating *maquiladoras*. This surge increased after the signing of the North American Free Trade Agreement (NAFTA) provided new access at reduced cost to the valuable American and Canadian consumer markets. Mexico emerged in the early 1990s as one of the world's largest producers of auto parts. Textiles were being produced all along the United States–Mexico border. At the end of this golden window, Mexico was the only developing country (other than China) to be ranked as one of the top ten exporting countries in the world.[3]

This strategy paid off for Mexico, just as it did for Taiwan, South Korea, and China. Mexico grew very quickly from a relatively poor country in the 1960s to one that was middle income by the early 1990s. This strategy worked so well that Mexico was widely expected to be the "next Taiwan." In 1990 the *Vancouver Sun* echoed common sentiment, reporting that "once-backward Mexico has fashioned the beginning of an economic miracle it hopes will propel it from the Third World into the ranks of developed nations." At the very apex of its rapid growth and development, optimism was so high that Mexico was admitted to the OECD. It seemed to deserve the name given to it by then-president Carlos Salinas de Gortari at the end of 1990: "the country of mañana."[4]

Then Mexico reached its turning point. Surplus labor gradually dried up because most young, able-bodied Mexicans were already working. That pushed up Mexico's wages right at the time when China was beginning to open its doors to foreign direct investment and trade. Since at that time China's wage rate was lower than Mexico's (in fact much, much lower), the low-wage jobs poured out of Mexico. From 2001 to 2004, Mexico lost an estimated 400,000 jobs to China. Over the course of just three years, the once-dominant Mexican textiles industry was supplanted by China as the number one exporter to the US market, and more than a third of Mexican factories assembling clothing were shut down. Many low-wage industries also contracted sharply. By 2000 "Made in Mexico" was fast disappearing from Walmart's shelves.[5]

As we've seen, this turning point is inevitable for any country riding this particular ladder of growth in a globalized world. There was no reason this turning point should necessarily have meant the end of Mexico's stellar growth. Mexico simply needed to pivot, like Taiwan and South Korea (and Ireland and Hong Kong and Singapore). But in Mexico that pivot never took place.

Instead, Mexico's progress broke down. As the factories began to leave, Mexico's economy faltered, then stagnated, and today has still never recovered. For the past two decades, per capita economic growth has hovered just above 1 percent (in the most optimistic accounting rules), much slower than would be expected for a country with Mexico's level of development. In the metrics that matter most for a growing economy, Mexico has also fallen behind. Rising productivity—getting more economic output from fewer inputs through new technologies and better management approaches—is a sign of a healthy economy. But productivity in Mexico has been consistently stagnant or declining across this period.[6]

The result is that Mexico has never broken free of the middle-income trap. In fact, taking into account the growth of other countries in this period, it is falling further and further behind. Along the way, Mexico has lost global power. Its people's lives have worsened by many metrics, with half the population living in poverty and crime running rampant. Today the idea that Mexico might have been the next Taiwan seems laughable. Mañana is now here, and Mexico's miracle never materialized. In spite of high hopes, Mexico is trapped.

I believe a big part of the reason for this divergence is exactly the set of circumstances I laid out above. At the time of its transition, Mexico had low general human capital in its labor force. In the early 2000s, when the factory jobs first began to disappear, only about 30 percent of the Mexican workforce had a high school education or higher. The average worker had only eight years of education at the time.[7]

More specifically, just like China's, Mexico's human capital was highly polarized. Mexico did have a contingent of the population with a high-quality, twenty-first-century education. When the transition came, those people were mostly able to find jobs. A large majority of the labor force, however, had no more than junior high school skills. Even today the distribution of education levels in Mexico's population has two peaks: one group averages at least fifteen years of education, the other group has eight years or less. That polarization in education led to labor polarization, setting off the exact set of dangerous economic and social effects that may be lurking in China's future.[8]

Investors pulling their factories out of Mexico in the early 2000s not only cited rising wages; they also said it was not worth staying in Mexico and upgrading their factories because of the low education level of the workforce. Given that the *average* worker had no more than a middle schooler's skill level, this should come as no surprise. How could those workers be expected to move up the supply chain or take on white-collar jobs? Why would any investor set up a new business in Mexico when there were so many other places to choose from where the people had better skills?[9]

Excluded from formal work, many in Mexico had little choice but to turn to the informal sector. Indeed, for more than two decades Mexico's informal sector has been steadily growing. Right as the factories began to leave Mexico in droves, employment in the informal sector rose, then skyrocketed. In fact, from 1998 to 2013, employment in that sector grew by an astonishing 115 percent. Today, fully half of Mexico's population is employed in the informal sector. In poor areas, things are even worse. In Mexico's poorest state (Chiapas), fully 80 percent of the population works in the informal sector.[10]

An article from *Mother Jones* in 2003 documented some of the paths people took when their factories suddenly closed. After Fela Contreras, fifty, was laid off from a Sony Corporation plant in 1998 (when Sony moved its factories to China), her only option was to start selling tacos and crafts at her local flea market. In the previously factory-filled border town of Nuevo Laredo, the exodus of the factories was accompanied by a sharp rise in the number of vendors and hawkers working the main street and windshield washers with rags hoping for a few pesos. This was life for Mexico's increasing number of informal workers.[11]

The rise of the informal sector has been a major drag for the Mexican economy (or shall we say a steep and slippery chute). Two influential economists—Santiago Levy at the Inter-American Development Bank and Daniel Rodrik, a Harvard professor—have argued that the growth of the informal sector has been a big factor in Mexico's lackluster economic performance. The informal sector is much less efficient than the formal sector, it actively undermines the formal sector, and it weakens the social safety net. The cumulative employment growth in Mexico's informal sector from 1998 to 2013, 115 percent, is much higher than the growth in the formal economy in the same period, 6 percent. Because it is much harder to tax, Mexico's informal sector has dramatically reduced the revenue the government can draw on to deal with social problems or to make long-run investments. In the state of Chiapas, for example, the fact that 80 percent of the local population is in the informal sector means that the state government can recoup only a paltry 1.5 percent of its budget through taxes. The result is major downward pressure on the economy by the forces operating among the unskilled masses.[12]

Mexico's problems did not stop there. As predicted, many other people who were excluded from Mexico's economy turned to crime. From 2000 to 2010, business theft and extortion increased dramatically. From 2007 to 2014, more than 150,000 people were killed in Mexico as part of the violence that now permeates large segments of the country. This is higher than the number of civilians killed in Afghanistan and Iraq over the same period. The murder rates in Mexico are three to four times the US rates (and the United States is already known around the world for its high murder rates). Today Mexico is known less for the quality of its innovations or technology than for the terror of its gang violence.[13]

The incentives to turn to crime were clearly strong. Back in the border town of Nuevo Laredo in 2003, when Braulio Pavon was laid off, all he could find to do to support his family was to spend his nights in the intersections, rag in hand, washing windshields. As he noted, while many people who were left out turned to these jobs in the informal sector, many more were driven even further outside the establishment. At the time Pavon said, "You're pushing me to be a robber." Sure enough, as the number of informal workers rose in his town, so did the crime rate. Joining a gang, too, is a choice that can start to make sense when times are hard. In Michoacán, a Mexican state where organized crime has a large and violent presence, an unskilled worker might earn about US$175 a month in difficult, unsteady work in the informal sector. But that same worker might earn three times as much by working for a local gang.[14]

The effects on the economy—and on human well-being—have been devastating. In Mexico, high levels of violence have pushed many to emigrate for safety. Rising crime rates have also suppressed investment, reduced consumption in the service sector, and in many cases forced people out of the labor market altogether, driving up unemployment rates. The government also has had to bear immeasurable costs of policing and damage repair, taking money away from more growth-oriented investments. With the rise of crime and the drug trade comes an associated rise in corruption of the police force and other government entities, making it that much more difficult to maintain the rule of law that a healthy economy depends on.[15]

The result is that the polarization of Mexico's labor force contributed to a vicious downward spiral. These effects were so big—so many people were stuck in this limbo—that Mexico got trapped. It didn't matter that there were some good companies and highly skilled people doing well at the top. The force of the structurally unemployable was too strong.

Here I have told the story of Mexico. But many other countries have followed a similar path, with very similar forces playing out owing to an insufficient foundation of human capital. Brazil's stagnation has launched both a huge informal economy and high levels of organized crime. South Africa is the same. Turkey is headed that way. Thailand cannot break out of the middle-income trap, and the economy is becoming dominated by the informal sector, undermining systematic efforts to promote formal sector growth. It remains to be seen whether China can avoid the same.

What about China?

Whenever I make this argument in a presentation, at this point I always get the same pushback: "China and Mexico are very different." "That could never happen in China." "China's rural workers will never turn to crime!"

It's true there are fundamental differences between Mexico and China. Mexico's rising crime was in part due to its proximity to the lucrative drug market of the United States. More recently it has been fueled by the emerging opioid crisis. That's a factor China might not have to face. In addition, there are of course cultural differences between Mexico and China that many people believe will prove significant. But overall I believe the forces that drove Mexico (and Brazil and South Africa) into the middle-income trap could very easily push China into the same position. This is not a cultural but an economic trap. Let's not forget, for all the talk of fundamental cultural differences between Mexico and China, Triads (China's version of the mob) first emerged thousands of years ago and have persisted ever since.

China has one more critical issue that may make a turn to crime or gang violence even more likely: about forty million extra men. What are "extra men"? Well, as most people know, for many years China's population was drastically curtailed through the One Child Policy. What is less well known is that this policy also led to a dramatic male-female sex imbalance in birthrates. The divide began to open up shortly after the One Child Policy was put in place in 1979, for a variety of reasons. One reason that has been shown to be significant is the traditional preference in rural Chinese culture for sons. Research has shown that as the One Child Policy was becoming more and more binding in many parts of the country—limiting families to only one child—many rural families took advantage of newly available ultrasound technology to have sex-selective abortions: aborting female fetuses at higher rates. This practice was unsanctioned and has since been made illegal, but it was sufficiently widespread to drastically affect demographics for an entire generation. By 2000, birth records showed that about 120 boys were born for every 100 girls. That ratio remained almost unchanged for the next ten years.[16]

The scale of this divide is hard to imagine, and once the children are grown, it may become a dangerous social force in itself. Many of these children have already come of age. The birth cohorts with the largest gender gap are now moving into adulthood as well. They are reaching marriageable age, and thanks to the numbers alone, it is almost inevitable that a huge share of men are going to be left out. The estimates vary (because of differences in the assumptions used to calculate the counterfactual), but it is conceivable that about forty million men will not have a wife or family.

That may have big consequences for China's future stability. Young unmarried men are more likely than married men to engage in crime and join gangs regardless of the circumstances. This is a well-established fact in criminology, and research shows it is also true in China today. But what if China's economy bottoms out? What if all these men do not have the education or the skills they need to find jobs? Jobs give people a sense of connection, a measure of dignity and respect, and status within their communities. If all these men lack the opportunity not only for jobs but also for marriage, what is to keep them from turning to crime in ever-greater numbers?[17]

This is not just speculation about some distant future. China's crime rates have already begun rising. From 1988 to 2004, criminal offenses increased by 14 percent every year. Over the same period, the number of arrests for both property crimes and violent crimes nearly doubled. A recent study showed that a substantial portion of the rise in crime was traceable to the increased male-to-female ratio in the young adult population. As the birth cohorts with the highest ratios reach adulthood, this trend may continue. If economic growth stagnates, unemployment rises, and a large number of unskilled workers are left out of the formal economy, the results could be catastrophic.[18]

In my travels around China, I have already started to hear stories of the first stirrings of this possible trend. Just last year I talked to a young man who had little education and was beginning to have trouble finding a job in his home province. After several minutes he told me directly that he was considering going into crime if he couldn't find a paying job in the coming months.[19]

The stories are bigger than that. In 2016 a friend told me about a town in southern China that is close to some of the biggest industrial centers in the country. This town—like many manufacturing towns in China—had a specialty: manufacturing synthetic materials. The whole town was full of similar factories catering to different markets and producing products of different qualities.

According to my friend, back in 2015 something changed. Who knows what drove the issue for this particular industry—wages were certainly rising, the economy was certainly slowing, and production in a number of China's neighbors was beginning to cut into business. For one or more of these reasons, several factories in this town suddenly closed. Before long there was only one factory left in the entire town—this one factory had a special deal with a group of firms in the United States, so the economic pressures that led other firms in the county to shut down did not affect this particular firm. It kept chugging along, business as usual.

When the factories began to close, the general workers packed up and moved on. They were migrant workers from all over the country and had no particular allegiance or any family ties to this particular town. Some headed off to Shanghai, some went to Chengdu, some to Shenzhen. For now, other places are still hiring—though jobs are not as easy to find as five years ago.

But another group of workers did not take job loss in stride. The managers and line foremen of the closed factories were all locals. They'd grown up in that town and had homes there. Their children went to school there. Many had never left their hometown in their lives. Some had been the foremen of production lines and managers of migrant workers for more than fifteen years. They weren't about to uproot their families and move somewhere else in search of new jobs. They suddenly went from having well-paid, stable jobs to having nothing—and little reason to believe things would get better anytime soon.

One evening after a long day at work, just as dusk had fallen, the managers from the one factory that was still operating got into a shared car to drive home, exactly the routine they followed six days a week, twenty-five days a month. But this time something different happened: a roadblock suddenly appeared. Out came a large group of the fired managers and production line foremen from the other factories. They surrounded the car and said, "Give us your money! We're entitled to it. You've taken what was ours. Now we get to share in the proceeds."

A year later, that one remaining factory is still in operation. But today it has high walls topped with barbed wire. It looks like a great palace surrounded by chaos. Guards escort its workers to and from work every day.

This could be China's future. It appears that the forces burdening Mexico and Brazil are already being felt in some parts of China, I shudder to think what might happen if things get so bad that there's nowhere else for those workers to go.

Mitigating Factors?

Still the question lingers, does labor polarization really matter this much? China is a big country, and it has a very accomplished class of elites. China's colleges produce more engineers than any other country. Several of its universities are among the best in the world. It sends more students to university abroad than any other country, to be educated at the highest levels. In 2018 Chinese students scored highest in the world on the PISA (Programme for International Student Assessment), this time including an even wider swath of citizens. Not for nothing is China seen around the world as a place that puts the highest priority on education. Based on all these factors, many people wonder if China might be able to get by without its uneducated masses. Sure, many people may find themselves structurally unemployable in coming decades, but aren't China's elites strong enough to power the economy on their own and pull the rest of the labor force along with them?

Unfortunately, I think this is unlikely. China may have a very well-educated and high-achieving class of elite workers, but it has far more people who are getting by with little education. As we've seen, our data showed that there are 300 million or more in the labor force today who have not been to high school. When their families are counted—those who rely on them—the number is probably more than 500 or 600 million. For all the reasons I have laid out above, I believe that is simply too many people to try to pacify while they are living with slowed growth, reduced employment options, and the loss of hope.

Perhaps things would be different if China could afford to directly pay off its workers who are soon to be structurally unemployable. One policy idea that has gained a lot of attention in recent years as a potential solution is the notion of a universal basic income. This kind of policy would guarantee that all citizens of a given country would be paid the minimum needed to survive and take care of their families. This would, so the theory goes, help to even out the inequities of twenty-first-century growth by taking some of the excess income of the elites and giving it to the poorest members of society, keeping them afloat and also promoting social and political cohesion. In fact, some countries are starting to talk seriously about putting such policies in place. Finland just undertook a high-level pilot program, whose results are just starting to become available. While its utility has yet to be proved in a real-world setting, universal basic income may be an important policy tool in the future.

Unfortunately for China, this kind of policy is imaginable only for a rich, developed country. China does have the second largest economy in the world today, which leads some people to think of it as a rich country. But in per capita terms, China is very much middle income. Based on its tax base, it simply doesn't have sufficient government revenue to provide for the economic needs of 300 million people. And no matter how strong the Chinese elite, I find it hard to believe there could be enough economic growth anytime soon to change that fundamental reality.

Spain and Portugal (and Greece) may be the exceptions that prove the rule. When Spain and Portugal emerged from decades of dictatorship, their per capita GDPs made them middle-income countries.

Today, of course, these countries are clearly within the category of high income. So what happened? Did they follow the path I laid out in this book, accumulating human capital early enough in their development pathway to keep growing all the way to high income? They did not. In fact, in the early 1980s the human capital levels of the people of Spain, Portugal, and Greece resembled those of a trapped middle-income country today. Far fewer than half of the workers in Spain, Portugal, and Greece had been to high school in 1980. Yet today Spain, Portugal, and Greece are high-income countries. They appear to have won the Chutes and Ladders game by some other route, in spite of low rates of human capital.

So why is it that these countries could make the transition without strong human capital and Brazil, Turkey, and Mexico could not? Of course, the reasons are complicated. But I would argue that the primary reason they made it to high income was by riding the EU's coattails. The EU provided massive subsidies to its new southern members in the late twentieth century. That meant that even though Spain, Portugal, and Greece were still middle-income countries and didn't have the revenues to support their struggling population themselves, the EU was available to help them fill the gaps. Those subsidies allowed these nations to invest in schooling and gradually raise the human capital of their labor forces. Economic integration into the lucrative EU market also boosted GDP.

What about the effects of job polarization? If Spain and Portugal had such low rates of general human capital at the time of their transition, why didn't they hit the "chute" of job polarization, with rising informal employment, rising unemployment, and rising crime dragging down the nascent economy? Why haven't they devolved into informality and crime as Mexico, Brazil, and South Africa did? Why doesn't it matter that they have so many structurally unemployable citizens?

Well, they do have high unemployment rates. The unemployment rate for people twenty-five and below is something like 35 percent. But they were able to overcome the social and economic costs by buying off their unemployed youth. EU transfers provide unemployment support for those who are structurally unemployable, keeping many from deciding to lead a work life outside the formal sector (or in crime). They provided government benefits—at tremendous cost—based on their EU membership to avoid the exact scenario I have laid out for China. That's what it takes to keep this from happening.[20]

China (with a huge population and no wealthy union members) certainly cannot afford to do the same. With a potential for 200 to 300 million unemployed (and when you count their families, above 500 million), the costs would be truly staggering. And at no point in the near future is that likely to change.

Global Spillovers

It is highly possible that China could soon join the ranks of the trapped. China is a massive country, home to over a billion people. If China is thrown into chaos, one-fifth of the world's total population will be in peril. The global share of human suffering will rise swiftly and dramatically. And if this worst-case scenario does come to pass, the social and economic repercussions are unlikely to remain within China's borders.

For the past several decades, China has been an engine of growth for the rest of the world. Its workers propel entire industries. Its consumers prop up business around the world. If China's economy stagnates, it will no longer be able to play that role. The economic reverberations from China's slowdown could wreak havoc on global markets for decades to come, affecting countries around the world. China's many trading partners will suffer, and global recession is likely.

The potential political costs may be even more dangerous. As a development economist, I am not in a position to predict what is going to happen politically. But other people are worried too. In a recent book, journalist Howard French has argued persuasively that economic distress could have particularly grave political ramifications under China's current leadership. He shows that in the modern era, the Chinese Communist Party (CCP) has depended on two key pillars for its legitimacy: fast economic growth and nationalism.

That nationalism has been very popular among the common people and is maintained through carefully managed public messaging campaigns.[21]

If one of those pillars of legitimacy—continuing fast economic growth—is irrevocably knocked down, what might happen? French predicts that the CCP might feel it has no choice but to bolster its legitimacy by doing even more to whip up nationalist passion. If China really starts to fall and people start to get angry, what's to stop the CCP from deciding that the time has finally come to make good on a lot of threats with the first overt military move to seize the Diaoyu/Senkaku Islands and thereby risk war with Japan? And if not Japan, then where else? The long-simmering skirmishes in the South and East China Seas might finally erupt, with grave military consequences for us all. These are only possibilities, but we must take them seriously.

I certainly hope this won't happen. I truly believe there will be some magic left in the reform bag of China's leaders so they can figure out a way to avoid such a catastrophic scenario. But I also argue strongly that it is entirely possible that China could go down the path of Mexico, with potentially devastating results inside and outside China. Knowing that this is a real possibility should be more than enough to motivate China's top officials to take action before they run out of time.

4: How China Got Here

As of 2015, fully 70 percent of working-age adults in China were high school dropouts. This leaves China's population less educated than the population of any other middle-income country and even worse off than that of many poorer countries. For instance, in that same year, only 58 percent of South Africans were high school dropouts. In the Philippines, only 42 percent had failed to finish high school. The truth is that the world is increasingly divided into two categories: countries that are well educated and those that aren't. China is clearly on the losing side.[1]

It might seem hard to believe that China could be so far behind. Indeed, from reading the news, one would think that education is China's great obsession. Press coverage of China is rife with stories of the intense academic pressure in Chinese schools, the huge tutoring industry, and the popularity of Math Olympiads for kids as young as preschool. In 2012 Shanghai-China famously outscored all the other countries participating in the OECD's testing program—an international academic test for fifteen-year-olds called the Programme for International Student Assessment, or PISA. In 2018 China's teens again topped the list of countries participating in the PISA. Even in the West, ethnic Chinese communities are known for their dedication to academic excellence. How could the breeding ground of the original "tiger mother" be putting too little emphasis on education?[2]

Even for those who live and work in China, this statistic can be hard to believe. In China's cities, everywhere you look there are high school students in their tracksuit school uniforms, carrying bags bursting with books as they shuttle between academic activities. Any urban Chinese will tell you that teenagers in China spend almost all their free time studying. In fact, forget high school. It sure seems as if almost everybody in China goes to college, too. Every year new universities are popping up around the country and existing universities are expanding their enrollments. Universities around the world struggle to keep up with the steady influx of Chinese students who want to study abroad.

This belief is ubiquitous in urban China. Just a few years ago, an Australian anthropologist doing fieldwork in urban Chinese schools wrote, "When I arrived in China to begin this research, entire rooms full of middle- and upper-middle-class Chinese parents roared with laughter when I said I was interested in studying youth culture. 'All teens in China do nothing except study to prepare for the [College Entrance Exam],' they explained patiently to me. 'There's no such thing as youth culture here!'"[3]

So why are our assumptions wrong? How can China be worse off in educational terms than South Africa and the Philippines, which look so much poorer? How can China, the "inevitable superpower" we hear so much about, be so far behind on this critical measure of success?

The question can be answered only by turning back the clock a few years.

Not Enough Time

Li Jie grew up in the mountains of Sichuan Province in the late 1980s and early 1990s. The son of rice farmers, he spent his days in school and his evenings daydreaming. His mother refused to let him help with the farm work—she wanted her eldest boy to spend his time studying and to have all the opportunities she'd had to pass up.

When he first started school, Li Jie attended the primary school in his village. Even though this was a public school, at that time public schools in China still charged tuition. His school fees were a heavy financial burden for his family, but both parents worked hard to make sure he could stay in school. They knew plenty of families who were not so lucky.

Li Jie did well in primary school. He was especially gifted in math. His fourth-grade teacher once lent him a book about space, and he was hooked. He would tell anyone who would listen that he was going to be the first Chinese astronaut. His mother would smile and ruffle his hair whenever he got going on a long description of a future spacewalk. He finished primary school at the top of his class.

A few months before Li Jie was to start seventh grade, his father called him into the house while his mother was out at the market. His dad grabbed two stools, set them on either side of a small plate of sunflower seeds, and beckoned him to sit. Cracking seeds between his teeth and avoiding his son's eyes, he told Li Jie plainly that they couldn't afford to send him to junior high school. This new school was also public, but it also charged tuition. The tuition was more than they'd expected, and because the school was in the county seat, far from home, he would have to board. Between the tuition, paying for his food and housing, and the cost of his books, there simply wasn't enough money.

Li Jie was shocked. He knew there was no way he could become a scientist, let alone an astronaut, without many more years of schooling. He tried to catch his father's eye, but his dad stared determinedly out the window. "Isn't there some way we can find the money?" Li Jie asked quietly.

His dad sighed, met his son's eyes, and put a hand on his shoulder. "I'm sorry, son. The truth is, we've already taken out a loan to help you get this far in your schooling. Now your grandmother is sick. The medicine is expensive. We simply can't make it work. You'll have to get a job or stay and manage the farm so I can go find work in the city."

Li Jie watched his father's face as he spoke, hoping to think of some way, some solution. But there was nothing. There was nothing more to say. And he never went back to school.

Unfortunately, Li Jie's story is all too common. This isn't a story from China's distant past. This was only the 1980s. And this recent history has much to do with China's current human capital gap.

One of the main reasons China has a human capital crisis today is quite simple: it's a fact of history. Simply put, China is a big country, it developed very quickly, and changing the human capital levels of an entire country takes a long time.

It was not so long ago that China was a poor country. Before the latest climb, China—like just about every other poor country in the world—had low education rates. When a large share of the population is living and working on small subsistence farms, there's no need for high levels of education. Li Jie's father received only a primary school education, his mother dropped out after three years, and his grandparents were entirely illiterate. That's just the way things worked in rural China for a long time. And that lack of education never really hampered their economic prospects.

Over the past few decades, China has radically transformed its economy. But not that much time has passed. It takes years to build up educational capacity to serve such a large population—to raise the funding, build the schools, train the teachers, and get people into classrooms. Even when all the resources are in place, it takes at least twelve years to fully educate a single cohort of children through high school. It takes far longer for that change to affect the economy. Indeed, boosting the human capital level of an entire labor force—full of older people who came of age before education was widely available—takes at least forty-five years, even if everything is done right. China simply hasn't had time.

China is not alone in facing this challenge. The disparity between the fast pace of development and the long time it takes to build up education levels is a big part of the modern middle-income trap. Thanks to globalization and the fast-moving development ladder of low-skilled manufacturing, it's now possible for a poor country to grow very quickly. A country can rocket from the bottom of the development game board up to the middle-income section in decades. But if the rate of human capital accumulation does not keep pace with that rapid development (or even stay ahead of it), countries soon find themselves unable to compete and stuck in a deadly trap.

As we've seen, however, some countries (the graduates) have managed to bridge this gap. The key to avoiding the trap is for the top levels of government to give priority to rapidly expanding education for the entire population even before the labor market demands it.

So why didn't that happen in China? The difference is that, for a long time, China's government did not emphasize education at all—quite the opposite. Mao Zedong ruled China for twenty-seven years. For much of that time, he worked actively to undermine the accumulation of human capital. For the ten years of Mao's Cultural Revolution (1966–76), for instance, all universities and most academic high schools were closed down for political reasons. Many of the most highly educated people in society were systematically humiliated and silenced. New schools were built across the countryside, but they taught Mao's Little Red Book (of Communist political thought) instead of math, Chinese, or English.[4]

Even under China's next leader, the reformer Deng Xiaoping, mass education—especially at secondary levels—was a low priority. In 1988, a decade after Deng took power, attendance in high school was lower than when he had taken over in 1978. Even as late as 1990, only 60 percent of all children in China were attending junior high school. In poor rural areas, many children like Li Jie went without the education their families wanted for them.[5]

A big part of the problem, as Li Jie and his family discovered, was the high cost of education. Throughout this period, public education was not mandatory (so children could drop out whenever they liked without consequences—unlike in most developed countries), and it cost money to attend. To go to primary and junior high school, students often had to pay high tuition. For rural parents, particularly in poor areas, tuition could be far more than families could afford, so many children (like Li Jie) simply went without.

The effects of these policy choices are still being felt. In the 1970s, 1980s, and 1990s, China invested far less in high school than almost all other middle-income countries. The result was that low education levels persisted for many years, even as China's economy continued its rapid transformation. And so China lost precious time in the (already tight) race to build up its educational levels. In short,

Percentage of 25-34 Year-Olds with Attainment Below Upper Secondary Education (2014)

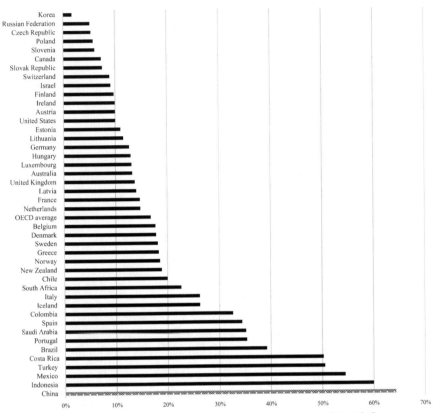

Figure 3. Educational attainment by country for youngest cohort (25–34). *Source: Organisation for Economic Co-operation and Development Staff, Education at a Glance: OECD Indicators 2015* (Paris: OECD, 2015), www.oecd.org/education /education-at-a-glance-19991487.htm.

China has a human capital crisis today in large part because it did not choose to give priority to the comprehensive accumulation of education as early as Taiwan and South Korea did.

This is not the distant past. Deng Xiaoping died only in 1997. Li Jie is in his early forties today. The legacy of low education rates remains dramatic across China's labor force, even for some of China's youngest adults. Figure 3, from the OECD, shows an international comparison of the proportion of the youngest cohort of adults—those twenty-five to thirty-four—with less than a high school education. With a high school dropout rate above 60 percent even among this youngest group, China is far behind every other country that has been measured. This historical oversight goes a long way to explain why China is facing such a crisis today.

Glimmers of Hope

Fortunately, China's recent leaders have dramatically reversed course. China's past several administrations—especially since the early 2000s—have stressed education to a greater extent than ever before. Their efforts have been remarkably successful—especially given the low starting point. In 2006, after years of rising tuition, public schooling was at last made mandatory and free from grades one through nine for every child in the country. By 2010 junior high school attendance was nearly universal—a truly impressive achievement, considering the 60 percent attainment rate of only twenty years earlier.[6]

At the same time, the government invested heavily in increasing educational opportunities at the highest levels. From the late 1990s to 2005, China's university system quadrupled in size, and it has continued to grow. Today several of China's universities are among the best in the world. China's universities now produce over seven million new graduates each year, and at least four million of them earn degrees in STEM fields. This is certainly the fastest expansion in university education that has ever occurred.[7]

Increasing the share of the population receiving a university education is certainly an important goal. But high school is just as critical. Much of my focus in this book has been on the importance of ensuring that all Chinese children receive at least twelve years of comprehensive education—through high school. This is for good reason. There is a lot of evidence that high school education is particularly important for economic growth today. For example, one study found that while it was *primary* education that drove economic growth in Great Britain before the Industrial Revolution, ever since the arrival of computing technology in the twentieth century, high school (and college) education makes the most difference. Since the start of the twenty-first century, the ongoing march of skill-biased technological change has made skills at the high school level (or higher) even more critical.[8]

China has also made strides on this crucial metric. As recently as 2005, only 53 percent of all fifteen- to seventeen-year-olds in China were attending high school. By 2015 high school attainment among all Chinese children had climbed above 80 percent, a staggering improvement in one decade. More than ten million new slots have been made available in China's high schools, the largest and fastest expansion of high school in the world to date. Efforts to expand access to high school continue: current president Xi Jinping has pledged to launch a national effort to make grades one through twelve universal for the first time by the early 2020s.[9]

This is wonderful news and all too necessary, but China's human capital challenge remains. Even this rapid rate of educational catch-up may not be enough.

What matters for China is the educational capacity of its entire labor force, not just today's children or young adults. The labor force includes everyone who is working: from age twenty-five all the way up to sixty-four. Emerging from poverty only recently and then living for several decades under leaders who did not make education a priority, China has a low starting point in its educational stock. As a result, the incremental increases—though impressively fast—have not yet reached the level needed across the entire working-age population. No matter how fast educational attainment increases among the children, the older generations remain as they were. They do not gain more education just because opportunity has expanded for youth. Even today, about 65 percent of the people in China's labor force came of age under the lackluster education systems of Mao and Deng.[10]

The result is that the improvements in recent years—while impressive—have not been enough. Even though, only decades after China's first steps out of poverty, many more children are being educated than ever before, the overall level of education in the labor force continues to lag far behind that of comparable countries. This historical legacy is a heavy burden that must be overcome as soon as possible. Before we can dig into the question of what China must do, however, we need to know where to look.

A Fundamentally Rural Problem

A big part of the reason China's human capital crisis has been unknown for so long is that it is rooted in a part of China that is often overlooked: the vast rural interior.

China is one of the world's most unequal countries. The fundamental divide in China is between people from rural and urban areas. In China the urban-rural gap is much more deeply entrenched than anywhere else in the world. Although everywhere in the developing world people from rural areas tend to lag behind those who live in cities, only in China is the urban-rural divide enforced by official policy and codified by law. Under the *hukou* (household registration) system, at birth all citizens are assigned either a rural or an urban identity. This status fundamentally affects every moment of life in China and is very difficult to change.[11]

Most critically for this story, all public services depend on one's hukou status. For example, rural and urban children move through almost entirely separate educational systems. Rural students, with few exceptions, are allowed to attend only rural schools, and urban students go to urban schools. Even if rural families migrate to the cities to find work—as hundreds of millions have done—in most places they are not allowed to put their children into urban public schools. Instead, most migrant parents must choose between leaving their children behind to live with relatives in the countryside so they can go to public school (the genesis of the infamous "left-behind child") or keeping their children with them in the cities but sending them to low-quality and legally provisional private schools for migrant children.[12]

Urban students are doing very well on the whole, but rural children are receiving far less education. According to China's census data, the high school attainment rate among the urban labor force (everyone from twenty-five to sixty-four) was 44 percent in 2010—four times the rate among individuals of the same age range living in rural areas (only 11 percent).[13]

This wide gap in human capital is not merely a historical divide. Even today urban children are being educated at much higher rates. Today, according to the 2015 microcensus, 97 percent of urban students attend high school and graduate—a rate higher than those of children in the United States and Germany.[14]

But rural children have lagged behind and continue to lag. As recently as 2005, only 43 percent of rural youth were attending high school. Thanks to the government's efforts to rapidly expand access to education, this number has soared since then. Today nearly 80 percent of rural children of high school age attend some kind of high school. As I'll show in the next chapter, this is not as good as it sounds, because many are attending low-quality vocational high schools. And that still leaves about four million rural children every year who are going out into the world without any kind of high school education.[15]

The gap is not just in educational *attainment*—defined as the share of people attending a given level of schooling. Urban and rural populations also show a large and persistent gap in how much they are *learning* when they are in school. Research by a team in central China in 2014, for example, found that rural primary school students in fourth grade were already more than two grade levels behind urban students in math. The research shows this gap widening every year the children are in school. The result is that rural kids are falling far behind on every measure.[16]

Although China's human capital crisis has its roots in rural communities, it has implications for everyone, both inside and outside China. When people think about China or read news stories, they generally imagine its cities. It's to the big cities that most journalists and foreign visitors go. The urban elites are the ones who make waves around the world: enrolling in overseas universities at mind-boggling rates, leading the companies that are remaking entire industries, and traveling the world as tourists in higher numbers than ever before. But for all the visibility and heft of China's urban population, it's actually a minority of the country. Most of the population—64 percent—has "rural" status in the hukou system, while about 36 percent has "urban" status. The "rural" category represents some 600 million to 700 million people. Most of those with rural hukou are still living in rural villages. Others are living as migrant workers on the outskirts of China's big cities. But wherever they are, they and their children are far less educated than their urban counterparts. And because there are so many more of them, that means China as a whole is in trouble.

Even more important for China's *future* economy, most of China's next generation is growing up in the countryside. China's countryside has long had higher birthrates than the urban areas. As a result, the share of the next generation that is rural is even higher. According to the 2015 microcensus, fully 75 percent of children up to age three are growing up with rural hukou. These children will face greater barriers to learning and, unless something drastic happens, are likely to end up with worse educational outcomes. Over time, therefore, rural children are going to matter more and more for China's overall economic outlook.

Because of the political realities of the hukou system, this gap may not be easily bridged. In China "rural" and "urban" are worlds apart—far more so than in almost any other country in the world. With such a large rural population, the problems of the poor cannot be allowed to languish on the periphery. The future of the economy depends on extending resources to those who are most marginalized—wherever they are. Instead, by walling off the rural population through the hukou system, China has chosen to keep the majority of its future workforce in the places that are hardest to reach, with the most poverty, the least parental education (an important determinant of child outcomes), and the least interaction with the outside world. This enforced urban-rural divide is another crucial contributor to China's human capital crisis. It must be overcome quickly, for everyone's sake.

The past two Chinese administrations have made major efforts to expand educational access to more of the population. The results have already been astonishing, but they may not be enough. If China is to remain free of the middle-income trap, its human capital levels must be brought as high as possible as quickly as possible. For the sake of all who call China home, and every other country that depends on China's economic strength and political stability, every child—and especially every rural child—needs to be given a quality education at the level of high school or higher.

So the critical questions that must be answered in the rest of the book are these: Why are rural kids falling so far behind? And what can be done to turn the tide?

The Final Barriers

Today Li Jie is grown up. Unsurprisingly, given that he never got beyond primary school, he did not become an astronaut. But he's been doing fine in China's growing economy anyway. He started out in construction as a teenager before moving into work in a series of factories. For a few years he even worked in a factory that made parts for rockets. In 2003 he proudly watched China's first astronaut launch into space. I met Li Jie in 2015, when I was doing a survey in a factory where he was working, and he told me his story.

Today, Li Jie has a son. Little Qiang, as his father calls him, lives back in his home village with Li Jie's aging parents. Because Li Jie works in Shanghai, he gets to see his son only once a year, for the Spring Festival. But he's proud to say his son has never wanted for anything. Because of the hard work Li Jie and his wife do in the city, Little Qiang has plenty to eat, doesn't have to work, and can stay in school as long as it takes to follow his dreams.

Li Jie's son is going through an education system that looks radically different from his father's. Tuition has been eliminated for primary school and junior high. There are better teachers, better facilities, and a better curriculum. More and more kids are staying in school longer and longer, even in rural areas.

And yet the research shows that Li Jie's son will still face big obstacles to finishing school, seeing out his own dreams, or even maintaining the better standard of living his father has worked so hard to provide for him. The Chinese education system is still leaving far too many rural children behind. What are the challenges that remain?

For one thing, although tuition has been eliminated for the first nine years of school, tuition is not the only expense that can impel a student to drop out of school. One factor that drives many rural students to leave before finishing high school is that dropping out early brings big financial rewards. Ever since China became a global hub for low-skilled manufacturing, there have been ample jobs for unskilled workers. The exact type of job that has earned Li Jie and his wife such a good living is also available to young teens who haven't finished high school. Indeed, research has shown that during the late 2000s virtually all young, able-bodied rural people who sought jobs in China's coastal provinces were able to find one. Particularly in recent years, as the unskilled wage rate has risen, many students have found the temptation to drop out and start earning a steady salary too hard to resist. This is no small temptation, especially for a young person from a poor rural village. The same study found that the *monthly* salary of the typical unskilled worker in 2008 and 2009 was comparable to the *annual* per capita income in poor rural areas. Thus, by leaving high school to enter the labor market, young rural Chinese could make higher wages than they might be able to refuse. For a poor family this makes going to high school very costly—they must give up what their son or daughter could otherwise have earned. In the language of economics, we could say there is a high opportunity cost to staying in school even though tuition has been eliminated.[17]

Note that this is a problem of mismatched short- and long-run incentives, and it's a critical contributor to the middle-income trap for any country. As long as a country is poor or middle income and low-wage jobs are easily available, poor children and their families have a clear incentive to forgo education in favor of making money today. It's only when development continues onward and those low-wage jobs start to disappear—as is just starting to happen in China—that they will discover they have made a regrettable choice. I hope Li Jie's son will not have to make this decision.

This incentive for poor students to drop out of school because of opportunity cost is part of the reason China's high school attainment rates aren't higher. But it's a factor that all upwardly mobile middle-income countries must reckon with. Indeed, the countries that have been most successful in boosting high school attainment at the middle-income stage have worked hard to overcome this opportunity cost. They have made schooling mandatory and free all the way through high school. In some places it has even become standard policy to *pay* families for students to attend school, through what is known as conditional cash transfers (CCTs). This tendency reflects the recognition by government officials, educators, and society that when children attend school, society as a whole benefits. In economics this is known as education's having large positive externalities. In other words, taking into account the economic effects of having a well-educated citizenry, educating a child is more valuable to *society* than it is even to the individual. So it's worth it for everybody to pay families to make the right choice today.

Many countries have put CCT policies in place for exactly this reason. CCTs ensure that a country's high school attainment rate will increase as quickly as possible, to everyone's benefit. For example, in Brazil today the government has a program that pays families to keep their children in high school. Families are given an estimated one-third to half of the income a child could expect to make in the unskilled labor market, so long as they stay in school. This program boosts high school enrollment, to the benefit of all—the families get the help they need to make it through the short-run disincentives to education while still reaping the long-run benefits of their children's having a higher education level and thus the ability to get better jobs. Likewise, the community (and the entire country) is better served by having more well-educated members.

China should consider taking similar steps, as well as eliminating the other barriers to attending high school that still remain. At this point, students in China still have to contend with opportunity costs—and, in many cases, tuition costs as well. Currently, China's educational system is compulsory (mandatory and free) only from grades one through nine. Even today children in China are not guaranteed access to high school, and high school is not mandatory.

For China's more prestigious high schooling track (academic high school), China continues to charge tuition. This may surprise many outside observers, but it's true. Although academic high school is a public schooling system, it is not free.[18]

There is a clear disparity between China and the rest of the world on this count. In most countries, twelve years of schooling are free. A few countries (Vietnam and Indonesia, for instance) do charge a nominal fee for high school. But China's high school tuition is far from nominal. A 2009 study estimated that the direct costs (including tuition, textbooks, and room and board) of attending three years of academic high school in China amounted to US$1,659. That may not sound like a lot to an American, but it's a staggering sum for rural Chinese families. Indeed, the same study showed that this is roughly ten to fifteen times the per capita net income in poor rural areas (three to five times annual income for each year the children are in school). These costs make China a clear outlier on the world stage—its tuition rates are the highest of any country in the world.[19]

This is a poor policy choice. As I said above, at this point China needs to work hard to get every possible student into a good high school program. No matter what China does, students will face opportunity costs. It certainly doesn't serve the nation's interests to add direct costs (in the form of high tuition rates) on top of that. Fortunately, there are signals that policymakers are thinking of reducing tuition or making academic high school free. They should do that immediately. In fact, I think China should follow Brazil's example and go so far as to use conditional cash transfers to increase its human capital stock as soon as possible.

Finally, it is of course true that China's future depends not only on increasing educational attainment (the number of kids going to school), but also on increasing how much students are actually learning (the quality of schooling).

First, the schools themselves need to provide high-quality education. As I'll show in the next chapter, a large subset of China's high schools (many of its vocational high schools, which are common in rural areas) are falling below this standard. In many vocational high schools, students learn next to nothing, and many are choosing to drop out and not finish school. In the best cases they are being trained only in narrowly defined vocational skills that will not prepare them for China's future. This means that resources are being wasted and children are not getting the foundation they will need to survive—let alone thrive—in the future. This issue needs to be addressed as quickly as possible if China's impressive gains in attainment are to yield results.

Second, the students who are being ushered into high school in larger numbers need to be ready to learn. Available research shows a persistent gap in learning and performance between urban and rural children. No amount of high school expansion is likely to close this gap without further action, because its roots are to be found at the very beginning of life. As I'll show in the following two chapters, the learning gap can be traced to a series of health and nutrition crises afflicting young rural children as well as to poor development among rural babies. I believe removing these early barriers to growth and learning is the single most important task China faces today. Certainly these issues need to be addressed if any further educational expansion is to truly improve outcomes in China's future.[20]

I only hope it's not too late. It takes time to raise the human capital of an entire country's labor force, let alone a country as large, and as historically undereducated, as China. Even if every child starts going to a quality high school as soon as the early 2020s, it will still be decades before the education levels of the labor force as a whole can be brought up to the level expected for a high-income country.

China's education system wasn't enough to help Li Jie achieve his dreams. And if something isn't done soon, Little Qiang may be left behind too.

5: A Shaky Foundation

Today China is poised on the edge of the middle-income trap. The Chinese Communist Party may have decreed that reporters and academics are no longer to mention the words "middle-income trap," but for all the bluster, it seems that China's top officials are in fact taking the issue seriously and implementing dramatic action to boost human capital and prepare China's labor force for new challenges.

The policy pushes I've discussed so far have focused primarily on education at the elite level: training the innovators, engineers, and entrepreneurs who will lead China's future economy. University access has expanded rapidly, and China has committed to expanding access to academic high school. But these remain strictly elite-level benefits. Even after all that university expansion, there are still slots in higher education for only 20 to 30 percent of each cohort of young people today. Even the most ambitious plans for academic high school intend to keep this path open only to the top students—those who can pass the difficult admissions exams (by official policy, about 50 to 60 percent of each year's youth cohort).[1]

What about the future common workers—the many young people who will simply not qualify for those coveted academic high school or university spots? As it happens, the CCP has a plan for them too. Beginning in 2002, China began to greatly expand a system of vocational high schools. This is the path designed for those who are excluded from academic high school and university.

Vocational education has different meanings in different places. Generally it is schooling focused on explicitly vocational or occupation-oriented learning. This kind of schooling is less common at the high school level in the United States than in many other nations. In the United States, all students are expected to complete traditional academic high school, but in many countries vocational schools are an integral part of the secondary education system. Germany, for example, has a large vocational high school system that has been widely praised as contributing to its strong economy. Indeed, the Chinese vocational education system has been explicitly designed to be similar to certain elements of the German system. Like Germany, China has two-track schooling where students choose between academic and vocational high schools.

China's vocational high schools are three-year programs, and students split their time between in-class instruction and professional internships. The curriculum is focused on a vocational major of each student's choosing. Some of the most popular majors in the past decade have been auto repair, welding, computer skills, preschool education, and nursing.

There have been steady increases in financial aid and reductions in tuition for these schools, which have substantially reduced the out-of-pocket cost of attending vocational school. Moreover, vocational high schools have lower academic requirements for admission than academic high schools do. Virtually everyone who seeks admission to a vocational high school is welcomed. Although the new schooling system has not explicitly targeted rural students, these measures ensure that rural students are enrolling in high numbers.[2]

Thus China has finally created a plan that will provide a place for all children to learn at the high school level. Students who are at the top of their classes in junior high school can pass the difficult entrance examinations for academic high school and receive a high-quality academic education. This will prepare them to go to university, to take the high-skilled jobs in China's future economy, and to drive national growth through innovation, design, and entrepreneurship at the elite level of China's transitioning economy. The rest of the students—all those who otherwise would have been left out of high school entirely—now can continue their studies on a separate educational track. Although they will not be able to attend academic high school or university, they can at least receive a vocational education at the high school level, with clear job prospects shortly after graduation. China now has an educational pathway open to all the students who are not prepared to follow in the footsteps of the elite. Perhaps this will allow China to avoid Mexico's fate.[3]

China's top officials do envision this expansion of vocational high school not just as a way to provide education, but also as a way to further the country's economic growth. Officials have championed vocational education as China's new "engine for growth." By educating a large cohort of students in concrete vocational skills, they say, China is preparing these workers for the next phase of development. They will be ready to say goodbye to the unskilled work of the factory floor or the mines (jobs that are rapidly disappearing as a result of falling demand, globalization, and automation) and instead be able to pursue higher-wage work in skilled trades. With a more highly skilled labor force, China will attract higher-value-added industries and transition to a new period of prosperity and stability for all.

This all sounds wonderful—as if it could solve exactly the problem I laid out in the first section of the book. Maybe the high school attainment rate will rise quickly and fewer people will be left structurally unemployable in the years to come. Maybe this will allow China to hold on until the skill level of the labor force catches up to demand. Maybe.

Unfortunately the new vocational high school system is not functioning as well as one might hope. Signs are emerging that some of these schools are riddled with serious problems.

First Days

Wang Tao grew up on the dusty outskirts of Zhengzhou, the capital city of poor Henan Province. His parents scraped out a living by farming a half-acre of land. As a boy, he took a few weeks off school every year to help bring in the crop of canola and watermelon.

Tao did well in school. In seventh grade his teacher made him the class monitor, a prestigious position in a Chinese classroom, reserved for the student the teacher trusts to model good behavior for the other students. Although few kids in his rural middle school ever got into academic high school, Tao's teachers had high hopes that his grades might be good enough. He studied hard for the high school entrance exam, but in the end his score was just below the cutoff. The academic high school offered to let him in anyway if he could pay an additional entrance fee of about US$3,000. His parents, who made only a few hundred dollars a year from their work on the farm, couldn't afford it.

Tao's middle school teacher suggested he check out the new vocational high school that had recently opened across town. Tao talked it over with his parents. They didn't know much about that kind of school, but they thought he was too young to give up on school completely. Since regular high school was not an option, maybe vocational high school would be better than nothing. In late August Tao went with his parents to look at the vocational school. He paid the small enrollment fee and signed up to major in something called "digital control." He wasn't sure exactly what that meant, but the administrator filling out his registration form told him it would help him find a good factory job someday.

When he arrived on campus a week later, he found himself in an unfamiliar world. Whereas his middle school had been orderly and regimented, here chaos reigned. The older students were tough-looking, with tight jeans, black pleather jackets, and spiked hair. As he walked to class on his first day, there were no adults in sight. He passed groups of kids hanging out in the courtyard, smoking cigarettes and laughing.

Class time was also different than he was used to. The teachers were cold and unfriendly. Some would lecture woodenly from the front of the room, writing on the chalkboard with their backs to the students, never turning around to see if anyone was paying attention. Other teachers would come into the classroom, mumble a sentence or two about the new assignment, and walk right out again. The few students who came to class spent most of the time sleeping on their desks, playing games on their phones, or listening to music through headphones. One girl in his class seemed eager to learn, raising her hand often to ask questions. Whenever she did, four or five of the boys would call out and ask what she was trying to prove. "Why don't you just relax?" they'd say. "We don't have to do that here."

Outside class, students spent their time in the dorms drinking beer or in the computer lab playing *League of Legends*, chatting online, or watching porn. Sometimes Tao's math teacher would stop by a group of students to sell them cigarettes.

Tao was confused and disappointed. He'd always liked school. Here it seemed no one cared about anything. He heard from older students that things in the higher grades weren't much better. It would be two years of the same meaningless classes, then one year on an internship in some factory somewhere. You didn't really get to learn anything there, you just worked day after day, standing for twelve-hour shifts at the assembly line with all the regular workers. Worst of all, when you graduated from vocational high school, you could get only the same kinds of jobs as everyone else you knew who had started working straight out of middle school.

Halfway through his first year, Tao decided he'd had enough. One morning, without telling anyone, he packed his bag and caught the bus back to his family's farm, never looking back.

Two years after he dropped out of vocational high school, I met Tao at his home. As we sat on small wooden stools in front of the house, I asked him to sum up his experience in vocational high school. He shrugged, shook his head, and looked away. "What a waste of time," he said.

Unfortunately, Tao's experience is all too common. Although vocational education has existed in China for several decades at a relatively small scale, since the early 2000s the dramatic expansion of vocational high school has become a major priority at the highest levels of China's government. Moving forward as quickly and resolutely as only a one-party state can, China has overseen a rapid educational expansion.

The new vocational education initiative began in 2002. Immediately thereafter, a flood of new schools was built. When the pace of expansion was not fast enough, policymakers added new incentives for growth. Beginning in 2007, local education bureaus were given cash subsidies for each new student they could enroll in a vocational high school. From 1990 to 2011, annual investment in secondary vocational schooling increased sixfold. By 2011 China was investing US$20 billion in vocational high schools every year. Each year from 2005 to 2010, according to government statistics, about one million additional students were filling the new slots in the vocational programs. As early as 2010 the government pledged that it would reach its target of enrolling half of all high school-aged students in the country (about ten million students every year) as soon as 2020. This is a staggeringly large target, set less than two decades after the project was begun.[4]

The speed and scale of this expansion have been jaw dropping, but little information has been available about the quality of the new schools. For a while the only evidence available was anecdotal. The state media reported that things were going very well. Every once in a while a school would show up in the news with astoundingly positive reviews. An official once told me he had discovered that the graduates of a vocational high school in his province were earning a higher monthly wage than some college graduates. Even the World Bank got caught up in the frenzy and invested enormous amounts in a small number of high-profile, "super-model" schools.

But questions remained. It was unclear how the new schooling system was faring overall, because no serious research had been done. So my colleagues decided to fill this vacuum. We planned a large-scale quantitative survey to get some answers. We kept coming back to this question: Is it really possible to build a functioning school system for thirty million students in a single decade?

The short answer is no. While many students have enrolled in these new schools—and some of the schools are doing very well—the system as a whole is plagued by serious problems. Wang Tao is not the only child who has been left sorely disappointed.

Quality Concerns

From my team's very first efforts in the early 2010s, something seemed seriously wrong. As we always do at the beginning of a survey, we went to the local bureau of education to get a list of about two hundred officially registered vocational high schools in the area. Several researchers from my team drove to each school to ask a few questions and assemble the basic information we would need to design a comprehensive research project.

To be sure, we did find some very nice schools. In these schools the facilities were attractive, the administrators and teachers seemed engaged, and the students appeared to be learning. But in two weeks of driving from school to school, we kept running into the same bizarre phenomenon. Not once, but many times, we drove to the address of a school on our list only to find there was no school there. Maybe there was a big empty building. Maybe there was a principal sitting behind a desk in a small office in a warehouse. But all too often there were no students to be found. One school was listed four times on the official record under four different names but had no real students. Another school was formally registering confused middle-aged farmers as students in order to receive the student subsidy. Curiously, there were no facilities. In one of the provinces, nearly 20 percent of schools on the list did not exist. They were listed in the administrative records and were presumably receiving government funding to educate students (though no one would confirm or deny that), but they did not really have any students. This was our first sign that something was wrong with vocational education in China. Things didn't improve as we began to look closer.

Another of our first steps in the research process was to go into classrooms (in the schools that did have real students) to observe the teaching. In some schools there were proper lectures, students were taking notes, there was time for questions, and homework was turned in at the end of class; in short, all the things you'd expect in a working school. But in far too many of the schools, we found complete apathy toward learning—from both teachers and students. We would call schools in advance to introduce ourselves as researchers and let them know we were coming. You'd think schools would want to put their best foot forward to impress visitors. But in no small share of the schools, when the principal led us into a classroom to observe, we'd find ourselves sitting in the back of the room watching the teacher ignore the fact that all the students were either sleeping through class or playing games on their cell phones. In two or three schools, students were smoking in class. Students in these classes were clearly not learning anything, and no one seemed to care if we saw it.

After those visits—some ordinary or exciting but many deeply troubling—my research team launched our formal research. In two separate studies from 2011 to 2014, we surveyed thousands of kids across hundreds of vocational high schools in three Chinese provinces: one province each from eastern China, central China, and western China. This survey covered all kinds of schools, including some that looked pretty good on paper. It also included some that were obviously in trouble. But because it was a randomly selected group, we can be confident that these data are fairly representative of the situation in the rural areas of the country as a whole. The results were grim.

First of all, let me reiterate that there are many good schools out there. We have surveyed them and found that they are doing well. Their teachers are dynamic, and their students are thriving. But many of China's rural vocational high schools are seriously struggling.

By official policy design, the first two years of vocational high school are spent in the classroom. Students are supposed to divide their time between general academic classes (like math, Chinese, and English) and classes for a vocational major of their choosing (e.g., mechanics, computing, hotel management). As part of our survey, we gave students standardized tests in two subjects: math and their vocational major. The tests reflected official curriculum standards for each subject and were proctored by my research team.[5]

The results showed that on average students in vocational high school are learning *nothing*. Across all schools, my team found that almost all students made no progress in math over the course of a year of vocational high school. In particular, 91 percent scored the same or worse after an additional year of schooling. Even in vocational skills—the official priority for these schools—students were not learning much. Students in the basic computing major were not learning anything about computers. No programming, no repair skills, not even how to use basic application packages like Word or Excel.[6]

Well, what about on-the-job training? That's another major goal of these programs. After two years in the classroom, vocational school students are expected to participate in yearlong educational internships in work related to their vocational majors. This is supposed to give them an opportunity to learn practical skills and prepare for future jobs.

Unfortunately, our data on internships were just as troubling. My team found that fully 68 percent of students were going on internships that had nothing to do with their majors. Students majoring in "graphic design" were spending their internships building smartphones on factory assembly lines. Students majoring in "natural gas pipeline design" were delivering gas canisters house-to-house or working as cashiers in roadside gas stations. According to our survey data, fully 56 percent of all students spend their internship working in low-wage manufacturing, doing the same work as any junior high school graduate with no specialized training at all. Certainly these internships were not helping them learn relevant skills.[7]

Perhaps the clearest indicator of the problem is that students are dropping out of school in astonishing numbers. In particular, the average school has a cumulative dropout rate (over three years) of 33 percent. In some schools, dropout rates were above 60 percent. Far too many students are encountering poorly run schools and, just like Wang Tao, are voting with their feet.[8]

These are obviously serious problems. Students are not having good experiences in the classroom or gaining useful skills or knowledge, and they are dropping out in huge numbers. Building a brand-new school system for thirty million people overnight is not easy, and there obviously are some real problems with how things are being run.

This problem likely stems in part from a simple deficiency in the way the system has been set up so far. Every educational system in the world depends on careful regulation and monitoring. At every other level of Chinese education (including primary schools, junior high schools, academic high schools, and universities), the government keeps careful tabs on school quality. Regulators evaluate schools according to objective standards of student outcomes, and schools are allowed to stay in operation only if they meet those standards. Only through such assessment and accreditation can schools be held accountable for providing a good education to their students. The prevalence of this accountability is no doubt a big part of the reason most of China's schools do such a good job.

But so far the vocational high schools have not been brought into this regulatory system. They are held accountable for the quality of their facilities, for the accreditation of their teachers, and (in theory) for the number of students they enroll, but up till now they have not been assessed based on student *outcomes*. There is no regulatory body that comes into schools to test students' learning. There are no explicit targets for students that schools have to achieve. No one even comes in to watch classes and make sure basic standards are being met. The result is that some principals and teachers get away with bad behavior.

This lack of oversight is bad for the students—many are left in schools that are not working. It's also bad for the vocational education system as a whole. Today the good schools struggle to distinguish themselves from the bad schools. Only with good regulation can the system as a whole be brought up to the level of those good schools.

Monitoring the schools and providing incentives for them to deliver higher-quality education would be an obvious first step. Evidence shows that setting higher standards and improving regulation can do a lot of good surprisingly quickly. Otherwise too many students are going to continue to receive a low-quality education and will be left no better prepared for China's looming transition than when they were fresh out of junior high school.[9]

Educating for the Future

China's vocational high school system is in dire need of reform. I believe that once the education officials figure out what is happening, reform will come. Regulation and oversight will increase. Surely the breakneck pace of the system's expansion is a big part of the problem. Over the next several years, China will likely take stringent measures to improve school quality, instituting rigorous assessment and ultimately establishing the high-quality schooling program that was originally promised.

Will that mean that China's vocational education system is on track to accomplish the goals China has set—to prepare a large cohort of common workers with the skills they need to contribute to China's new economy? I fear not. Even if school quality can be improved, China's vocational high school system may still be in trouble, because the new schools are almost solely focused on teaching the wrong kinds of skills. That means that the vocational education system—even if it is brought up to code—may not be enough to pull China out of the path of potential economic and social crisis.

Let me back up for a minute to make sure this point is clear. Throughout this book I argue that China's future depends in large part on the skills and aptitudes of its common workers. Only with higher skill levels will these workers be able to handle the kinds of jobs that will define China's future economy. Only with a more highly skilled labor force will China attract new investors and new firms to replace those that are leaving or automating. Indeed, China's top leaders have used a very similar argument to explain why and how they have chosen to expand vocational education. They are hoping to boost the skill levels of all workers as a way to improve China's development prospects.

But an underlying question needs to be answered. What do I mean by "skills" in this context? Just what skills will determine whether China's workers can be successful in the coming transition?

Two kinds of skills are useful for a worker looking for employment. The first type of skills is purely vocational or professional: the ability to do a certain job well. Examples include knowing how to weld, how to type (before computers), or how to fix a car. The key is that these are skills that can be immediately used to get a certain job, but only that specific job. The second type I refer to as general or academic skills. These are taught in a traditional academic junior high school or high school. They include skills like math, reading comprehension, writing, science, logic, information technology (IT), and (in much of the world) English. These are the skills that teach a person *how to learn*. They give a student the foundation for any subsequent study and the ability to take on many alternative future skills—vocational or otherwise.

The problem is this: today China's vocational high school system is being run in a way that emphasizes vocational skills to the exclusion of almost anything else. But I believe China's future depends much more on the ability of all children in China to learn general skills.

There is plenty of reason to believe general skills are more important. True, vocational skills can be used to find a job immediately, which is certainly valuable. But a vocational skill is useful only so long as a certain industry is doing well, paying well, and hiring enough people. If an industry changes, that vocational skill can be rendered obsolete. In the past several decades, the march of technological progress has seen that happen again and again across industries. General skills, by contrast, give a person the ability to learn new things, to switch industries as needed, and to take on a variety of vocational skills for the rest of their lives.

China's future will certainly include lots of change. As is one of the main premises of this book, China is hoping to become a high-income country, and high-income countries are far more dynamic than poor or middle-income countries. Workers are expected to take on new jobs, to switch jobs or tasks as needed, and to learn quickly as they do so. The jobs that command higher wages are thus referred to in the economics literature as "nonroutine": they expect a worker to handle many new things in a day, a year, and a lifetime. To make those adjustments, workers need skills in math, computers, critical thinking, and creativity. Above all, they need to know how to learn. If they cannot handle such demands, they will be relegated to low wages in dead-end jobs. They may turn in increasing numbers to the informal sector or to crime. If enough people are left out, China is likely to follow the path of Mexico.[10]

In the twenty-first century, as technological change marches on, the need for flexibility will only increase. The fierce competition of globalization ensures that innovation and the creation of new technologies and industries will continue unabated. It's hard to predict how technology will change, of course, and which industries will survive. But you can be sure that many existing ones will be rendered obsolete, and many new industries will require skills not yet imagined. This means it's impossible to predict the specific vocational skills that will matter in the long term, or even the middle term. It's unlikely that any of China's workers can expect to do any one job from now until the end of their careers. They need to be ready to learn new skills and to adapt. That's why I believe the single most important contributor to these children's long-term success is a general education in academic skills (math, reading, language, and IT).

This is not just my own intuition—it's been proved with long-term data. Research shows that students given a broad education in general skills do better in the long run no matter what industry they end up in. And ensuring that the entire population is given access to these general skills has been shown to be the most reliable predictor for a country's long-term growth and prosperity. Investing in general skills thus is crucial both for the individual and for the entire nation.[11]

But in China, students in a large number of vocational high schools are not being made ready to learn. Their education is focused almost completely on narrowly defined vocational skills. Although academic skills are ostensibly part of the curriculum, they take up a very small portion of students' time and attention. Policymakers in China have stated that vocational high schools need spend only 30 percent of their time on academic skills. That attitude has been passed down the line to principals. Our studies have shown that 82 percent of vocational high school principals say that teaching academic skills is their *last* priority: 10 percent of school administrators in our surveys admit they don't offer general academic classes at all. Student feedback suggests the number may be even higher. The evidence from our tests in schools suggests that many of these are teaching academic skills at a troublingly low standard. Recall that 91 percent of students in our survey made no improvement or did worse in math over the course of the year.

It might make sense for these kids to focus solely on professional skills if they already had a strong foundation in the general skills they will need for a lifetime of work and adaptation and learning. But that's not the case. These are high school students, not college students. When they enter these schools, they are fifteen or sixteen years old and junior high school graduates. Considering that most of them ended up in vocational high school because they were already struggling to learn—they couldn't pass the academic high school entrance exams—you can be sure that many of them are not even armed with the skills of a junior high student. Thus their general skill levels are remarkably low when they enter vocational high school. Under the current system, they are not learning anything further.

The result is that these students graduate from vocational high school with the same general skills they started with, or even fewer. Whether or not they have learned to weld, to repair cars, or to operate a digital control machine, in their foundational skills—the skills that will allow them to grow and change and learn new things over a lifetime of employment—they're just as clueless as if they'd never finished junior high school. The vast majority are not being prepared for the future that China needs.

The risk of focusing solely on vocational skills is not just hypothetical. Some of the vocational majors on offer in these schools are already mismatched to the market, since they're chosen by policymakers developing curricula rather than through market relationships. For example, researchers found that students in the bookkeeping major spent a full year learning how to calculate on an abacus—a device that hasn't been used in a century.[12]

But even the majors that are well suited to the *current* market are unlikely to be of much use in five, ten, or twenty years. Indeed, the recent history of some vocational majors shows this clearly. In 2005 a colleague of ours went into a vocational high school that was encouraging students to major in telephone booth repair and maintenance and repairing VCR machines. These skills, though taught just a few years ago, are already completely outdated. The list of these outdated majors is long and tedious: internal combustion engine repair, desktop computer repair, pencil-and-paper bookkeeping, tube television repair, and more.

All this means that even if China's vocational schools can be brought up to their intended standards, the students will still be graduating with only one vocational skill. At age eighteen, they will be sent off into the world with no more than a junior high school foundation in general skills. If the vocational skill they chose happens to experience a change—if that industry is pushed out by a new technology or if there is less demand for that skill than the education officials expected—those students will be back to square one. They'll be left with none of the foundational skills that would allow them to learn a new trade.

At that point either they will be permanently excluded from the formal sector by their lack of skills or they can go back to school to learn a different vocational skill in an adult retraining program. These retraining programs are necessary and have some use in a dynamic economy, but they can't fill the gap entirely. Because these kids were left ignorant when young, without strong foundational skills, they'll be much less able to learn.

If I make this argument in a presentation, at this point I often get a specific question. "What about Germany?" many people ask indignantly. "Germany has vocational high schools, and they have one of the strongest economies around."

These questioners haven't looked closely enough. It's true that Germany has a program known as the vocational high school. But unlike China's, Germany's vocational high schools do not *solely* teach narrow vocational skills. Those schools are primarily focused on giving their students a strong academic education in general skills, with a small helping of vocational skills on the side. They are high schools first and vocational training institutions second. Rather than spending 30 percent of their time in academic classes (as in China), students in German vocational high schools spend 70 to 80 percent of their time in general academic classes. The Germans know that their vocational high school graduates need to know how to learn. China needs to understand that too if this system is to be brought to its full potential.

Investing so much money in a lackluster system of vocational high schools is setting millions of kids up for future disappointment and unemployment—or worse. The China of the future will have to foot the bill for this oversight—in the most hopeful future, by paying for major adult retraining programs that, if they work at all, will work much less effectively than had children been given a proper education. China will get a much better return on investment if it provides a general education while people are young and at their highest potential. In the darkest prospective future, the costs will be unemployment, slowing economic growth, crime, gang activity, and perhaps even the loss of social and political stability.

China has taken a bold first step in seeking to expand high school education to all children in the country. That step is to be commended, but it's not enough. If China is to keep moving ahead, the vocational high school system needs an overhaul. First, proper regulation and oversight must be put in place so that school quality can be improved. Too many children are being abandoned in schools that are not accomplishing even their most basic goals. This is a real problem, but it's also easy to fix. I fully expect that China's leaders will soon take the necessary action.

But beyond this oversight, China's vocational high school system needs to be reimagined. Rather than trying to pump out ever-larger numbers of students with specific vocational majors that are doomed to be short-lived, China needs to emphasize general skills for all young people. If vocational high school is going to continue in China, it needs to be rethought as academic high school with vocational electives. This is what Germany has, and it's the only type of vocational high school that makes any sense in the twenty-first century. That way kids can learn how to learn, and if industries change and they need to acquire a new vocational skill in the future, they'll be ready to learn it through an adult retraining program. But just giving them one basic, narrow skill and sending them out into the world is a recipe for disaster.

In the meantime, as long as vocational high schools are beset by disorder and poor outcomes, China should consider expanding access to academic high schools. The country already has one of the world's best systems of academic high schools, and access to them could be expanded at far less expense than it takes to build a new vocational high school system from scratch. Regardless of what policy is chosen, China needs to prioritize students' learning and long-term benefit as soon as possible. There is too much at stake to fail. China's rural children are already fighting an uphill battle.

6: Invisible Barriers

In the late 1980s and early 1990s, when I first started working in rural elementary schools in China, the poverty was visceral. I would go into rural villages with my collaborators and find kids in one-room schoolhouses with dirt floors and mud walls, sitting at broken desks with one dim lightbulb swinging from the ceiling. Often we'd find no teachers. In many cases the students didn't have books. They would sit four to a desk, huddled around a single textbook with torn or missing pages and no cover, straining to see in the dim light.

In those days the extreme needs of China's rural elementary schools couldn't be missed. Whenever I brought potential collaborators or donors into one of those schools, they came away shocked, dismayed, and eager to do whatever they could to remedy the serious problems. They'd seen the problems for themselves.

Today, China's rural elementary schools look a lot better. Since two-thirds of China's children are rural, that's an important shift, and the government deserves a lot of credit. Supported by grants from the National Ministries of Finance and Education, local school districts have made enormous investments in infrastructure over the past decade. Now almost all rural elementary schools, except in the very poorest parts of China, have modern buildings with concrete walls, sturdy desks—one for each child—and adequate lighting. Dormitories for boarding students and apartments for teachers have also been upgraded.

Teaching quality has improved greatly as well. Absence of teachers used to be common (in the 1980s and 1990s), in large part because cash-strapped local governments didn't have money to pay teachers regularly. In 2006 the national government took over responsibility for paying teachers' salaries across the country, creating a reliable and stable payment scheme. Three years later teachers' salaries were raised across the board. Now all teachers—even in the poorest, most remote areas—are paid just as well as all Chinese civil servants, and teachers' absence is almost entirely a thing of the past. The government has also been pouring money into teaching colleges and subsidizing higher education for future teachers through a number of policy channels. The result is that today almost all new teachers are college educated. At a recent on-campus job fair for graduating seniors in a teaching college in Xi'an, I was told by several school district human resource managers that it was a "buyer's market." For every open teaching job—even in the many remote rural areas—there were three qualified applicants.[1]

Finally, whereas textbooks used to be hard to find, today books are provided free to all rural schools. Rural students use the same curriculum as kids in the prosperous coastal cities. Critics may say it's not the most dynamic curriculum, but it's the same one used to teach the Shanghai students who outscored the world on the international PISA tests in 2012 and 2018.[2]

Thus the visible signs of poverty have been all but eradicated from most of China's rural elementary schools. Now when I bring visitors to these schools, they look around and smile. "Wow," they say, "I thought rural China was poor." One visitor, a professor from Stanford University's Graduate School of Education, observed that many of the classroom facilities are better than those in the San José Unified School District in the heart of Silicon Valley. This colleague quipped, "China's clearly fixed its rural education problem. Let's go home."

If only that were the case. For all the visible improvement in conditions in rural elementary schools, rural students are still falling far behind. Studies consistently show a large and persistent gap in learning between children in China's rural and urban schools. For example, one study from 2014 found that rural elementary students are more than two grade levels behind urban students in math, and this gap widens every year the children are in school. This early learning gap has far-reaching implications. In a competitive school system like China's, where promotion to each level depends on test scores, once a child falls behind it's nearly impossible to catch up. In fact, I believe this early gap lies at the heart of China's human capital crisis.[3]

This presents something of a mystery. All the educational resources are there: adequate facilities, better teachers who come to school and teach every day, and the same curriculum that is used in the thriving cities. Yet rural students are still falling far behind. The truth is, for all of the investment into rural education, the most important contributor to learning has been almost completely overlooked: students' health.

Simply put, rural children are not learning because they are sick. Until this issue is addressed, it won't matter how much rural schools improve. As long as they are sick, rural students are going to remain stuck in place.

Three Invisible Epidemics

On the surface, the students at this primary school in a mountainous rural community in southern China look like a normal group of kids. The children in the classroom have curious faces, dirty hands, and colorful backpacks. But a closer look reveals some fundamental differences. These students, mostly on the small side, look one to two years younger than their actual ages. As they walk out of the classrooms after the bell, there's none of the pent-up energy kids usually have after sitting in class all morning. No running, no playful shouts, no steady rhythm of skipping rope. It's as if a blanket of weariness has descended on them.

It was 2005, and I was visiting the school as part of a survey of rural schools. I struck up a conversation with Li Jun, the principal. While the rest of the group was still gathering around the conference table, Li told me about his recent experience spending a year as a visiting principal in a school in the suburbs of Xiamen, one of China's prosperous coastal cities. I asked him what, if anything, was different about the two schools. Li responded immediately by pointing out the window. I got up and looked out. Thirty minutes after lunch, the schoolyard was quiet and still. Puzzled, I asked the principal what I should be looking at. Li said, "Exactly. There's nothing. There are no children out on the playground."

The biggest difference between the urban school and the rural school, as Li saw it, was in the kids themselves. When Li first arrived at the rich coastal school, the energy of the urban students shocked him. In the morning before school, at recess, after lunch, and after school, the schoolyard was always full of noise, with exuberant children running, laughing, and playing. Back in his poor rural school, after lunch the children—by their own choice—would search for a quiet place to nap.

More than a quirk of rural life, this difference speaks to a fundamental problem in rural areas that is going undiagnosed. Studies across the Invisible China—by my team and others—have shown that elementary school students in poor rural areas are beset with a series of health conditions that sap their energy and interfere with their ability to learn. These health conditions may be the biggest barrier to learning in rural schools today, one of the primary obstacles preventing students from getting the education they need to succeed—and help China succeed—in the long run. Unless students are prepared to learn at young ages, no matter how much China increases access to education (such as by making high school universal), the human capital crisis will remain.

First, research has shown that millions of children across the Invisible China have iron-deficiency anemia. Anemia has grave physical and cognitive effects, interfering with the body's ability to carry oxygen to essential organs, including the brain. As a result it causes fatigue, poor attention, and long-term cognitive impairment. Generally it is caused by insufficient nutrition (often a lack of iron).

Most important for this story, anemia is known to critically inhibit learning: studies have shown that anemic children around the world have worse grades, lower school attendance, and higher dropout rates than healthy children. The data are clear—not only is anemia correlated with worse school outcomes, but a causal relation has been shown. In particular, research by my team (and others) has found that when children are given a micronutrient supplement so that anemia rates fall, test scores improve significantly relative to a control group.[4]

This problem is widespread in rural China. According to the World Health Organization, anemia prevalence above 5 percent in a population is considered a serious problem. Meanwhile, a series of studies by my research team from 2009 to 2012 revealed that more than 30 percent of elementary school students in the Invisible China suffered from iron-deficiency anemia. In spite of some policy efforts to address the problem in the intervening years, studies from 2016 and 2017 found that anemia levels were still high, with rates of about 25 percent among rural children in both central and western China. The high rate of anemia even today in poor areas of rural China constitutes a serious educational crisis. Students are being expected to learn—and to compete in one of the world's most competitive schooling systems—without even basic health.[5]

A second major health crisis can be found by looking carefully in an obvious place: on the faces of rural children. Everywhere in the world, no matter how rich or poor, there are kids who have poor vision. For most of these kids, the solution is simple and effective—give them glasses. With properly fitted glasses, they would be able to see and learn just as well as anyone else.

But in rural China it's very rare to see a child with glasses. This isn't for lack of need. In fact, in rural China many more children are nearsighted (and suffer from other vision problems) than in most of the rest of the world. International research has established that in most normal populations of elementary school kids, between 10 and 20 percent will have some problem with their eyesight. In rural China the rate of nearsightedness (myopia) ranges from about 10 percent among third graders to 30 percent among fifth graders and 40 percent among sixth graders. In other words, the rate of poor vision in rural China's schools is two to three times that in other countries.[6]

In fact, rural China is not alone in having elevated rates of poor vision. Research suggests that poor vision is disproportionately common in East Asian countries in general. There is debate about the reasons for the epidemic. There are several theories, including differential exposure to outdoor light, study time, screen time, and other factors. There may also be a genetic component. Still, rural China has one crucial difference. Myopia is common everywhere in East Asia, but it is only in rural China that the rate of treatment (providing eyeglasses) is so low.[7]

A higher rate of poor vision wouldn't be too much of a problem so long as kids were being given the glasses they need. But in rural China, despite higher-than-average levels of poor vision, there is almost no access to vision care. Most students are suffering from "uncorrected myopia"—they need glasses but don't have them. The problem is of large proportions. According to our five-province dataset, fully 9 percent of all third graders have uncorrected myopia. Because the rate of myopia increases faster than the rate of providing glasses, the overall rate of all children (those with and without poor vision problems) with uncorrected myopia rises steeply as they age. By sixth grade, fully 32 percent of all children in rural schools have uncorrected myopia (figure 4). This means that a third of rural sixth graders need glasses but don't have them.[8]

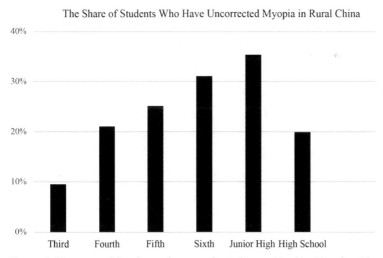

The Share of Students Who Have Uncorrected Myopia in Rural China

Figure 4. Unmet need for glasses by age cohort. *Source:* Yue Ma, Xiaochen Ma, Yaojiang Shi, Nathan Congdon, Hongmei Yi, Sarah Kotb, Alexis Medina, Scott Rozelle, and Mony Iver, "Visual Impairment in Rural China: Prevalence, Severity, and Association with Income across Student Cohorts," REAP Working Paper, 2018.

As you might expect, uncorrected myopia is hugely significant for learning. When you can't see clearly, it's a lot more difficult to learn. Research by my team and others has shown that simply putting properly fitted glasses on nearsighted students leads to large and rapid improvement in student test scores. When students were given glasses and wore them in class, their test scores nearly doubled. Eyeglasses can thus cut the achievement gap between rural students and urban students in half in only nine months. This is the single biggest improvement in learning I have ever seen in my decades of fieldwork. Yet, across rural China, about twenty million students don't have the glasses they need to see what's written on the blackboard. This is another crisis of epidemic proportions.[9]

There's one more major health crisis among elementary schoolchildren in southern China. A 2013 study in Guizhou Province revealed that more than 40 percent of students in rural elementary schools were infected with parasitic intestinal worms. That means more than four out of ten children in rural southern China were attending school—and living life—with worms in their bellies.[10]

Studies by other researchers have confirmed the 2013 study, documenting rates of intestinal worm infection of 40 percent and higher in rural areas of Sichuan, Fujian, Hunan, and Yunnan Provinces. Childhood intestinal worm infection appears to be endemic across large swaths of rural southern China.[11]

Invisible to the naked eye, intestinal worms steal valuable nutrients from their human hosts. This leads to malnutrition, poor appetite, nausea, dizziness, and compromised physical and cognitive development. Intestinal worms are also associated with anemia. Between the poor attention and cognitive effects of anemia and the negative health consequences of the worms themselves, this condition can be devastating for educational outcomes. Infected children stay home from school more often and come to school with less ability to focus and learn. According to my team's research, intestinal worms in rural China are clearly associated with worse academic performance, lower scores on memory and intelligence tests, and lower rates of school attendance.[12]

Based on all these project findings, one source of China's per-

Table 2. Health data on elementary schoolchildren

	Children affected
Anemia	27%
Uncorrected poor vision	20%
Intestinal worm infection	33%

Source: C. Zhou, S. Sylvia, L. Zhang, R. Luo, H. Yi, C. Liu, Y. Shi, P. Loyalka, J. Chu, A. Medina, and S. Rozelle, "China's Left-Behind Children: Impact of Parental Migration on Health, Nutrition, and Educational Outcomes," *Health Affairs* 34, no. 11 (2015): 1964–71; Ma Yue, Xiaochen Ma, Nathan Congdon, Alexis Medina, and Scott Rozelle, "Prevalence of Visual Impairment by Overtime among School-Age Children in China," REAP Working Paper, 2016.

sistent rural-urban education gap has become clear: rural students in today's China are sick. They are anemic, they can't see the blackboard, and they have worms. These health conditions make them tired. They make it harder to concentrate in school. They make it harder to understand what the teacher is saying and to read what's written on the blackboard. Visitors to the Invisible China are impressed with school facilities, but they can't see the obstacles to learning and growth that are plaguing rural students from the inside out.

Table 2 summarizes recent findings on these three issues from empirical studies across the country. Based on health data for 133,000 students from diverse regions, I estimate that about 60 percent of the elementary school children in the Invisible China are suffering from at least one of these three conditions.

These specific health problems may be only the tip of the iceberg. Anemia, uncorrected myopia, and intestinal worms are all easy to screen for and easy to treat, but our studies have shown that they are still being left untreated. This suggests that rural health is being systematically neglected. There may be many more serious health conditions running rampant in rural schools that have yet to be discovered.

China's elementary schools have transitioned from a system with highly visible problems to a system plagued by invisible epidemics. Huge strides have been made to improve educational resources, but not nearly enough has been done to help the students themselves.

As long as rural kids are sick, they will have no chance of catching up. So is it any wonder they're falling so far behind? Is it any wonder they don't have the energy to play at recess?

The Roots of the Crisis

The scale of this public health crisis seems hard to believe. The problem isn't that these health conditions are too difficult to address. Quite the contrary: all three have cheap and easy solutions.

Anemia is caused (in most cases) by a lack of iron in the diet. Hence it can be cured through changes in diet or, even more simply and cheaply, by giving each child a daily multivitamin that contains the recommended dose of iron. This means anemia is incredibly inexpensive to treat: an effective multivitamin can be purchased for only ten cents per child per day.

I've already mentioned the solution to poor vision. More than 90 percent of vision problems can be corrected by a proper pair of glasses. At about thirty dollars per nearsighted student, this solution is a bit more expensive but still within the budget of the average rural family. In fact, given today's wage rates (two to three dollars an hour), a pair of glasses costs about two to three days' wages for a rural family. Moreover, since glasses will usually last two years or so, the annual cost is not high (one day's wages of one parent per year); overall, the daily cost is even lower than the solution to anemia.[13]

There is a very cheap and well-established solution for intestinal worm infection as well. Good sanitation and healthy eating practices prevent children from contracting parasites. But even where sanitation practices are insufficient (as in much of rural China), the problem can be all but eliminated if children are given deworming medicine twice a year. This medicine is safe (safe enough to be given to all children, whether or not they are infected) and effective (worms are almost completely eliminated within one to two days). The medicine is also cheap; it costs less than two dollars to deworm a child for a year. This is only an hour of a parent's time each year.

The problem is one of information. These health challenges exist because no one knows about them. Anemia, poor vision, and intestinal worms are all invisible to the naked eye. Anemia is also known as "hidden hunger" because the effects are so hard to see. Intestinal worms are hidden in the bowels, often with no visible signs of sickness.

In discussing these problems, many people are quick to say that caring for children and feeding them nutritious meals is a private matter. They conclude, often on philosophical grounds, that a child's health and nutrition are rightfully the job of parents and families alone. Based on what I have seen, however, I don't believe that parents and grandparents in rural China have the capacity to resolve these problems on their own—at least for this current generation. Without specialized knowledge or experience, no parent can diagnose them. Especially in communities where anemia or intestinal worms are endemic, why would parents think twice because their child takes a lot of naps? Most parents in rural areas have received only a very basic education, and grandparents, the primary caregivers for many children in rural villages, are often almost entirely illiterate. Of course they want to help their children; they simply don't know how. Besides, it's a lot easier, cheaper, and more effective to manage these issues as public health problems and treat all the children at the same time, when they're concentrated in schools.

Our interviews with parents have revealed their lack of information about all three health problems. If the proximate cause of anemia is poor diet, the root of the problem in rural China is that parents just don't know that good nutrition is important for children's health and development. When my team surveyed caregivers in rural areas, more than 70 percent had no idea what anemia meant. I asked one rural grandmother how she decided what food her granddaughter needed to grow strong. "I make sure her belly is full," she said. "What more is there to worry about?" She chuckled at the obviously silly question. In most rural homes, children are given little to eat but rice, noodles, or steamed buns, with at most a bit of pickled vegetable. Most important, they have little or no source of iron or other key vitamins or minerals in their regular diets. Having meat, fish, tofu, and vitamin-rich fruits and vegetables (to help the child absorb iron) would go a long way toward staving off anemia and other micronutrient deficiencies.[14]

Knowledge about vision problems is just as limited. In one study my team asked parents and grandparents whether they thought their children had trouble seeing. Nearly half of the parents with nearsighted children (we knew because we'd already done a visual acuity and refraction exam at their school) did not know their child had a vision problem, and most did not think it needed solving. Even had they realized their child couldn't see well, many wouldn't have known what could be done about it. Parents laughed when we asked if they'd ever been taught about vision health. "Who is supposed to tell us? When we were children no one had glasses," one parent said.

Parents are similarly ignorant about the dangers of intestinal worms. Most mothers do not know that worms are passed on through human night soil. Grandma still rarely washes her hands before cooking. No one tells children or grandchildren they should always wear shoes outside, even though these parents do recognize the importance of deworming livestock. In a qualitative study of parents' knowledge about worms, almost every one of the families surveyed (98.7 percent) reported that they regularly dewormed their pigs. Meanwhile, 35 percent of their children were suffering from intestinal worms. They never thought about deworming their children.[15]

Beyond a lack of useful knowledge, many parents (and grandparents) in rural China distrust modern science in favor of traditional beliefs that are detrimental to children's health. The myths about eyeglasses are harmful and intractable. Despite research proving that eyeglasses do not hurt children's eyes—and in fact likely slow the decline of vision—most rural principals, teachers, and parents believe eyeglasses are harmful to children younger than twelve. "Glasses hurt children's eyes," they tell us. "Not wearing glasses make the eyes tougher, and they get better on their own." Of course none of this is true. Instead of eyeglasses, most rural families favor a Chinese-developed practice of "eye exercises" popular since the

1950s. Every day in school, children are required to massage their temples and the muscles around their eyes to ward off vision problems. Researchers have shown conclusively that these eye exercises are clinically worthless. They do nothing to help students, and they distract from the solutions that actually work.[16]

The folk wisdom about intestinal worms is also harmful to children's health. When you ask adults in rural Guizhou why they don't deworm their children, they frequently state outright that "worms are not bad for you." Some even say something like "You need them to digest your food." In a recent project, my team worked with local doctors to deworm children. We gave each child two high-quality, super-safe deworming tablets with simple instructions: "Take these two tablets before you go to bed tonight." In no small number of our households, the caregiver had the child take one pill and throw the other away. Why? "Too many worms is not good, but everyone needs some of them," they said. But if the deworming is not completed, the worms will almost immediately reproduce again in the child's intestines, and the effort is wasted. Thus myths are preventing children from getting healthy.

Another crucial part of the crisis is that even if parents do want to help their children and believe in modern medical care, in rural areas there is often almost no reliable source of health information. Most mothers say their main source of advice on how to care for their children is their mothers-in-law. But these grandmothers, though well-intentioned, simply don't have the latest information about children's health. Many of them have raised four or five successful subsistence farmers, but they know little about how to prepare their grandchildren for a modern knowledge-based economy.

Even supposed experts in China's rural areas aren't reliable sources of information and solutions. In most rural areas the most accessible health workers are the so-called village doctors. These doctors, also known as "barefoot doctors," are widely available, but they have highly variable levels of training and knowledge, so rural families can't always count on getting good information or good treatment from them. For example, in a recent survey in rural villages with a high rate of intestinal worm infection, my team sought out village doctors to ask about their knowledge of this health issue. In half the villages surveyed, there was no village doctor at all. In the villages that did have one, the village doctor had no relevant knowledge. Doctors in worm-infested villages said that intestinal worms were no longer a problem in their area. Some doctors shared the same inaccurate beliefs we had found to be so prevalent among the parents and grandparents: for example, that deworming medicine was harmful to children. In one village the rural doctor said, with full conviction, "I never recommend that young girls take deworming medicine because deworming medicines reduce fertility." This lack of understanding of the basic problem at the local level is appalling. It shows how difficult it is for parents to get good information about children's health, even if they seek it out.[17]

The problem of unreliable rural health care is widespread and serious. Starting in 2013, my team has conducted a series of innovative studies to assess the quality of rural health care. Rather than asking doctors to fill out survey forms or answer questions in a formal setting, we trained ordinary rural people to go into health clinics and ask for help for pretended health problems according to a script designed by the researchers—a kind of experiment known in the public health world as "standardized patients." The "patients" then recorded what the doctors told them, and the researchers compared those answers with the medically appropriate responses. The results of these studies were shocking. For very common symptoms and illnesses, including diarrhea, angina, and tuberculosis, doctors correctly diagnosed the illness only a small fraction of the time. Even when they got the diagnosis right, they prescribed the wrong treatment more often than the right one. In some cases, therefore, those seeking care from the rural health system have a higher probability of being hurt than helped.[18]

Overall, our research findings have shown that the situation is dire: parents and grandparents in the Invisible China do not have the knowledge or resources they need to help their children get healthy. Too often they hold on to myths that prevent them from curing their sick children in ways that have been proved to work. Even if they want to learn how to cure their children, they have no reliable source of information. The result is that millions of children are being surrendered to a future that is less than their full potential. And because two-thirds of China's future labor force is growing up in the Invisible China, improving the health and education of these children is literally an issue of national concern.

Health as the Foundation

It's not just China. This kind of problem—pervasive, invisible health issues that prevent kids from learning—is something that all countries at China's current stage of development must reckon with.

All three of the health crises cataloged in this chapter are endemic to middle-income countries generally. In Mexico, for example, about 30 percent of preschool-aged children suffer from anemia. Anemia rates are just as high in Thailand and Turkey: 25 percent and 33 percent, respectively. In Brazil the preschool anemia rate is fully 55 percent. For context, in a rich country like the United States, anemia rates among preschoolers are only 3 percent.[19]

The same is true for vision problems. The reasons myopia occurs at much higher rates in East Asia than elsewhere are still being debated, but the result is that a higher overall proportion of kids need glasses in rural China than in middle-income countries outside the region. Still, across the entire middle-income world, it's very common for children's vision problems to go undetected and unaddressed. A study in Chile, for example, found that only about 25 percent of children who needed glasses had them.[20]

Intestinal worms are rampant in other middle-income countries as well. Overall, worm infections are most prevalent in the poorest countries, among people who live on less than two dollars a day. Still, middle-income countries carry high burdens of worm infection. Intestinal worm infection rates are estimated to be as high as 26 percent in Brazil, for example, and 39 percent in Venezuela.[21]

So why is it that middle-income countries are still saddled with issues that most people probably associate with the poorest parts of the developing world? In part it's because they tend to have high rates of income inequality. As a country moves up the Chutes and

Ladders board, average incomes do increase, of course. This allows many people to finally afford better food and health care. Still, with the high rates of inequality, many others continue to live in poverty or hover just above the poverty line. In China in 2009, for example, only about 12 percent of the population were still below the extreme international poverty line (US$1.25/day), but fully 30 percent were living on less than two dollars a day. Thus, in spite of the improvement in average incomes, many people—especially in rural areas—still face the same barriers to basic health and nutrition that affect poor people around the world.[22]

Another part of the problem is that most middle-income countries do not have strong social safety nets or particularly well-developed public health systems. Their governments often do not provide the health screening and advice that we in high-income countries depend on to catch these problems and tell us how to address them. Moreover, because of the underdeveloped social safety nets, particularly in rural areas, families cannot rely on loans, health insurance, old-age pensions, or other economic and social institutions that we take for granted. Instead, they must pay out of pocket for all of life's biggest costs—catastrophic illnesses, children's education, and their own retirement. Thus, even if they know there's a problem, they simply don't have as much income to buy high-quality food or invest in preventive health care.

Finally, many people in the rural areas of middle-income countries simply don't have the knowledge or education to understand that nutrition and health play such big roles in children's educational success. They know enough to keep their bellies full and to seek help when they're very sick, but they don't know to look out for these invisible, but significant, health crises. This situation can be traced to the rapid pace of development in most middle-income countries. If development happened quickly (as it did in China), then many of the people who are raising children today still have poor-country levels of knowledge and education. They often don't know about nutrition or worms or glasses. This factor is magnified when many of the people doing the child-rearing are from the previous generation—the children's grandparents. In many middle-income countries, including China, the demands of the expanding economy bring about a large migration to the cities, so many children are left to be raised by grandparents who grew up when the country was poor. They generally have little education and not enough knowledge of what will be needed to succeed in the long run.

Thus a big part of the problem is that China, and many other middle-income countries, simply developed too fast. In the case of China, in one generation people across the country moved up the income ladder a distance that took four or five generations in most of the world's developed countries. In countries such as the United States, which grew at the slow but steady pace of only 2 to 3 percent a year for more than one hundred years after the Civil War, there was time for ordinary citizens to learn about nutrition and health and how to educate their children for a new higher-wage economy. China's families—especially those in poor, remote areas—have not had the same chance to catch up. Yet their children and grandchildren will be asked to compete in a global economy that demands twenty-first-century skills and knowledge and ability to learn.

When today's rural Chinese grandmothers were raising their own children—not so many years ago—they were raising subsistence farmers. Now these same grandmas are raising grandchildren who will need to go to high school and college and to thrive in an advanced economy. These children will have to learn algebra, English, and Chinese literature if they are to acquire the skills to take on more demanding jobs. Perhaps having anemia or worms or being nearsighted didn't matter in the past, but now it does matter. In a newly competitive and more technology-intensive economy, it may mean the difference between success and failure.

I believe these invisible health crises are not just critical for learning but also unrecognized contributors to the middle-income trap. They are fundamental to why so many middle-income nations can't make it up the last segment of the development game board.

For any middle-income country to be successful, its policies must go beyond the visible problems—whether school buildings or large infrastructure projects—and address the invisible barriers to students' learning and ultimately to economic growth. That could be said to be the primary lesson of this book. In fact, middle income could be described overall as a period of moving from visible to invisible (but still deeply significant) problems.

Take nutrition, or more broadly hunger. In poor countries, many people can't get enough food to keep their bodies strong. In many of the world's poorest countries, the average person still can't afford the 2,200 calories per day that scientists estimate is the bare minimum for a healthy life. For example, average residents in Haiti, Chad, Democratic Republic of Congo, Ethiopia, and Kenya must survive on fewer calories per day than their bodies need.

That kind of hunger—common in poor countries—has highly visible effects. You see children with the distended bellies of starvation. Parents are well aware that their crying children aren't getting enough to eat. The effects of childhood hunger can be clearly measured in reduced height (stunting) and reduced weight (wasting).

In middle-income countries, by contrast, the most basic form of hunger has been eliminated for most of the population. Higher average incomes mean that most people can afford adequate calories. People in Brazil, China, Mexico, Thailand, and Turkey, for example, can afford more than 3,000 calories a day on average. That's plenty to ensure that they can avoid starvation and many of the worst health effects of insufficient food. Of course, even in middle-income countries (and high-income countries, for that matter), some people still go hungry. But this is still a monumental shift for the average person at the national level.

Yet even in middle-income countries, the issue of hunger persists: the hunger simply has a different form. While people in middle-income countries generally can get enough *calories*, they still often struggle with poor diets—often starch-based with little nutrient-rich food. They can't afford to buy much meat or many vegetables. Maybe they can't afford the refrigeration required to keep such foods fresh. Maybe they were forced to survive on insufficient food earlier in life, so now that they can afford to eat well, they want foods, like grains, that are cheap and easy to prepare so they can eat their fill. Or maybe they simply don't know that many micronutrients are vital to basic human health and cognition.

Whatever the reasons, many people in middle-income countries are still lacking the fundamental nutrients their bodies need. They don't get enough vitamins or iron, for instance. This lack of nutrition continues to fundamentally affect their ability to take care of themselves and to perform at their highest level—for all that it's harder to see. Not for nothing is anemia known as "hidden hunger"; the effects are hard to detect. But in spite of its invisibility, hidden hunger is just as important to address as the visible burdens more prevalent in poor countries.

Traditional hunger (insufficient calories) is understood in the development world to be one of the major impediments to growth in poor countries. People who aren't getting enough to eat are less able to work, less able to take care of themselves, and more likely to get sick. This effect is so important at the national level that one of the most important contributors to a poor country's national growth strategy is often just ensuring that everyone is getting enough to eat. Once they have enough to eat, their lives improve, they're able to work harder at their jobs, and the productivity of the entire economy increases.

But hidden hunger (and the other invisible health crises I've discussed in this chapter) at the middle-income phase of development is just as critical in determining a country's long-term growth. The future prospects of middle-income countries depend on their ability to arm their citizens with the skills and education they'll need to find work in a higher-wage future. A country's most crucial resource during the middle-income phase of development is its children's ability to learn. Anemia, uncorrected myopia, and intestinal worms are all hard to see, and they often go unaddressed. But because all three conditions interfere with children's ability to learn, they form a critical barrier not just to individual wellness, but also to national economic growth.

I therefore believe that invisible child health issues are a crucial (and underexamined) reason so many countries are not accumulating the human capital they need quickly enough to keep up with the rapid pace of development. It is surely a factor that China—and other middle-income countries—must take seriously if they are to find a way out of (or around) the middle-income trap.

That's why health and nutrition are the foundation for everything else. That's why China's effort to combat the human capital crisis must start here. When many people, apparently including Chinese policymakers, think of "human capital," they think of education. They think of improving teaching, improving facilities, or improving the curriculum. Those are all important elements. But the most important factor China needs to address is the people themselves. They need basic health and nutrition if the rest of that investment is to pay off.

A National Policy Plan

Today, despite the best intentions, China's huge investment in rural education is in some sense being wasted. It will cost billions of dollars to get all children into high school. Hence it only makes sense to prepare them as much as possible before they are high school age so that they will be ready to learn—and thrive.

Researchers have shown again and again in countries around that world that many of the popular educational programs that are expected to improve students' learning do not work well. Policymakers can invest in reducing class size, upgrading equipment, or improving student health, yet students' learning will not change. The reason so many programs fail is usually that the other resources students need to succeed—good schools, good teachers, and good curricula—are lacking. In China all those building blocks are there. The only major thing still missing is student health. So for once the solution to the problem of poor learning is actually simple and even cost effective.[23]

In fact, my research team has proved through the highest standard of experimental evidence—the randomized controlled trial (RCT)—that all three health epidemics could be easily and cheaply addressed within the school system. What's more, the interventions not only improved health and nutrition, they also led to significant rises in students' academic achievement.

Randomized controlled trials have become increasingly common in social science research during the past decade. The theory and utility are easy to understand. We work with local policymakers and international experts in health, nutrition, and education to develop scalable, low-cost interventions that might improve student health. Then we randomly sample a group of schools in the very communities we're trying to help. Half of those schools are randomly chosen to receive the pilot policy, and half act as a control group. After a year (or two) of implementing the policy, we return to all the schools to see whether the policy was effective, by comparing outcomes in the treatment and control groups. RCTs are considered the gold standard in public policy because they allow for potential policies to be rigorously tested in real-world settings.

In the course of our research on anemia, intestinal worms, and visual health, we have conducted fifteen RCTs in the field to find the best, most cost-effective policies that can resolve these conditions. For each study, we administered the proposed solution in one group of schools (the treatment group) while leaving another group of schools unchanged (the control group). We have successfully identified real-world, workable solutions that can be brought to scale and are proved not only to improve health but also to boost educational performance. If the government decides to take responsibility for student health, to fix the last major barrier to students' learning in rural elementary schools, we have a toolbox ready for them to make big improvements very quickly.

Since my team began working on anemia in 2008, we have conducted a total of eight RCTs. We tested the effectiveness of several varieties of multivitamins, of supplementing students' diets with a range of food items, and of giving school principals incentives to improve student nutrition. This work showed that the most effective and cost-effective solution to China's anemia problem is to provide a daily multivitamin supplement. This program was shown to reduce the anemia rate by 25 percent. The daily multivitamin also raised the test scores of formerly anemic students significantly. The size of the effect was equivalent to reducing class size by half or to adding nearly a semester (or half a year) of schooling, just by adding a daily vitamin. Our work also showed that a nutritious school lunch, while more expensive, is also effective both in improving health and in raising educational performance.[24]

What about vision? We have conducted six RCTs targeted at finding the best ways to ensure that all students can see well enough to learn and succeed. Across all studies, we have shown unequivocally that putting glasses on a nearsighted child immediately and significantly improves academic performance. Glasses' effect on learning is one of the highest I have observed in decades of educational research. For the subset of children who regularly wore their glasses in class, test scores increased by a stunning 0.74 standard deviations—almost the equivalent of doubling the pace of learning of children affected by uncorrected myopia.[25]

In our work on vision, we have experimented with a number of ways to get glasses to children. If the government wanted to take the most charitable approach (handing out free glasses to all nearsighted children), the expense would be large, but not prohibitive for a country the size of China. A pair of glasses costing about thirty dollars can last a rural child about two years. Thus, if there are fifteen million children in grades four, five, and six in China's poor rural areas, and if 30 percent of them need glasses, this travesty could be averted for an investment of only fifteen million × 30 percent × fifteen dollars = sixty-eight million dollars a year.

We have shown that this is not the only way to get glasses to children who need them. We are in the midst of a project that is training local vision experts to go into local schools to test students' vision and refer nearsighted children to county hospitals. The program gives the first pair of glasses free to students in grades four to six, sells glasses to students in higher grades who can afford them, and offers them free to any student whose family doesn't have the money. In this way innovative new organizations can get glasses to every child who needs them without the need for large government subsidies or large charitable donations.[26]

Eradicating intestinal worms is similarly feasible through coordinated government action. In many developing countries, governments have had remarkable success in reducing or eliminating intestinal worm infections by passing out deworming drugs en masse in schools. In China, until the 1980s (and even into the 1990s in some provinces), every student would be dewormed twice a year in school. China knows how to do this effectively and efficiently. All it takes to keep a child worm-free for six months is two tablets, for about fifty cents each. Yes, you read that right: for a total of two dollars per child per year, Chinese children could be entirely worm-free. This devastating health problem could be averted for only fifty million dollars a year (if every student in every poor county—all twenty-six million—took their deworming medicine).

This is an opportunity to spend less money in smarter ways to ensure that young people are prepared to learn and thrive. And it's a chance to ensure that all children in China are given the chance to achieve their dreams before it's too late.

Human Scale

In 2018 I was visiting one of our vision programs. The team was on its third visit to a school in rural Gansu Province. The first two visits were for screening—figuring out which children were having vision trouble and assessing the proper prescription for each. On this day the kids would receive their new glasses.

As I watched the fifth graders form a line at the front of the classroom, I noticed that one boy in particular was hanging back. Unlike his friends, he wasn't pushing to get to the front. He had his eyes on the ground and his hands clasped nervously behind his back. It would be a while before it was his turn, so I wandered over to talk with him.

I asked how he was doing and how he felt about getting glasses today. He looked at me searchingly for a few moments, then looked away.

"It's OK," I told him. "I won't be offended. You can tell me what you're thinking."

He sighed. "Well," he told me. "I don't want glasses. I think I can see fine. And I think they'll make me look funny. And when I told my grandmother about the people coming to check our eyes and saying

I needed glasses, she told me it was a bad idea. She says the glasses are going to make my eyes worse and it's all a waste of time anyway."

I listened and nodded along. He had a stubborn expression, so I didn't try to convince him of anything. "Well, I guess you might as well give it a try," I said after a few moments. "Maybe they'll surprise you. It seems like it's worth a chance."

He nodded, looking thoroughly unconvinced. I went back to the rest of the team and left him to his waiting.

An hour or so later, I came back into the classroom and saw that this boy was now at the front of the line. The doctor handed him the glasses made with his prescription and told him to try them on and take a look out the window. Still frowning, he did so. Almost immediately, his face changed. His eyes widened, and he stumbled and almost fell. At first, he was confused. "Why is the light so bright?" Then a huge smile broke out. For the first time, the world wasn't blurry. For the first time, he could see the leaves on the trees.

It was a wonderful moment, one I cherish. Truly, the glasses project is the most fun to see in action. But the real impact of that day became clear only when our team returned to his school a few months later to assess the program's progress. We did a few home visits, and this boy's family was selected for one of them.

It had been six months since he got glasses. I walked with him to his house down the lane from his elementary school. There I met his grandma, the only adult he lived with, who had been so skeptical of the glasses program at the beginning. Tears came to her eyes as she told me her experience. "He's almost at the top of his class now. The teacher is so happy with his work and progress. I can't believe what a difference it's made."

She told me the change had been more than academic. "He used to be so isolated. No friends ever came home with him from school. Now, every day he stays after school and plays Ping-Pong and basketball with his friends. When he comes home he sometimes likes to take walks with me. He would never ever do this before getting his glasses. He actually smiles every time he puts them on. I can't believe how great the change has been." She shook her head and looked down at her hands. "I can't believe we almost kept him from this. I never knew how much he needed it."

This is what it looks like to make change at the micro level. And it's this kind of micro change that may make the difference for China in the coming decades. Starting with young children and individual families is the key to macro change. In fact, as I will show in the next chapter, the roots of China's invisible challenge start even earlier.

7: Behind Before They Start

In a small village in southern Shaanxi Province, terraced fields of green chives contrast sharply with the dry hillsides rising steeply on each side of a small concrete house. In the front yard Wang Jinjin sits on his mother's lap, staring across a low table at Meichen, a graduate student who has come to visit for the day. Jinjin is bundled up against the autumn chill, a warm woolen hat tucked down around his large eyes and plump, wind-burned red cheeks. He is just eighteen months old.

From all appearances Jinjin is a very lucky baby. Whenever he cries, someone picks him up and comforts him. Whenever he is hungry, someone brings him enough to eat. Although his father is often away working in the city, Jinjin has a stable family life, with parents and grandparents who love him very much. He has never known violence or hunger or real distress. But for those who know where to look, there are subtle signs that Jinjin is in trouble.

Meichen is here to give little Jinjin a test. The Bayley Scales of Infant and Toddler Development (Bayley test) was first developed by American psychologists in the 1960s. Today it is used internationally to assess babies' and toddlers' cognitive and motor development. You can think of it as an IQ test for babies.[1]

The test evaluates Jinjin's awareness. Does he notice when Meichen puts a colorful toy in front of him, waving it back and forth to get his attention? The test also checks whether Jinjin can follow simple instructions. "Put the block in the cup, Jinjin," Meichen tells him. "Like this, you see?" she says, demonstrating what she means, before handing him the toys to try for himself. She tests whether he has learned the basic rules of the physical world. When she takes a toy he likes and covers it with a cloth, does he know the toy is still there? Does he stare at the spot and reach to move the cloth away? Or does he look around helplessly and start to cry, thinking the toy has disappeared?

This test is based on decades of systematic research on human development and is carefully standardized. It has been adapted and administered millions of times in scores of countries around the world, including three Chinese-speaking countries or territories: Mainland China, Taiwan, and Hong Kong. Normal, healthy babies master these tasks in a predictable order and at reliable age milestones. Of course individual babies have good and bad days and, as any parent can tell you, some babies just learn more quickly than others. But scientists now know what behavior is within the broad normal range for each age group. If babies are far below the normal range, that's a sign that something is going wrong.

Something is going wrong here. Little Jinjin just failed his IQ test. He struggled with tasks designed for babies half his age. Although Jinjin is already eighteen months old, he hasn't yet said his first word. He hasn't learned to interact with anyone outside his immediate family. When Meichen asks him a question, he stares at her uncomprehendingly. When she holds out a shiny new toy, asking him to play with her, he takes the toy and turns away, watching her with solemn eyes as he sits curled and silent in his mother's arms.

This doesn't bode well for Jinjin. And the problem is much bigger than this baby, or this family, or this village. In spite of his unremarkable appearance, little Jinjin, and the ten million other babies like him, are the fulcrum on which the future of China will turn.

First Clues

It was on a winter day in Xi'an in 2012, with the western Chinese city's familiar dust and pollution clouding our view of the mountains, that

I first learned the importance of infant development. Reynaldo Martorell, a leading nutrition scientist at Emory University's School of Public Health, was visiting to consult on one of our research projects. A native Honduran and a keen observer, Rey has distinguished his time as a faculty member at Stanford, Cornell, and Emory by his unceasing dedication to helping the poor. He has probably spent more time in rural villages in the developing world than any other academic.

On that day in Xi'an, Rey was in town to work on a joint project, assessing nutrition in rural Chinese primary schools and evaluating whether improving nutrition might help ten- to twelve-year-old rural students do better in school. Four professors and twenty graduate students were gathered in a conference room, with the latest survey data projected on a screen in front of us, trying to stay focused with the help of instant coffee and cheap takeout. As Rey bent over his notes, he looked up, deep in thought. "You know," he said, "you've done all this research looking at barriers to education among school kids. You work with kids from primary school all the way up to college. But have you ever worked with babies?"[2]

I shook my head, an obvious no. I'd worked only with school-aged children. Rey responded, "The kinds of problems you're finding in these schools—the struggle to learn and the persistent achievement gap—well, it could be that the trouble is actually starting much earlier than you think. I've learned that babies' development is really sensitive to shocks. If kids don't get what they need when they're really young, the effects can be irreversible."

With plenty to do, we turned back to the task at hand, but Rey's comment stayed with me. Late at night, after long meetings on other projects, I would lie awake and wonder. I'd been working for a decade to try to close the gap in learning between rural and urban kids in China. Could I have missed the most important issue of all? As I continued my other work, I started asking around and searching online. In fact, there was a lot of recent work on this subject, even in many developing countries. But I quickly learned that no one had any idea how babies in rural China were doing. There was absolutely no research on that. Zero. There weren't even news stories or personal accounts about the issue.

In 2014 and 2015, my team began our first research project to get some answers. With the help of Rey and a few other experts in psychology and neuroscience, we trained a team of over a hundred graduate and postdoctoral students, including Meichen, in administering the Bayley test to babies. We had no clear agenda. We didn't even know if this was an issue in rural China. The results were certainly the most shocking of my career.

First, in 2014 our study of nearly two thousand families in rural Shaanxi Province revealed that 53 percent of babies in our sample had failed the Bayley test. That's right: more than half of the infants and toddlers in our sample were measured as cognitively delayed. Just like Jinjin, they were missing important milestones. Just like Jinjin (who was one of the babies in that sample), they were falling behind in their most basic abilities. This was not a minor delay—these babies were scoring more than a standard deviation below the average for babies their age. In a normal distribution of a typical population, only 16 percent of babies would score this poorly. In other words, the failure of these rural toddlers in rural China was astounding in scope and scale. I could hardly believe it.

We did studies in other parts of China to see if this was a general problem and found it was even worse in other places. A second study in 2015 and 2016 in rural Hebei Province, only a two-hour drive from rich, prosperous Beijing, found that 55 percent of babies were delayed. The lowest scores we found were in remote Yunnan Province, where more than 60 percent of babies failed the Bayley test. We aren't talking here about the poorest of the poor, those in remote minority communities. The babies we tested were mostly Han, China's largest and most prosperous ethnic group. This means the problem is probably even worse in the poorest communities.[3]

In 2017 we extended our study to nearly all other types of communities that are full of rural hukou holders: rural communities in central China's plains region, communities of rural-to-urban migrants in China's largest cities (Beijing, Zhengzhou, and Xi'an), and large migrant resettlement communities. Of all rural communities, these are the most prosperous, full of ambitious parents who dared to seek opportunity beyond the village and close to the worldly urban elite. But in these more successful, cosmopolitan settings, babies are falling just as far behind. On average, more than 50 percent of these children were shown to have delays in cognition, language, or social-emotional skills.[4]

This problem appears to be limited to rural China. Several studies from cities across China have found that urban Chinese babies are well within the normal range. In particular, as I mentioned above, the Bayley test is scaled for about 16 percent of babies in a normal, healthy population to fall into the "low development" category. The data show that urban Chinese babies actually perform a bit above average: studies found that 5 to 13 percent of urban Chinese babies were falling into the low development category. As a reminder, over 50 percent of rural babies fall into this category. Overall, this research shows that urban China is not facing a problem of delayed infant development—this is, again, a fundamentally rural problem.[5]

That does not mean its insignificant. Recall that children with rural hukou (including those living in villages and the children of rural-to-urban migrants) make up about 70 percent of all China's children today. I believe our work on the problem of infant and toddler delay is representative of nearly the entire rural infant and toddler population. From all available evidence, it seems delayed infant development is endemic across China.

As the results of these studies began to sink in, I was overwhelmed by the scale of the problem. How could so many babies be so far behind? How could no one know about this? As I began to share the results with experts from other disciplines and to learn more about psychology and neurobiology, my concern grew. Just as Rey Martorell had warned me years before, infant development is critical.

This isn't a story of late-blooming babies who will catch up in a few years. Without immediate help, the evidence suggests, Jinjin and his peers will be left at a lower level for life.

The Importance of Early Childhood

For most of human history, child-rearing was an art rather than a science. Like other species, we did our best to raise our young, drawing on a combination of instinct and the example of our own parents, relatives, and neighbors. For most of human history, that method worked just fine. We taught our children the skills we knew. We showed them how to feed themselves, how to make a living, how to protect themselves as best they could against illness and external threat.

Then the world changed. With the rise of the scientific method, we began to base our opinions more on facts established through the isolation of variables than on our best guesses at the workings of complex mechanisms. Among the great things we learned in this way—lifesaving medicine, new ways of controlling our environment, new methods of propelling ourselves through the physical world—we also learned that certain ways of raising children work better than others, especially in a modern world that places high intellectual and social demands on them once they're grown.

I don't want to overstate this point. As a father myself—and as an observer of this literature—I know just how many questions come up in the course of raising a child that have no good answers. There is no perfect way to parent—no comprehensive guide and no single scientific formula. But rigorous research in biology and developmental psychology has established beyond doubt that there are certain foundational elements that all children—particularly infants and toddlers—really do need if they are to reach their full cognitive, linguistic, motor, and social-emotional potential. Without these resources, kids can fall behind and remain negatively affected for their entire lives.

Since the 1960s it has been widely recognized that, on average, children from different family backgrounds begin school with different abilities. In particular, children from wealthy families generally start kindergarten with better cognitive and language skills than poorer children do. For many decades most scientists and educators chose not to question their inherited prejudices, interpreting this divide as evidence of the genetic superiority of certain groups. Leading theorists made arguments based on sloppy science that certain social classes—or certain races—were just inherently "smarter" or "better" than others.[6]

As more objective researchers began to investigate this question more rigorously, however, the old arguments quickly fell apart. Evidence has now conclusively shown that, on average, all people, regardless of racial identity or economic class, are born with about the same innate cognitive ability. Instead of genetic differences, research shows that poor children fall behind primarily as a result of differences in their early environment and experience. Simply put, the way we're treated during our first years of life has a tremendous effect on our fundamental capacity to learn and thrive and our chances of success throughout our lives.

This is because the environment of early childhood profoundly influences our most essential tool in life: the human brain. From conception to about five years of age, our brains build their fundamental architecture, laying the groundwork for a lifetime of learning, thinking, and social skills. At this age the brain forms up to a thousand synapses each second. For the basic brain networks that allow us to think, to learn, and to develop our cognitive abilities across our lifetime (including numerical understanding, language ability, and understanding of symbols), the most critical brain growth happens before age three. After this peak, it's more and more difficult to acquire these fundamentals. Because these skills build on one another over time, early deficits can accumulate, leaving children in trouble for their entire lives.[7]

This means there is a finite window of opportunity during which young children can develop their core cognitive and social skills. Children who fall behind early in life, as Jinjin and others have in rural China, are (to a very high level of probability) left with a much lower lifetime capacity. If the critical resources are missing for too long, the window of opportunity can close, leaving children with lower ability for the rest of their lives. Before they are old enough to say their own names, they are set on a trajectory toward lower IQ, more behavior problems, worse school outcomes, higher likelihood of criminal behavior, and lower lifetime income.

So how badly are Jinjin and other babies in rural China doing today? According to our results, at least half the babies in China's rural villages are scoring low enough on cognitive tests that it is unlikely that (without immediate intervention) they will ever reach adult IQs above ninety. IQ is scaled such that an IQ of ninety or less puts the bearer in the lowest 16 percent of a normal population, unable to learn many of the basic skills taught in the junior high curriculum in China's school system. In the United States an IQ below ninety or so is generally enough to place a student in special education classes. Babies like Jinjin, twenty to thirty million of them across China today and five to ten million more each year, are likely to end up in this category if nothing is done.

Thanks to Rey's prompting, I had stumbled on the single greatest crisis China faces today. And this problem—even more than intestinal worms in school-aged children or uncorrected myopia in rural villages—was truly invisible.

Left Behind

Just a few hundred meters up the valley from Jinjin's home is another house that looks much the same as the first. It has the same white paint, the same sloped wooden roof, and the same tattered red and gold banners hanging along the door, remnants of the Chinese New Year celebration a few months before. The family living in the second house is also much the same. Like the Wang family home where Jinjin is growing up, the Li home houses two hardworking parents, two loving grandparents, and one son. The son, Li Xiaofei, learned to crawl in the same sandy soil as Jinjin and attended the same schools Jinjin will go to once he's old enough. But Xiaofei hasn't been around much recently.

On a windy spring day, I met Xiaofei at a bus stop on the outskirts of Xi'an—a couple of hundred kilometers from his rural home. Across the street, a new complex of luxury condominiums was just opening its doors. But Xiaofei led me in the opposite direction, along a narrow dirt road lined with small noodle joints and shops selling plastic tubs, mops, and cheap toys. With his well-worn work boots and black-and-tan pleather jacket, Xiaofei blended with the crowd of migrant workers. Only his face gave away his age. He'd just turned sixteen.

Five years ago Xiaofei was just a normal rural kid, living with a family who loved him and had high hopes that he could succeed in school and go on to a life much more stable than their own. Every morning Xiaofei would race his friends down the path to the village elementary school, eager to get to the classroom. His grades were pretty good. He liked school well enough.

Then, right after he started seventh grade, his grades started to slip. Every week his teacher would post the scores from the latest test on the blackboard for everyone to see. For several months he watched his name slip down the list. By mid-October, he was toward the bottom. When he saw his name there, he felt shame well up inside him.

As his grades fell, his teachers became increasingly hostile. "In class the teacher would make us write English words up on the board," Xiaofei told me, as we settled into a corner booth and ordered two big bowls of noodles. "And every time I got a word wrong, the teacher would smack me across the head and yell at me in front of everyone. It was so ugly." Finally in the spring of his seventh-grade year, Xiaofei decided he'd had enough. He left a note for his parents and bought a bus ticket. The next day he arrived in Xi'an with a canvas bag and a job flyer. He was just thirteen.

There are a million and one reasons for a rural kid to drop out of school. Xiaofei's family was poor, and getting to his junior high school was inconvenient, a two-hour commute there and back each day in a rickety van. But in Xiaofei's mind, the reason he left school was always clear: "I just couldn't learn," he tells me. "No matter what I did, no matter how hard I tried, I just couldn't get it. I decided I'd do anything to get away from that place."

After Xiaofei's mother found her son's note, she phoned him

every day for a month and begged him to come home. She warned that he was throwing away his only chance to make a better life for himself. She reminded him how hard they'd worked in the hope that he might have all the opportunities—college, a safe and steady job, a chance to see the world—that they were forced to go without.

But Xiaofei had run out of patience—or maybe hope. "Some kids are good students and some aren't," he told me, his jaw set stubbornly as he stared into his noodle bowl. "I thought I was, but now I know I'm not. Nothing made sense no matter how hard I tried or how many hours I studied. I don't see why I should keep wasting my time."

How common is Xiaofei's story? In fall 2017 my research team traveled to some rural junior high schools. We were there to do an unrelated study—looking at the effect of teacher payment schemes on students' learning. However, since we were going to be working inside more than a hundred junior high schools across a large area of rural China, we took the opportunity to try to understand what was going on with rural students' cognition. I had an idea I wanted to test.

Ever since I started working with babies and discovered the crisis of delayed development, I'd been wondering how this would affect kids when they grew up. According to the theories of developmental psychologists and neuroscientists, if half the children in rural areas were suffering from cognitive delays when they were babies, then (as long as nothing had changed for the worse over the previous ten years or so), we should expect to find roughly the same share of students in junior high school with poor cognitive skills. I also wanted to know if this cognitive delay was negatively affecting their schooling.

To test this theory, my team administered two different tests of cognition to five thousand randomly selected seventh graders in the one hundred rural junior high schools in our sample. Over the whole group, we found that more than 40 percent of kids had low IQs. We also gave them a standardized math test, like the ones Xiaofei had been failing. The correlations were striking. Low cognition and low math scores moved in lockstep. Higher math scores were closely associated with normal levels of cognition. In my mind this was quite likely Xiaofei's problem. He wanted to learn. His family wanted him to learn. But he just couldn't do it. He is probably who Jinjin will be fifteen years from now—if Jinjin doesn't get help.[8]

What became of Xiaofei? For a while, he was doing all right. He didn't have a junior high school degree, so many career paths were closed to him and probably will be forever. But at first it wasn't hard to find paying work. Within several days of arriving in Xi'an, he was able to find a job on a construction site. He was supposed to be at least sixteen, but no one really cared.

For the first two years, he worked on the bamboo scaffolding around the upper stories of Xi'an's rising skyscrapers. It was hard and sometimes dangerous work. He was talking to his mother again, and she wanted him to find something safer. But he thought he could last a few years at least, and the job paid more than he could make anywhere else without a degree. But in 2015, without warning, his construction site closed down. For a while he worked on an assembly line in a local factory, making electronics of some kind—he wasn't sure what they were used for. Then that job closed down too. He looked for another job, but no one seemed to be hiring.

Xiaofei has been out of work for the past three months. For now he's living on the money he saved. He hasn't told his parents. Recently he's been talking to a few other friends from his construction days. One of them has found a way to make some money, but it's dangerous and Xiaofei's not sure he's up for it.

"What's the job?" I ask, as I finish my lunch.

"Well, you probably wouldn't like it," he says, fidgeting in his chair. When I don't look away, he sighs and continues. "Well, so, for a few months this guy's been involved in a gang that has been kidnapping girls from the prefectural seat . . . and selling them as brides to rural farmers who live way up in the mountains in another province."

As I try to keep the shock from my face, Xiaofei lowers his face over his bowl. "I know that's not right. I don't want to do that," he tells me, shaking his head as he slurps up the last few noodles. "But I really need to find something."

On that spring day I paid for our lunch and shook Xiaofei's hand. I thanked him for his time and wished him well. As he walked out the door and back up the busy street, his shoulders hunched and his hands deep in his pockets, one question kept returning to my mind: Where did it all go wrong?

Parenting for the Twenty-First Century

Early development experts like Rey will tell you that when something is going seriously wrong with infants' cognitive development, one of two culprits is usually to blame. The first is malnutrition. The second is the way babies interact with their parents in the earliest years.

My team has found evidence that part of the problem in rural China can indeed be traced to malnutrition. Iron-deficiency anemia, one of the three types of malnutrition proved to permanently affect brain development in young children, is rampant among babies in the Invisible China. A large study including data from babies in eleven Chinese provinces found the average infant anemia rate across all rural areas was 33 percent. My team's own survey research has found anemia levels ranging from 40 percent all the way up to 70 percent in rural mountain communities. Our recent research found that anemia was almost as serious a problem among the young children of rural migrants in Beijing and other large cities. Internationally, anemia during infancy has been linked to long-run lowered IQ, more mental health issues, more grade repetition in school, and a gap in cognitive and learning abilities that widens through at least nineteen years of age.[9]

Rural China's widespread infant anemia problem is therefore likely part of what is preventing Jinjin, Xiaofei, and others like them from developing as they should. Indeed, we found that improving nutrition by giving each baby a daily iron supplement—a micronutrient powder called Sprinkles (Yingyangbao in Chinese) with their cereal led to small but immediate (and statistically significant) improvement in Bayley test scores. This program is not expensive or dangerous, and research suggests that if implemented more widely it would likely have a long-term positive effect for a large share of the children now suffering from micronutrient deficiencies. Our research with this age group, like our research with schoolchildren, showed that such an effort to stave off and treat anemia would be both inexpensive and hugely beneficial. China, in fact, launched an experimental program in 2012 to deliver Sprinkles to rural families with infants and young toddlers. This is a good sign and seems to demonstrate that policymakers are beginning to realize the benefits of this kind of program, but they need to expand it across as many villages as possible.[10]

We also found, however, that the nutrition program made a difference on cognitive outcomes only for very young babies, and it resolved only a small part of their slow development. After they reached twelve months of age, no matter how much their nutrition improved, their cognition remained low. Remember that addressing the problem of anemia does still have positive effects on learning outcomes for schoolchildren (as we've seen in the previous chapter). Still, this finding among young children suggested that another factor was contributing to the delayed development. It turns out the problem can be traced back to something that might seem very subtle: the way parents and grandparents interact with their children at the youngest ages.[11]

Almost everywhere I go in the world, I see parents taking care of their young children in much the same way. It goes something like this. When you pick up a baby, you smile, you coo, you try to get the baby to laugh. You point out things in the world around you, narrating in a way that will engage a curious mind: "Look at the blue sky! What color is the cloud? It's white!" you say, nodding and smiling down at the child. Every night before bed, you read your child a story or sing a lullaby. You surround the baby with toys that have bright colors and moving parts. You sit and play with her and ask her to name the colors of different parts of the toy, to move the toy in new ways. When the child is old enough, you hold her hands as she takes her first stuttering steps, or you sit on the floor a few steps away, spread your arms wide, and call encouragingly, "Come on, you can do it! Walk to me!"

I raised my own sons this way in California's Silicon Valley over thirty years ago. My young granddaughter is being brought up the same way today. Last June, on a train passing through the German countryside, I saw a young couple parenting this way too, holding their toddler up to the window, pointing out the trees, farms, and castles they passed, smiling and encouraging her as she repeated the new words. In fact, this is the norm in all developed countries from Norway to Canada to Australia.

This parenting style is not ubiquitous only in rich countries. In urban China, parents interact with their children exactly the same way. On a flight across China in December, I watched a young woman from Beijing set a toy on her tray table, a plastic tower stacked with colored blocks of different shapes. With her young son on her lap, she held up one of the blocks. "What color is this one?" she asked. "Red!" he squeaked joyfully. "And what shape?" "Square!" "Good!" she said, beaming at him.

Hence, to parents in developed countries, and even to parents in urban China, this style of parenting seems ubiquitous. It feels natural. Babies love it, and most parents probably cannot imagine any other way of interacting with their kids. "Everyone does this. What's there to question?" you might think. But in rural China (and in fact in many other developing countries), the picture looks very different. Rural families love their children, but they don't engage in these practices.

On driving up to a rural household, one often sees a grandmother silently going about her work in the fields with a baby strapped to her back. The baby is close to Grandma, safe and warm, but immobilized and staring up at the back of her head for hours on end with no mental stimulation or social interaction. Mothers stand on the side of the road with babies tucked up on their hips. They chat with their neighbors or other family members, but you almost never see them talking to their babies.

The first time I visited Jinjin and his family, I found his mother chopping vegetables at a low table, with Jinjin sprawled on a chair next to her. Over the sixty minutes I sat in their home, Jinjin's mother didn't once speak to him or play with him. When he began to fuss, she handed him to his grandfather, who held him silently on his lap while he watched TV. Both family members loved Jinjin, and it showed clearly in their faces. Jinjin's grandmother told me she really hoped he could go to college. But it simply never occurred to them to interact with him in the ways that are common in other places. Hard as it may be to believe, this subtle difference in parenting style lies at the heart of China's current crisis.

Research has shown that to develop healthy brains, babies must have dedicated mental and emotional engagement. They cannot learn how to express their emotions without seeing those emotions modeled and mirrored on an adult's face. They cannot learn the names of the colors, or understand the concepts of "sky" and "cloud," without having some adult take the time to introduce the ideas. They cannot develop the basic brain architecture they need for a lifetime of learning and personal development without sustained, mentally stimulating one-on-one engagement from a loving adult.[12]

The first evidence for the importance of mental and emotional stimulation came from some of the most tragic episodes of child neglect. In the 1950s, researchers studied children who had been raised in a particularly grim orphanage in Lebanon. For the first several years of their lives, the orphans were almost entirely confined to their cribs. They were fed and changed but given little or no individualized care or attention. The researchers discovered that this absence of one-on-one interaction had a devastating effect on the children's mental development. The orphans displayed stark developmental delays that persisted for the rest of their lives. This finding was duplicated in other orphan studies in Korea and Romania: early neglect can become destiny if not remedied in time.[13]

This research has shown that the most extreme cases of neglect (as in institutionalized orphans) leave children with severely stunted emotional and cognitive abilities (and in the worst cases even starkly shrunken brains). But even in otherwise normal, loving families—like Jinjin's—development can differ markedly depending on the kind of stimulation children receive when they are very young.[14]

For example, striking differences in child outcomes have been traced to a very simple source: how much parents talk to their young kids. Researchers working in the United States showed that in the first three years of life, babies from richer families hear thirty million more words than babies from poorer families. By age three the two groups had a disparity in their vocabularies that was almost directly proportional to the difference in word frequency at home. What's more, that early disparity was linked to long-term achievement gaps, with early delays in language skills predicting lower cognitive scores and worse school outcomes a decade later, all because of a slight difference in parenting practices.[15]

In rural China, babies are systematically missing out on the mental stimulation they need. When we asked rural families if they ever talked to their babies, we were met with blank looks or bemused smiles. "Why would I talk to my baby?" one young mother responded, giggling into her hand. "She can't talk back!"

I spoke to one grandmother who thought my question was very strange. "Why would we talk to the baby? He's a baby!" When I didn't immediately agree with that statement, she slowed down to make sure I was following. "You see, the baby can't understand words. He can't even follow basic instructions like 'don't go outside.' So how could he follow a story?" She shook her head at my wild questions. And yet research clearly shows that speaking directly to infants helps them learn the basics of language and improves their cognition even before they are old enough to respond in any obvious way.

My favorite way to describe this to people outside rural areas—let's say an audience at a talk I'm giving in Shanghai—is to go through the following dialogue. As I said, when a member of my research team asks rural parents if they ever read to their children, the most common response is a giggle. Then I ask the audience if they've ever had a goldfish or a turtle. Always a couple of people raise their hands. I then ask them to stand up and answer my question out loud: "So did you read to your turtle every night?" "Did you sing to that goldfish?" Their response? Almost always that same giggle. In fact, the entire audience would chuckle. I think they finally understood. Asking a rural mother or grandmother if they had read a book to their baby was as silly and unthinkable to them as asking if they told stories to their goldfish or sang songs to their houseplants to help them grow. Most rural parents in China today simply can't imagine the point of treating a baby that way.

For those used to the modern way of caring for young children, this can seem hard to believe. Is it possible to hold a child you love and care for and not talk to him, make faces at him, try to get him to smile? Who could be so cold, so unloving?

To be clear, the difference I am describing in rural China has nothing to do with intensity of love. Families in these villages love their children more than anything. When Jinjin's mother is cooking, she straps the baby to her back so he's close and safe and will not get burned by the sizzling oil in her wok. When the weather turns cold, she bundles him up in so many layers that he looks more like a marshmallow than a baby. Every day she feeds him as much as he will eat. She would rather go without a meal herself than withhold anything from her young son. Just like Xiaofei's mother, she has big dreams for Jinjin. She hopes he will go to college someday and pledges she'll do whatever it takes to get him there.

But the point remains. Jinjin's parents are not interacting with their son in the ways that have been proved to promote his long-term development. This problem is systemic across villages in the Invisible China. The results of our first study on parenting showed that only 5 percent of families in rural villages ever read to their children. Only about 10 percent tell their babies stories. Only 30 percent ever use toys to play with their children or sing to them.[16]

What's more, we found a clear link between these parenting practices and children's scores on the Bayley test. The few families who did engage in these beneficial practices were raising children who were doing fine. In the families where the parenting practices were the most lacking, the kids were falling the furthest behind.[17]

In spite of their best intentions, most rural families just don't know what their kids need to thrive. How could they know? Jinjin's family doesn't have access to any of the tools that teach other families around the world how to interact with their children. When I found I was going to be a father, I bought out the entire parenting section at our local bookstore. I went with my wife to Lamaze classes and took harried notes about everything we were supposed to do or to avoid. Every time we went to the doctor, we'd come home with a new pamphlet explaining how to master some critical parenting skill. Nowadays modern parents have access to all that and more on the internet.

But Jinjin's parents have none of that. They don't have a library or a bookstore or a computer with access to the internet. They don't have books about parenting or access to web forums. No one in their village offers classes in parenting. They probably took Jinjin to a village doctor once or twice, but that doctor certainly never gave them any parenting advice or helpful flyers to take home. No one they know has ever had access to these things either.

Instead these families—Jinjin's family among them—have been left to rely on the wisdom of tradition, the way things have always been done. When Jinjin's mom doesn't know how to help her son, she asks her mother-in-law, a woman who has spent a lifetime working the fields as a poor farmer, unhampered by never having spent a day in school. Living on tiny farms among the mountains, much as their ancestors have done for generations, they are living—and parenting—for a bygone era.

A Changing World

Is this a new problem? One of the things I think about when considering China's current infant development crisis is that this has probably been a problem in China's rural villages for decades. Certainly our IQ testing in rural junior high schools suggests that the problem has been around for a while. I think if we had done this same Bayley test in rural villages and the same IQ tests in junior high schools forty years ago, the scores would have been even worse. But for a long time that really didn't matter.

Forty years ago, it didn't matter if half of rural peasants had below-average IQ—they were going to spend their lives farming anyway. Even twenty years ago, low cognition didn't get in the way of a rural villager's ability to thrive. As we've seen, the jobs that turned China into the factory of the world in the past three decades—working on assembly lines or construction sites—put relatively low demands on a worker's cognitive abilities. Just look at Xiaofei. He may not have been able to handle the demands of junior high school, but he has no trouble working on a construction site or an assembly line, doing the same repetitive action day after day.

But now the challenges are steadily increasing. As China's wages rise, there will be fewer and fewer assembly line factories to choose from. Low-wage, low-skilled jobs will lose out to either offshoring or automation. That is going to happen: the question is when, not if. For China to become a prosperous, stable country, it's going to need workers who can handle a wider variety of jobs. Today's China needs kids who can grow up to be college students, or at least high school students, so they will be flexible enough to take on whatever's next. There's no point in expanding access to high school if children aren't given the foundation they need to learn once they get there.

The modern parenting style that has become common from Los Angeles to London to Tokyo feels natural to many of us, but it had to be learned. It took generations of slow social change, rising economic fortunes, increases in education, and intentional efforts to give people access to modern information to help parenting practices keep pace.

In rural China change happened too fast. In one generation, living standards for many in rural China increased by a factor of one hundred—a staggering rate of change. In most of today's rich Western countries, the same amount of growth took four to five generations. Because the process there was slow, ordinary citizens had time to learn how to live in their changed world and how to prepare their children to live and thrive in that new world.[18]

Think about the families in rural China today. When Jinjin's grandma was raising Jinjin's father, China was still poor. If she did her job right, she could hope her children would survive long enough to become peasant farmers. For a peasant, the nutrition and parenting practices used in traditional rural China would be more than enough. It didn't matter if kids had the nutrition or the parenting they needed to eventually learn algebra and foreign languages: they'd never have the opportunity anyway.

But that's not true anymore. It's easy to romanticize the rural way of life, to wax poetic over the beautiful hills, the simple schedule, and the freedom from the stresses of a twenty-first-century existence. But even in these remote farming communities, the times have already changed. Whatever his parents experienced before him, if Jinjin is going to survive in a thoroughly modern world, he's going to need the cognitive skills that will allow him to take on twenty-first-century challenges. Now that we know just how critical early childhood experiences are for lifelong capability, Jinjin, as much as anyone, deserves to benefit from all that modern science has revealed.

In fact, the world is beginning to discover that the problem of poor infant development is indeed common throughout the developing world. A recent special issue of the prominent medical journal the *Lancet* demonstrates the breadth of this problem, estimating that across all low- and middle-income countries approximately 250 million children below age five are at risk of long-term reduced development. An earlier *Lancet* study in the same series concluded there is ample evidence that inadequate cognitive stimulation (due to insufficient parenting practices) is one of the most important contributors to the problem of delayed early childhood development worldwide. That study estimated that only 11 percent to 33 percent of parents in developing countries undertake cognitively stimulating activities with their children. Thus this is a common problem across the developing world, and much of it can be traced to parenting practices that have not kept pace with the needs of young children.[19]

As we saw with invisible health issues in the previous chapter, delayed infant development is not limited to the poorest countries. Many other middle-income countries are also saddled with high rates of development delays due in large part to insufficient parenting practices. For example, in Colombia a research team from the University College of London undertook a study of 1,400 rural mothers and babies in ninety-six poor towns and discovered rates of delayed development similar to my team's results in China. In particular, from 30 to 40 percent of the babies at the baseline were cognitively delayed. Anemia was also widespread among this group of children. In their subsequent field experiment (RCT) they found that the parenting intervention (a weekly parental training session and access to toys and books) yielded dramatic results. In particular, over the eighteen-month study, children in the treatment group showed significant improvement in language and cognitive development over the control group. Indeed, this Colombian study had findings remarkably similar to my team's work in rural China, in the prevalence of the problem, the description of the parenting environment at home before the study, and the effect of the interventions. Similar work has been done in Jamaica, again with very similar findings.[20]

Fortunately, in some of the countries most at risk, there has started to be a response. Attention to this long-overlooked issue is finally gaining traction among policymakers, scholars, and development professionals who are interested in the economic development of (middle-income) countries in Latin America, southern Africa, and other regions of the world. The Inter-American Development Bank (IDB) is funding loan program after loan program and investment after investment to help local country officials direct resources to this critical issue. The most high-profile response so far has come in Brazil. With the intense support of Marcela Temer, then first lady of Brazil, a nationwide training program for parents of children from birth to age three was launched. The program has prepared thousands of primary parenting trainers and invested hundreds of millions of dollars into this effort to lay the foundation for breaking out of the middle-income trap. When the new president of Brazil, Jair Bolsonaro, took over in 2018, he decided to keep this program running. Today more than three million families are participating across thousands of municipalities.[21]

A book written by an influential scholar at the IDB makes it clear that the organization is strongly committed to, and has high hopes for, broadening this new undertaking for the sake of the many middle-income countries in his bank's region. In short, it says the parents are not to blame. They want more than anything for their children to thrive. The problem is that they just haven't had time to learn how one can raise children to prepare them for the twenty-first century. When the information is presented to them in a digestible way, they learn and adopt the lessons, and their children improve markedly. In other words, this campaign is completely in line with the conclusions I have drawn based on similar work within China. This work is urgently needed, especially for countries at risk of falling into the middle-income trap.[22]

Hope for Dramatic Change

On a summer day just a few months after Meichen's first visit to Jinjin's village, I'm back for another visit. It appears that Jinjin is already doing a lot better. Today Jinjin and his family are hosting a man named Liu Xianju. About thirty years old, Liu is dressed simply in a black hooded sweatshirt and well-worn jeans. At the moment, he and Jinjin are having a tea party. Holding tiny plastic teacups, they sit on either side of a wooden bench. "Let me pour you some tea," Liu says theatrically, pouring water into the tiny cup set out in front of the baby. "Careful—it's hot!" he cautions, his eyes cartoonishly wide and locked on Jinjin's face. "Mmm, delicious!" he says, sipping from his cup as baby giggles and plays along. Sitting just behind her young son, Jinjin's mother is trying to hold back a giggle of her own. It's her turn to play next.

Contrary to appearances, Liu Xianju is here on important business. Just a few months ago, Liu was part of the first class of "parenting trainers" to graduate from my team's new training program, based at our research center in Xi'an. As part of this program, Liu was trained in a new curriculum we developed with the help of experts in child psychology. The curriculum consists of a series of activities carefully tailored to each age and stage of child development and designed to progressively stimulate children's language skills, boost general cognitive function, enhance motor skills, and teach social skills. The goal of the program is to teach rural parents how to care for their young children in ways that will promote their long-term growth.[23]

For the past few months, Liu and a contingent of these trainers have been back in the villages. Every week Liu appears at Jinjin's house with a sack of toys and picture books slung over his shoulder. Each time, he teaches Jinjin's parents a new game from the curriculum, observes the way the parents interact with their child, and offers tips and encouragement.

The tea party exercise is this week's activity, and it works on many levels. The exchange of dialogue helps Jinjin develop his vocabulary even before he's able to talk. The motions of pouring tea and sipping out of little teacups help Jinjin develop his fine motor skills. Acting out the social graces helps the baby develop his ability to navigate real-life interactions and to regulate his emotions. Activities on other days include reading storybooks aloud, singing simple nursery rhymes, playing pretend doctor, stacking blocks, and naming the colors of toys. The activities are all carefully targeted to each baby's current abilities and stage of development.

There's a lot of evidence that this kind of program can do wonders for young children who are falling behind. Just as a huge swell of research has revealed how catastrophic early cognitive delays can be for children's long-term prospects, other research has demonstrated that taking action to address these barriers can have huge payoffs.

As far back as the 1960s and 1970s, studies in the United States have shown that investing in early childhood programs can have enormous effects in the long run. In the famous Perry Preschool Study, for example, poor babies who were enrolled in a short day care program that focused on cognitive development and nutrition showed immediate improvement in cognitive and social skills. What's more, when scientists followed up with the children decades later and compared them with a control group of similar children who had not participated in the program, they found that the Perry graduates were doing better on a wide range of outcomes. They stayed in school longer and had better high school test scores. As adults they had higher income, were more likely to own their own homes, and were less likely to be on welfare. It's this work that had so caught Rey's attention when we first talked about infant development in western China.[24]

These results are also being duplicated in other contexts around the world, including other developing countries. In 2007 the *Lancet* published a review of international evidence on the effectiveness of early childhood programs in developing countries. The authors reviewed evidence from high-quality evaluations of early child education programs, parenting training, and home visits for young children in countries as diverse as Guinea, Cape Verde, Bangladesh, Myanmar, Nepal, Vietnam, Colombia, Argentina, Jamaica, and Turkey, among others. Nothing yet on China—although the national government is currently, for the first time, in discussions on what should be done to support early childhood education.[25]

The vast majority of studies found significant positive effects on children's cognitive and noncognitive skills. For example, evidence from a longitudinal study in Myanmar showed that early childhood stimulation had a significant long-term effect on school grades. A parenting program in Turkey was found to have long-term positive effects on children's school attainment, school grades, and test scores, attitudes toward school, and family and social adjustment a full seven years after the program finished. Perhaps most relevant, a study in Colombia that used an intervention similar to the one we have been using in China had large effects on cognitive outcomes. For most of these studies, the effects from the early childhood stimulation were approximately equivalent to raising IQ for the average child by two to three points (already a large effect, on average) and had much larger effects when the children were developmentally delayed as they entered the program and the parents participated actively. Many of the studies found that these improvements in cognitive outcomes persisted for years—with one study documenting effects lasting as long as seventeen years.[26]

These results have led experts to conclude that the single most effective thing we can do to spur lifelong success and reduce inequality throughout the world is to invest in programs that target the youngest children. International health experts using the most conservative figures estimate that at this very moment at least 200 million children around the world are growing up without the basic nutrition and mental stimulation they need to reach their genetic potential. This may be the single greatest opportunity we have to reduce human suffering on a global scale.[27]

In addition to the humanitarian benefits of these programs, Nobel Prize–winning economist James Heckman has also made the case that investing in early childhood programs is the best choice we can make from a purely *economic* perspective. Because people who do better in early childhood do better for the rest of their lives, the economic returns to investing in early childhood programs are astronomical. Heckman estimates that the economic return to the Perry Preschool Program was as high as 10 percent per year. Put another way, this means that for every dollar we put into programs like this, we get a return of about seventeen dollars by the time children are in their thirties. That's a seventeen-fold return on investment. By reaching children while they're still young, we can reduce the need for other programs that seek to reduce the same disparities later on, at higher cost and with less effectiveness.[28]

These types of programs are working in rural China as well. In 2015 my team conducted the first randomized controlled trial of a parenting training program in rural China. We randomly selected three hundred toddlers and their families to participate in a six-month program of parenting training—the work Liu Xianju is doing in Jinjin's home today. An identical group of three hundred babies was selected to serve as the control group, without any intervention. After six months, by comparing the babies in the parenting group with the babies in the control group, we can see how much the parenting training is actually helping.

Jinjin has already made great progress. The first time Liu visited, Jinjin hid behind his mother's leg, peeking out at Liu with wide, frightened eyes. When Liu and Jinjin's mother tried to engage the little boy with some modeling clay, he would only play silently with it on his own. Once in a while he uttered an incoherent phrase. Three months later, when I joined Liu in another visit to Jinjin's house, the boy's transformation was dramatic. As soon as he caught sight of Liu, Jinjin smiled and waved, calling out, "Uncle! Uncle!" He looked eagerly to see what new toy Liu had brought him. Jinjin's test results also reflect this improvement. After failing the test only months before, he is now almost within the normal range for a baby his age.

Our careful evaluation has shown that the program is working for many children. After six months, we found on average young children whose educated mothers participated in most of the parenting sessions showed a significant rise in Bayley test scores. This may translate into an eventual rise of five to seven or more IQ points in adulthood. This alone is enough to set these children nearly back on the course of normal development. These findings demonstrate just how critical it is to improve parenting practices in these areas.[29]

These findings from the Qinling Mountains were not a one-off discovery. Our team evaluated a similar intervention run by Save the Children in Hebei and Yunnan Provinces. Similar positive effects on cognitive and language outcomes were found from teaching mothers how to interactively parent their children. We are repeating the interventions now in another setting and waiting to see how the children fare.

Babies in rural China have many more advantages than other poor children in the world. Like Jinjin, they almost all have a safe house. Most have two loving parents and four loving grandparents. They are not in dire poverty. Their nutrition is not great, but it's not terrible. They aren't starving orphans. They aren't indigent refugees. They aren't destitute slum dwellers. All they need is cognitive stimulation. Give them stimulation, and they thrive just like kids in Beijing or London or San Francisco.

To the top leadership's credit, early childhood education is finally on the national agenda, but I believe expanding this program should be one of the government's top priorities in the coming decade. The stakes couldn't be higher. Of the fifteen to twenty million babies born every year in China, five million or more are in danger of becoming developmentally delayed for the rest of their lives. If this program can be brought to all families, then over the next ten years it has the potential to change the lives of fifty million children—in a single decade. From a national human resources perspective, this would mean that in the next decade China can produce fifty million additional productive citizens to ensure the continued prosperity of all. If not, the costs may be immense.

Conclusion

In the next several years, China either will prove itself the inevitable superpower some have predicted and reach the top of the development game board, or it will succumb to the invisible challenge described in this book, ending in economic downturn and stagnation or even in collapse.

Right now it's difficult to imagine that the Chinese dream could ever end in failure. But one near truism in macroeconomics is that it's always hard to foresee an economic slowdown. In the 1960s no one would have predicted that the juggernaut Soviet economy, which inspired so much fear across the Western world, would collapse two decades later. In the 1970s everyone viewed Brazil as an upstart with unlimited potential; few imagined that fifty years later it would remain stuck in middle-income status. In the 1980s the world was betting on Japan's economy as other nations opened Japanese-language programs and envisioned a Japan-centered world; yet today that nation is entering its fourth straight decade of almost zero growth. And no one expected that the Mexico of the early 1990s, "the next Taiwan," could turn into the Mexico of today.[1]

Much of the evidence suggests China could be headed for similar trouble. Although China is not the Soviet Union or Brazil or Japan or Mexico, the middle-income trap still looms. Regardless of the optimism of the government and many observers, there are no guarantees that China will not sputter and fail. Most countries that have reached this point in the past seventy years have done exactly that.

Still, in many ways China is unique. Observers have been predicting imminent disaster for the past four decades, but China has

proved the skeptics wrong again and again. In the 1980s it under-
went a radical transformation by successfully decollectivizing its
moribund agricultural economy and converting it into a strong
driver of growth. In the 1990s China managed to reform its state-
owned enterprise sector, in spite of every expert's assumption that
this would be impossible. Completely cut off from the rest of the
world for decades, China joined the World Trade Organization as
one of the least trade-protected countries and shocked the world by
succeeding—integrating itself into world markets and increasing its
share of global trade. China now has more major trading partners
than the United States has. Each time, China has figured out a way
to accomplish a seemingly impossible transformation and continue
to grow and thrive against the odds. Might China be able to pull off
another shocking success? Can it be the first country to graduate to
high-income status with such a low human capital base?

I certainly hope China will defy the odds. As I've argued, the entire world will be much better off with a thriving China. But the risks
of failure are significant. Even the best-case scenario holds considerable downside risk for China, and for all of us who depend on
China. A deep understanding of what is happening in China today to
bring about these risks—and how those same issues may be at work
in other countries that are hoping to climb the Chutes and Ladders
board—is critical.

China's Unique Structural Barriers

Several structural issues within China's political system may have
made it more susceptible to a human capital crisis than other
middle-income countries. Of all the sources of the country's current
crisis, one in particular is a purely Chinese problem: the hukou system. Recall that hukou (the "household registration" system) forms
a high and mostly impenetrable wall between China's urban and
rural people. While many countries have great inequality between
rural and urban populations, China is the only country in the world
that maintains and reinforces that inequality through law. Though

few outsiders realize it, hukou in China is like a state-sponsored caste system.

Hukou dates back to the state planning era of the 1950s, and even now it divides China's population into two essential categories—the small privileged minority with urban status (about 36 percent today), and the large excluded majority with rural status (64 percent). This status is assigned at birth and depends on the status of one's parents. Those with urban parents have urban hukou, those with rural parents have rural hukou. For many decades urban and rural people lived in entirely separate economic systems—allowed to live, work, and receive government benefits only in the place of their hukou registration. Even to travel within the country required paperwork—something like a visa. In the 1980s reforms allowed rural people to come to the cities to work, a change that allowed for China's massive rural-to-urban migration and has played a critical role in its record-setting growth rates. But even today social services are allocated throughout the country based on hukou, with serious ramifications for inequality and rural human capital accumulation.[2]

To understand the depth of this divide, think of China as two separate countries. Rural people are residents of the Republic of Rural China, and urban people are residents of the Republic of Urban China. Since the reforms in the 1980s, it's as if a Free Trade Agreement between the two republics allows for the flow of goods and people across boundaries without customs fees or security checks. However, for the provision of social services—health care, education, housing, unemployment benefits, and social security—they are still like separate countries. Rural children have access to social services only in rural areas. Even if rural children accompany their parents to the Urban Republic, with few exceptions they aren't allowed to use urban services. Most critically for the issue of human capital, education and health services are almost fully dictated by one's hukou. Even if rural parents move from their villages to the big cities for work—as more than 300 million people have done—they are not legally entitled to send their kids to urban public schools (at all) or to access urban public hospitals (without paying unaffordable fees). Children with rural hukou are guaranteed access to public school—or to public medical facilities—only in their hometowns and villages.[3]

Rural parents thus must make a devastating choice between three undesirable options. If they stay in their home villages with their children, the family will remain intact and their kids can go to proper schools. But because the average farm in China is so small and other job opportunities in the villages are few, they will be forced to live in relative poverty. Their kids will get an education in rural public schools, but they will have little money to invest in the home or in health care and other things that will give their children the best chance for a better life.[4]

The second option is for rural parents to leave their children behind in their home villages while they live and work in the city. They will be able to earn more money and send that money home to help with childcare, but the children will be left for years at a time to be brought up by relatives. This is the story of the millions of "left-behind children" (LBCs) around the country whose parents are urban migrants. Today it's believed that more than sixty million children in China have been left behind in rural villages by at least one migrating parent. In some poor areas more than half of all kids are left behind, and by some estimates as many as two million of these children are living completely on their own, without even a relative to watch over them. These children have access to public education in their villages, and because their parents are working in the prosperous cities, they generally have greater fiscal resources than rural kids whose parents stay home. But these families are split up for long periods, at great social and emotional cost. Indeed, research suggests that the psychological effects of being left behind can be considerable and long lasting.[5]

Finally, rural parents can choose to bring their children to the city in spite of the barriers they'll face. If a particular family is lucky, rich, and well connected, they may find ways to get their children into an urban public school. Only a small minority of migrants succeed in this. Otherwise they have no option but to pay to send their kids to a private school that caters to the migrant population. This choice, too, comes with grave costs.

These schools are largely unregulated, and they suffer from serious problems of quality. Research by my team found that private migrant schools have systematically higher student-teacher ratios, less-qualified teachers, and higher teacher turnover than urban public schools. Moreover, these schools frequently charge high tuition for these inferior services. Another study by my team found that on average the students in migrant schools were one to two years behind their rural school counterparts and had worse mental health outcomes as well. What's more, the longer students remained in migrant schools, the further their test scores deteriorated relative to staying in normal rural schools. Finally, not only do migrant schools provide a much lower quality of education, they are also fundamentally unstable. Because they aren't recognized by the government, they can shut down at any time. In 2011 Beijing closed down twenty-four migrant schools just days before the school year was supposed to start, leaving 40,000 migrant students with nowhere to go. Overall, then, families making this choice can stay together, but what education their children receive will be of poor quality, providing little hope of success in the long run.[6]

The hukou policy thus causes unnecessary suffering, both for individuals and families and on the national level. At this point in China's development, it is in everyone's interests for all children to receive the best possible education, nutrition, and health care. Instead, the government is maintaining artificial barriers that make it more difficult for rural children—the majority of the future workforce—to receive these things. This is a serious strategic mistake.

The hukou system is also highly inefficient. As we've seen, China has poured a lot of resources into improving conditions in rural schools. It has upgraded the facilities, paid extra to bring in qualified teachers, and standardized the curriculum. This is progress, but it is also enormously expensive. And after all the investment, rural students are still falling far behind their urban peers. The obvious answer, both for the rural kids and for the sake of the country, is to bring more rural students into urban public schools. That is more cost effective and more likely to be successful. The urban schools already have good facilities and good learning outcomes, not to mention that good teachers are much more willing to live and work in big cities than in remote rural areas. If the state could come to understand the full benefits of boosting broad-based human capital, the decision would be obvious.

Indeed, in most countries, instead of blocking students from coming to urban areas for schooling, the state creates incentives to draw more students to the city. This is one of the major policy achievements of Taiwan and South Korea. In the late 1970s Taiwan's education department began an aggressive program to attract workers and their families to Taipei, the capital city. The new rural migrants were welcomed. They were free to buy or rent houses, they had access to public hospitals, and everyone (no matter what their origin) could buy municipal bus passes at the same subsidized rate. Most important, every child was fully welcome to attend public school in Taipei. Unlike China, where municipal governments often take draconian action to discourage families from bringing their children to the city, in Taiwan they were welcomed. The logic was simple: in Taipei, children could get higher-quality schooling with better teachers and better facilities at lower cost for everyone. China needs to take these steps today. Instead of actively working to keep rural students out of urban schools, it needs to do everything in its power to ensure that every child has access to a high-quality education with no strings attached. This is one of the key policy failures that has given rise to the human capital crisis, and it is a purely Chinese problem. No other country in the world has such a system.

Another structural factor that has contributed to the neglect of rural education and health in China is the nature of the fiscal system. Simply put, China's social services, including education, are almost entirely decentralized, which perpetuates the large-scale underinvestment in education and health at local levels—especially in the poorest areas. We might assume that China, a one-party, officially

Communist state, has centralized all functions of the state—but in some cases, ironically enough, the opposite is true.

Decentralization presents a barrier to human capital accumulation because it generates a fundamental incentive problem at the local level. Educating children is costly—it takes a lot of effort and money to educate a child from preschool through high school. Sure enough, education is one of the biggest expenditures in China's rural counties, taking up a large share of the available budget. The problem with decentralization is that the high costs of education fall mostly on the local leaders, while the benefits of educating a child have a large social externality that accrues not locally but at the national level. Ensuring adequate health, nutrition, and education for every child is of great importance for ensuring the continued health of China's entire economy, but for local leaders there are fewer benefits. If the rural education system is successful and children make it all the way through high school, that education then enables them to move far from home to pursue further opportunity. Few students who have been educated through high school or higher choose to live and work in their poor home counties. From the perspective of local leaders, then, after spending scarce fiscal resources on these students, they provide almost no benefit for the local economy and contribute very little to local society beyond remittances to their aging parents.[7]

The problem is that, under the decentralized fiscal system, the decision of how much to spend on education, health, and nutrition is made by local officials rather than the national government, creating a fundamental incentive problem. The costs accrue locally, but those at the local level receive little of the benefit. In contrast, large benefits accrue at the national level, but national leaders are not making the ultimate funding decisions. The result is systematic underinvestment in education and health, especially in poorer rural areas.[8]

Decentralization is thus a second major contributor to China's human capital challenge. Of course China is not alone in having a decentralized system of social services. For geographically large, populous, and fiscally constrained countries, decentralization may be all but inevitable. Back when China was impoverished, the central government had control only over meager fiscal resources and needed to fund and manage education across a wide geographic area for a large population, without the ease and low cost of modern communication and transportation technology. It was easier (or even the only option) to delegate authority to local leaders. Other large developing countries struggle with this issue to varying extents for similar reasons. Indeed, in the post–World War II period, the United States also had a decentralized education system, and the incentives were similarly misaligned. The benefits of educating America's rural youth accrued to the entire US economy, but the costs were borne by the local school systems, which had much less to gain. The result was underinvestment in education. This was one of the messages of Michael Harrington's *The Other America*. So we can see that, unlike the hukou system, decentralization is a problem that many countries must grapple with.

However, while decentralization may have been necessary at one point in China's history, that's no longer true. Today China has sufficient government revenue to guarantee education for all, not to mention the cost savings of instant communication and convenient transportation. Thus the decentralization issue is a question of political administration that it's entirely within the power of China's leaders to change. In fact, the United States confronted—and ultimately overcame—this same challenge. In the 1960s President John F. Kennedy and President Lyndon Johnson developed and implemented a national War on Poverty. Among the most high-profile and ultimately successful policies was the decision to assign the federal government the primary role in funding and administering rural education. I believe China will need to similarly realign its fiscal system and fully centralize the funding of rural education. And this needs to happen sooner rather than later.

A third structural factor that has contributed to China's potential crisis, after the hukou system and decentralization, is a strong focus on short-run growth. For the past several decades, the official priority in Chinese politics has been to ensure growth at all costs, and this approach is baked into the system at every level. At least until recently, the top three categories for which leaders were rewarded were growth, fast growth, and faster growth. When growth occurred, leaders got promotions and were granted larger staffs and bigger offices and the recognition of being successful contributors to China's miracle. Local leaders do not stay in place very long; those who are successful in the short run get promoted. And, by design, they cycle through various posts—around departments within a jurisdiction and around towns, counties, prefectures, or provinces. In every way, China's political system emphasizes immediate returns. With short-term thinking rewarded, long-term thinking is rare.

Over time this attitude that only growth matters has begun to attenuate. As China entered the twenty-first century, more of the policy rhetoric began to center on ensuring social stability in addition to growth. In the past five years, the state has also started to put much more emphasis on addressing environmental issues and waging anti-poverty campaigns. These new priorities seem likely to attract more attention going forward. But the growth targets set by the top levels of government are hugely ambitious and emphasized at every level of government even today. Locally produced growth remains a top priority—especially in an era when the economy is slowing and external forces are seen to be holding back China's growth. And it is almost a given that rewards accrue to officials who are successful on a relatively short timeline.

This focus on short-run growth is another reason human capital is still largely being overlooked. Investments in human capital take a long time to show dividends in economic growth. Who can blame officials for declining to increase their jurisdictions' investment in primary school education, or health and vision screenings, or even parental training and nutrition programs, when they are far more likely to be rewarded for showing short-term gains in purely fiscal terms? Putting glasses on children in primary school will help their grades, but these children will not enter the prime of their working life until 2045. Investing in infant cognition will not pay off until 2050. Meanwhile, most of the current leaders will retire long before

2040. Those who are still around then will have moved to a different ministry or jurisdiction. And they certainly won't be rewarded for those choices under the current system.

This special focus on short-run growth is a problem many countries must reckon with. In the United States, for example, education is often seen as a low political and social priority compared with immigration issues, social security, health, drugs, and police protection. Again, short-run incentives are a major part of the problem. Presidents serve only eight years at most. Members of the House run on two-year cycles. Mayors and governors likewise face short-term accountability from voters.

Thus education investment suffers in many countries around the world owing to the absence of long-term incentives for those who make the crucial decisions. All countries must overcome the same problem (to varying extents) as they seek to boost human capital. But it's also true that China has elevated this focus on short-term growth to a level that is rare on the world stage, which may be one of the reasons it is now facing such a dramatic human capital crisis.

Risk Factors Inherent to Middle-Income Status

These three structural issues—the hukou system, decentralized funding of education and health, and short-run growth incentives for local leaders—are integral to the Chinese political system and need to be addressed if progress is to be made in boosting rural human capital. These issues are unique to China—or at least especially potent there. But many of the critical issues that brought about China's current crisis exist in all (or at least many) middle-income countries. Thus many other countries are at risk of falling into a similar crisis and would benefit from studying China's example.

As we have seen, the most fundamental reason for China's crisis is the time inconsistency between its human capital gains and its human capital needs. There are different human capital requirements in different development phases (at different times). The basic economic health of a rich country depends on a high level of human capital for a large share of the labor force (in terms of education, health, and nutrition). But this broad-based human capital is much less important for a poor country, or even a middle-income country. Yet broad-based human capital is a resource that must be produced and consolidated far in advance of when it is needed—indeed, at least forty years in advance. This discrepancy introduces a time inconsistency. The country (and individual people) may have made rational decisions on how much education to acquire in the short run, but those decisions don't hold up in the long run as the needs of the economy change. That is, levels of general education below high school during the poor or middle-income stage are no constraint on the smooth running of the economy, but if education levels are not being built up in the background among a large enough segment of the population, the labor force's poor human capital will eventually put a major brake on growth and prosperity, possibly preventing the transition to high-income status. This issue is inherent in this phase of development, and I believe it is a key contributor to the middle-income trap that is often overlooked.

This time inconsistency is heightened because, in our globalized world, it is now possible for middle-income countries to grow so much more quickly than ever before. Countries that successfully ride the ladder of low-skilled manufacturing are able to bring about massive economic growth very quickly, with little in the way of human capital investment. But if that economic growth is not accompanied by a strong government effort to boost human capital even before it is demanded by the marketplace (which is still offering low wages and happy to hire those with low skills), then the country can easily find itself between a rock and a hard place—with wages too high to bring back low-skilled manufacturing and skill levels too low to attract higher-value-added work. In other words, with fast growth it is more likely that human capital accumulation will be outpaced by economic growth, leading the country to the turning point before the population is ready to handle higher-skilled jobs.

Countries are even more likely to fall behind because so many of the issues that stand in the way of rapid human capital accumulation in this phase of development are largely invisible. Investments in broad-based human capital may not be easily recognized as important to the economy. Among economists and in development circles, it's now well known that building up human capital is critical for a country's long-term growth. But beyond the academy, the importance of human capital is often not appreciated. Even if a country does make building up education a priority, many of the most serious barriers to human capital gains in middle-income countries are poorly understood and difficult to detect. This can lead a country to lose valuable time in the already tight race to build human capital before the transition.

For example, the biggest hurdle to long-term growth and stability in many middle-income countries (including China) is the epidemic of stunted cognition, language acquisition, and social-emotional skills in infants and toddlers. This problem is difficult to detect. Indeed, the invisibility is so complete that this challenge has only recently begun to be more fully understood—even within the scientific community—although it has been shown to profoundly affect lifetime outcomes. Likewise, anemia is widespread among schoolchildren in middle-income countries, but though it has a devastating effect on children's ability to learn, it is so hard to identify that it is widely referred to as "hidden hunger." These barriers to human capital accumulation are difficult to detect even in the best circumstances, let alone by poorly educated and disconnected rural parents.

As I've said in earlier chapters, I believe these invisible impediments to growth are another overlooked contributor to the middle-income trap. While poor countries face barriers to human accomplishment that are easy to see, middle-income countries must face significant invisible barriers to the accumulation of human capital and to basic human health. This is the transition from the highly visible wasting and even starvation of children in a poor country to the hidden hunger of a middle-income country, or from the deadly disease epidemics of a poor country to the slow, inexorable drag on productivity caused by infection with intestinal worms in a middle-income country. These problems are subtle, but they still represent major impediments to growth in the middle-income phase of development because they get in the way of much-needed accumulation of human capital. And their invisibility is a big part of the problem—their very subtlety makes them difficult to address.

Of course, that there is a trap does not mean every country is destined to get stuck. As we have seen, several of China's policies (hukou, decentralization, and short-term incentives for growth) are making it more likely that the nation will succumb to these issues. A few other factors may have made China more likely than other countries to develop a human capital crisis. For instance, China had faster-than-usual economic growth, which may have made it more likely to fall behind in the race to accumulate human capital before it was too late. Consider China's emphasis on physical infrastructure. The state invested billions in roads, but not enough in rural education. The focus on physical infrastructure at the expense of schooling may have been counterproductive: had there been less road building, the pace of development would have been slower, and China would have had more time to build up its human capital before it reached the current crisis.

China also had the bad luck of a few long-tenured leaders who did not make amassing human capital a priority. Although the past few administrations (since about 2000) have grasped the importance of broad-based human capital and have begun the urgent work of raising educational attainment across the country, most of the people in China's current labor force came of age under administrations that put much less importance on broad-based, modern education.

During his long tenure as China's helmsman, Mao Zedong valued Communist indoctrination over math, Chinese, and English and subjected the country to his Cultural Revolution, perhaps the largest intentional destruction of human capital the world has ever seen. After Mao's death, China's new leader, Deng Xiaoping, was a noted reformer and did much to improve the economy, including expanding elite education. Deng deserves great credit for orchestrating the Chinese economic miracle, but mass education (beyond literacy and numeracy) was not part of his grand plan, so several of the decades when China should have been steadily accumulating higher levels of human capital were wasted. The low levels of education among the current labor force owe much to these long-dead leaders. Indeed, a large majority of China's current workforce (65 percent or so) came of age under the education systems of Mao and Deng, which did not stress high school education and teaching the general skills that workers need to thrive in a modern, developed economy.[9]

I am thankful that China's recent administrations have made strong and successful moves to boost access to higher-quality education across the country. I believe China's top leaders do understand the fundamental premise of this book: China is facing a huge human capital challenge. Indeed, in the past two decades, China's government has achieved truly incredible expansion, making nine years of education compulsory and free for the first time, quadrupling the number of university slots, creating a massive new system of vocational high schools, and raising high school attainment among today's rural children from about 50 percent to over 80 percent. The efforts continue—policymakers are now hoping to ensure universal high school education within the next few years. But even this effort may not be enough. Owing to time inconsistency, the transition to high-income status was always going to be difficult, even without decades of underinvestment in education by the highest authorities. China is now far behind. Recall that even today (after all this effort by the recent and current governments), China has the lowest level of human capital in the middle-income world. Its labor force is simply too large, and too historically uneducated, for these recent improvements at the margins to clearly lift China out of danger.

So we can see that a human capital crisis is a real possibility for all middle-income countries in the modern world, and China has additional risk factors that made its eventual human capital gap far more likely. But these risk factors also exist in other countries. Like China, many middle-income countries have had leaders who (for many reasons—often purely rational) do not make human capital a priority, or did not do so in the recent past. For all that hukou is uniquely Chinese and constitutes a particularly high barrier to providing rural education and other services, many other countries also have wide divides between rural and urban populations (crumbling slums, unequal land tenure, and a lack of social services) and underestimate the importance of the rural poor for future growth. Indeed, middle-income countries are generally beset with greater inequality than countries in other parts of the development game board.

Overall, then, many of the key issues that have led China to this point are not specific to China. They can (and do) play out in similar fashion in many middle-income countries. All middle-income countries face the problem of time inconsistency in amassing human capital before the transition to high-income status. Since growth can be so fast (and rates are accelerating in today's world) in many middle-income countries, time inconsistency is all the more urgent. For all middle-income countries, many of the issues that are most critical for maintaining growth are "invisible." For the most populous middle-income countries, decentralization is all but inevitable, at least when an education system is first being expanded, distorting incentives and making it harder to prepare all kids for the future.

There is a real risk that other countries might be susceptible to the exact crisis China is facing today. If China can find itself there, so can many other countries. As we know, most countries that make it to middle-income status do not make it out the other side. For every Taiwan, Ireland, or South Korea, many more places have gotten stuck. Getting stuck in the middle-income trap is the rule rather than the exception, and I believe the human capital crisis is a big part of that equation. Thus, considering China's options (and risks) may provide lessons other countries can learn from.

Lessons for Other Countries

The most obvious lesson from my analysis of China's crisis is that all countries need to be building up human capital for as much of the population as possible, and as quickly as possible. In the twenty-first century it is vital that all governments recognize that human capital has become the most fundamental building block for long-term economic health. As automation progresses and the march of skill-biased technical change continues, human capital is likely to matter more and more.

This book also holds lessons for countries that are eager to build up human capital but don't know how. We've seen that one of the most important tasks—particularly for middle-income countries—is to address the opportunity costs (in the form of a temporarily high unskilled wage rate) that keep families from investing in education and encourage kids to drop out of school before they've learned all they'll need to know in the long run. Many countries seem to have learned this lesson already, as is clear from the widespread elimination of school tuition, and even the use of conditional cash transfers, to encourage all children to stay in school.

Another takeaway is that barriers to education need to be eliminated for all children—not just the rich or the middle class, but the poor as well. Many countries remain plagued by wide disparities in educational access between urban and rural communities. Certainly countries should avoid explicit structural barriers to rural education such as China has in the form of hukou. But beyond that, countries should learn from the examples of South Korea, Ireland, and Taiwan (and other graduates) and make public, high-quality schooling available to all, both in rural areas and among migrant communities.

Another lesson is that human capital can't be built up without moving beyond what we usually think of as the educational realm. School facilities and quality teachers are important, but nutrition and health and other invisible contributors to learning are just as significant and far more likely to remain neglected. Schools are highly efficient places to screen for health conditions and even administer treatment. Countries looking to maintain long-term growth rates should put their highest priority on eliminating the barriers to human capital accumulation that occur at the very beginning of life—in infancy and early childhood. These barriers can be addressed only within a narrow window of opportunity. If left unaddressed, the costs are considerable and long-term. Thus no educational (or indeed growth) policy will be fully successful unless dealing with these invisible problems is a central part of the strategy.

Finally, I believe perhaps the most critical lesson of this book has to do with the timing of such policy efforts. Countries need to invest in human capital on a wide scale and with careful forethought *before* it is actually needed in the marketplace (before rising wages make businesses demand workers with higher skill levels). That means that even poor and (especially) lower-middle-income countries need to be making the biggest push. Countries can't afford to wait until they reach upper-middle-income status. By that time in today's world, it will be too late. Unless they start earlier, they may find they are already stuck in the middle-income trap.

Who needs this advice? Certainly all middle-income countries could still benefit from it. As we have seen, many remain far below the educational attainment they need to reduce the risk of remaining stuck in the middle-income trap. Not only that, many middle-income countries also remain saddled with the invisible health and nutrition issues that keep a population from gaining human capital as quickly and effectively as possible. A nation with high rates of anemia and other health conditions that are easily treatable but devastating for learning, and with high rates of delayed infant cognition, will find it difficult to boost educational attainment. Some of the countries in question have at least started to take this issue seriously and are investing in early childhood development on a large scale. For example, there has recently been a sweeping trend in Latin America to prioritize early childhood development (birth to age three).

That's a good start. But as we've seen, because of the timing problem, these issues are even more critical for countries that haven't yet made it to middle income (or are still in its early stages). If countries wait until they have achieved upper-middle-income status to start focusing on infant cognition, on invisible health barriers to learning, and on getting kids into school, that may be too late. They may already be in the trap. The lessons in this book thus should have the most significance for countries just starting to move into middle-income status.

India is a prime example. Today India's per capita GDP is about US$7,000—right in the middle of middle income. India is growing at about 7 percent a year, a rate that will undoubtedly slow slightly over the next decade or so as the nation moves into upper-middle-income status) and has its sights set on high income. Assuming that India is moderately successful (which will of course depend on many factors beyond education and health policy), India will be at upper-middle income or lower-high income (a bit higher than China is to-day) in about twenty years or so (let's say about 2040). If India makes it to that point, will it be able to continue growing and become a developed country, or will the poor human capital of its labor force undermine that growth, leading to stagnation or even collapse?[10]

Based on its current levels of educational investment, India might be headed for trouble. Today about 20 percent of India's overall labor force has been to high school. According to the World Bank, about 40 percent of youth in India now attend high school. Hence if India only continues to raise achievement on trend, the education level of its labor force will be near the average for a trapped country (about 40 percent). If India is aiming for education levels near those of developed countries (50 to 70 percent) by 2040, it must dramatically increase educational attainment today. In the 2020s, 60 to 70 percent of India's youth need to attend high school. By the 2030s, 70 to 80 percent or more need to attend.[11]

If India is to meet these mileposts, huge investments are needed now. Given that India, like most other rapidly developing countries, is fiscally constrained, it will have to make some hard choices. Almost certainly, simply following China's example of investing vast sums in transportation, communications, and agriculture is not the best option for India. Investment is needed in these sectors, and they are a key part of a nation's growth strategy, but China's example shows that India should perhaps slow—though certainly not stop—its pro-growth investments so that the country's growth doesn't outpace the accumulation of human capital in the labor force. I don't mean to downplay the importance of economic growth. But I want developing countries to fully enjoy the benefits of long-term economic growth, and that requires increasing human capital along the way. Paying attention to human capital early on is the only way to reach greater long-term growth and stability.

Today's most stable, highest-income countries—the nations of

Western Europe, North America, and Australia—grew much more slowly over a much longer time. Perhaps their slow but steady growth allowed for a balance between physical investment and human capital investment—the key to their long-term growth and stability.

If India and other countries like it (including Peru, Ecuador, Ethiopia, and Vietnam) don't take a new tack now, with their youngest children in mind, they may struggle to avoid ending up where China is today. For China it may already be too late.

The Way Forward for China

What must China do to avoid the worst-case scenario? First, and most critically, it needs to ensure that all young children, from birth to age five, are given everything they need to develop healthy cognition for a lifetime. In China today, every six seconds the window of opportunity closes for another child. This is a tragic waste of human potential and a drag on the economy that China cannot afford. Investing in early childhood development is the single most effective way to boost long-run human capital and likely the most cost-effective strategy for achieving high-income status overall. Thankfully, there are solutions at hand. The program of parental training and nutrition supplementation my research team piloted is showing results. Other groups in China are carrying out similar programs, and their efforts also appear to be succeeding.[12]

There are already substantial resources available to establish this program on a much wider scale. For the past thirty-five years, China has employed family-planning inspectors in every village in the country to enforce its One Child Policy. As of 2015 that policy has been brought to an end. Under a new partnership with my research team (REAP) and the National Health and Family Planning Commission (NHFPC), that once fearsome bureaucracy is being put to a much more appealing purpose: training rural parents to better care for their children. Over the next ten years, this program has the potential to change the lives of fifty million children. And so China's harsh One Child Policy can be turned into a gentle and highly effective Fifty Million Children Policy, focused not on quantity but on quality and designed to prepare China for the twenty-first century at last. I firmly believe this is the single most important thing China can do to prepare for the future.[13]

Second, China needs to ensure that all rural children have the health care and nutrition they need to learn. Invisible health issues in rural schools are a critical factor contributing to the persistent gap between rural and urban learning, and as long as children remain sick, no amount of investment in rural schools (or expanded access to education) will make a difference. Childhood nutrition—and the epidemic of anemia—need to be recognized and addressed. There are effective and cost-effective ways to make this change. Other health problems also need addressing. In the past (through the 1970s and 1980s and even into the 1990s), China's government had remarkable success in reducing or eliminating intestinal worm infections by passing out deworming drugs en masse to students in schools. With all the children gathered in one spot every day, this is an ideal way to ensure that large numbers are treated cheaply and effectively. Given the high levels of intestinal worms that still affect rural Chinese children—especially in the worm-friendly tropical climate of southern China—this kind of deworming program should be relaunched all across the region. Students in rural schools also should be screened for vision problems and fitted with eyeglasses as needed. These are not purely private-sector investments that primarily benefit the families of the affected children. The overall social benefits are so high that the central government must take more concerted action now.[14]

Third, China should work to overcome the pervasive issue of poor-quality vocational high schools—especially in rural areas. A robust system of regulation and monitoring needs to be put in place. There are many good vocational high schools. National and provincial and local education officials need to ensure that all schools are brought up to this standard—especially in rural areas—for the sake of the students themselves and for the sake of China's basic economic health. In addition, the curriculum should be adjusted to ensure that all students are being given a chance to learn not only specific vocational skills but also the general academic skills that will prepare them for a lifetime of learning.

Fourth, China should ensure universal (and tuition-free) education for a full twelve years. Right now it provides free, compulsory education only for grades one through nine. That is simply not good enough if China hopes to move up the Chutes and Ladders board in the twenty-first century. Ensuring that all children are getting a proper twelve-year education is in everyone's interest, and China needs to dedicate the resources to eliminate any barriers—such as the high tuition rates for academic high school—that stand in the way of education for the poorest. In fact, the government is now moving rapidly in that direction. The stated policy goal is to universalize high school education by the early 2020s. I totally support this move and hope that China's government will not only make high school free, but also creatively think about how to persuade students from poor rural areas (and their families) to embrace the idea of going to high school.[15]

Fifth, China should eliminate the artificial political barriers that keep rural children out of the highest-quality schools. The hukou limitation that guarantees children access to public schools only in the place of their registration (their home villages) should be eliminated so that all children can receive the best education possible. This will improve outcomes and reduce costs for the government. Just as it was for Taiwan (and South Korea), this would be a win-win for China. I know this policy move will be difficult to realize in the short run. I also know there have been gradual movements toward relaxation over the past decades. I support all efforts to continue this liberalization.

Finally, at the structural level China should centralize funding for education from grades one through twelve so that the wide gap in the education it provides can be bridged and all children can be given a good education regardless of where they happen to live. The problem is that local governments have neither the funds nor the initiative to provide high-quality education for their rural students, since they do not fully capture all the benefits when newly educated youth leave the county and never come back. The national government, on the other hand, has access to greater revenue and will capture the benefit of the higher human capital of all Chinese. The United States undertook this policy in the 1960s, with great success. If I had to choose one policy shift to push the hardest, it would be this one.

All this sounds expensive. Can China afford to do this? The answer is a definite yes. It just needs to recognize the stakes of the human capital crisis and reshuffle its investment priorities. Indeed, with the scale of the potential costs, these steps can be seen as insurance against the worst possible outcomes.[16]

Three Scenarios

What does China's future hold? Based on the evidence available, I envision three possible scenarios. In the best-case scenario, China gets the message (which in no small part it already has) and throws all its ingenuity and resources into successfully boosting human capital levels quickly and radically. If, for example, China can really get all children into high school by the early 2020s, ensure that all high schools are providing a high-quality education, and substantially reduce the incidence of poor health and delayed development among rural children, then it might just have a chance to escape the middle-income trap.

This scenario might seem too optimistic. After all, about half of rural students are growing up with reduced cognitive capacity. Even if every baby gets the help needed starting tomorrow, many children have already passed the window of opportunity to ensure they reach their full genetic potential. Many may not have the capacity for academic high school. Building more schools is not going to solve that underlying problem. It may be that little can really change for China's human capital before today's babies enter high school. That means that even in the best-case scenario it could take fifteen years before all children have a real opportunity to succeed in China's high schools.

But this scenario is still possible. It's clear that China will soon face a major economic transition, with rising wage rates greatly increasing the demand for higher skills. But it's possible the economic transition will move more slowly than I expect. Wages could rise more slowly than economists have predicted, or companies could be a bit slower to move offshore. Automation could take longer to achieve or could require a construction boom, keeping unskilled workers in jobs. In short, it's very difficult to predict how quickly this situation will deteriorate, and several factors could buy China time in the race to build up human capital. Some combination of these factors could render the best-case scenario a real possibility.

Still, even in the best-case scenario, owing to China's very low starting point, it will likely be 2035 before China's labor force reaches an average high school attainment of even 42 percent—and remember, no country has avoided the middle-income trap with high school attainment below 50 percent. Thus it's still likely, even at best, that growth rates will fall and much of China's population will struggle to find formal employment for many years to come. Even if everything works out as well as possible, economic stagnation and the middle-income trap cannot be ruled out.

At the next level, which I'll call the worse-case scenario, China's efforts to get children into quality high schools would be less successful. Perhaps it would take a few more years to make the transition to a free twelve-year education for all. Or maybe the top leadership would not get the message about rural China's invisible problems and so investments in education and health would be delayed. If this happened, human capital would become an even bigger hurdle to overcome in the race to high-income levels. This outcome could also become reality if all youth were enrolled in high school but the instruction was poor because of inadequate teaching or the students weren't ready to learn because of poor health, nutrition, and development. In either case, growth would slow dramatically and unemployment would quickly rise. Social problems would become more serious. China's leaders would be forced to divert resources and attention into mitigating these second-order problems, and growth would slow further. China would then find itself at the beginning of a vicious downward spiral. The probability of "not making it" and suffering a serious collapse or long-term stagnation would rise—maybe to a fifty-fifty chance. There would still be hope: perhaps some miracle would come along, allowing China to keep hanging on while it battled to get its human capital levels right at last. But it would be a much tougher fight.

In the third possible outcome, which I'll call the catastrophic scenario, China would fail to increase its human capital at all from today's level. Things would quickly spin out of control. China would experience an economic nosedive, a huge rise in unemployment, negative economic spillovers across global markets, and large negative feedbacks owing to falling world growth that put more and more pressure on China's own growth, and hence on its labor markets. This is the worse-case scenario with added speed and depth of impact.

All these scenarios are possible. And none of them are good. This is why it's so important for countries to do everything possible to increase human capital before they get to where China is today. Indeed, the countries that have made it past the middle-income trap (Taiwan, South Korea, Ireland) all made this transition *before* they were where China is now.

In China's case, even were the state to succeed in improving human capital, this is no guarantee of success in reaching high income. In fact, the "worse" or "catastrophic" scenario could be set off by something other than the human capital crisis itself. Let's imagine that China's growth fails for some other reason. It might be a monetary or banking crisis or a more traditional economic crisis. The COVID-19 pandemic of 2020 might even prove to be the trigger. By mid-2020, the pandemic-induced economic slowdown had left more than 100 million rural workers still at home without employment off the farm. It's hard to say at the time of writing, but the indirect and longer-term effects of the events of early 2020 may be even greater and more permanent. Regardless of the immediate cause, unemployment will rise. If the crisis is severe, the revenue available to address the problems created by the crisis will also fall sharply. Fiscal reserves would be used to stave off the original crisis. With reduced employment and without unemployment insurance, there would be an upsurge in the informal economy. People would likely find it difficult to scratch out a living, because the massive number of new entrants would push down wages (or returns to the petty businesses). There are no social benefits to tide people over. If Mexico's history holds any lesson, it may be that an extended period of slow growth (or structural transformation) may result as the informal economy begins to outcompete the formal economy.

It could get even worse. Tens of millions (if not hundreds of millions) of newly unemployed men and women might become dissatisfied with washing windshields at intersections or selling kebabs on the side of the road, especially if they begin to lose hope for the future. As soon as people believe that no matter how much effort they put in, the future will never get better, crime can easily begin to seem worth the risk. Gangs can start to form. And with forty million unmarried men (maybe more) roaming the cities without adequate work, the situation could become truly ominous. These young, mostly uneducated bachelors would have little to lose by turning to crime. They may also be the ones most likely to direct their pent-up energy, frustration, and anger toward something even more dangerous.

At that point, if not before, the crisis would no longer be confined to China. This is one of the hardest things for people who are not Chinese to grasp. When I give presentations outside China, I often get the same question: Shouldn't you be worrying more about the education of kids in the United States? Aren't there babies in California who need your attention? Who cares about China? I hope that at this point the answer is clear. This is not a remote problem: the issues plaguing rural China today are of huge significance for all of us.

Any steep fall in China's growth will certainly have major ripple effects both inside and outside China. If China's economy stagnates, it could well trigger a humanitarian crisis within China. But it could also affect demand for imports, for example, with a huge effect on all of China's trading partners—basically everyone, since China is the largest trading partner of more countries in the world than any other nation. In other words, a failure of China's economy could lead to huge economic shocks around the world. Given China's outsized importance as a major exporter (and, increasingly, importer) of goods on the international market, this outcome would also likely drive up prices around the world and thus decrease standards of living almost overnight. In summary, then, economic slowdown or stagnation in China could easily plunge the world into a global recession. The ensuing slowdown of world growth would of course have further negative feedback that could make this truly devastating the world over. And, of course, economic decline in China would likely lead to increasing political instability that could have still more devastating effects on the world stage.

In short, it's in all of our best interests for China to keep growing, remain stable, and thrive. In the Western media, much of the discourse about China presupposes a sort of competition between East and West, assuming that any gains in China's power and prestige will come at the expense of American interests and pose grave risks to the current world order. But I believe that a growing, thriving China is good for the world. A floundering China would be far more dangerous.

Why Might I Be Wrong?

As always, the questions linger. Have we thought of everything? Why might the predictions I've made in this book end up being wrong? The world is a complicated place, and few things are harder to predict than macroeconomic trends. When I propose this argument at conferences or in academic presentations, I'm often asked similar questions about factors I might be leaving out.

One question that often comes up is whether China really needs to have its entire labor force gainfully employed. Given that China is such a large country, and that it has successfully nurtured an elite class of workers who are educated at the highest levels, does China really need its many less-educated workers? Can't China float its economy on the industriousness of its millions of elite workers? Can't they pull the rest along?

I find this argument unconvincing. As I detailed in earlier chapters, a huge number of workers (as many as 300 million) might be left out of China's next economic phase for lack of sufficient education. That is a whole lot of people who will need some way to support their families. No matter how productive China's educated elites are, it strikes me as unlikely that they could carry the economy for everyone. Not only that, as we've seen, labor polarization can be a hugely divisive social force. People rely on jobs not just for a paycheck to buy the things they need, but also for a sense of meaning, respect, and belonging within their communities. Take away their jobs, and many people will be bereft. Without education, they will have few attractive alternatives. The informal sector will be an option, but it will offer little respect or stability. The loss of hope—the belief that life will be better tomorrow and that one's children will have a brighter future—could be an even more destructive force. If too many people are disappointed, a rise in crime is likely. A crime spike would undoubtedly lead to further economic stress, requiring more spending on policing and regulation, making China less attractive to investors and potentially driving up out-migration of those very skilled elites. In short, China can't afford to leave out the majority of its labor force.

Things might be different if universal basic income was an option for China. This policy idea has gained a lot of attention in recent years as a solution to inequality. It proposes to deal with structural unemployment by paying all members of society an income sufficient to meet poor families' basic needs and to help maintain the social fabric of the nation. This policy idea may prove to work. Political momentum has been building to try it soon in a number of relatively rich, developed countries, and it may be very successful. But it isn't an option for China. Even though China's economy is the second largest in the world, in per capita terms the country is still relatively poor. In per capita income, China currently ranks about 106th out of 228 countries in the world. At no point in the next few decades is China likely to have sufficient revenue to support the majority of its population on public assistance no matter how well the elites do. And that means any future instability from a polarized labor force can't easily be bought off.[17]

Another buzzword that some bring up as a potential solution to China's current challenge is the Belt and Road Initiative (BRI), a massive project in developing countries around the globe that seeks to bring Chinese investment capital, materials, and labor to help other countries build up their infrastructure. The program has been touted as a boon to Chinese relations abroad as well as a good way to stimulate the economy at home. Even if China has built all the bridges, roadways, and skyscrapers it needs in the past few decades of monumental growth, surely those construction workers (and miners, and all the other industries that support the construction industry) can be put to work abroad.

Again, this seems to me unlikely to avert China's human capital challenge. BRI has already met many serious obstacles, and there is even talk that it may be scaled back in coming years. I also find it unlikely that many developing countries will be willing to bring in large numbers of Chinese laborers to do work (largely unskilled) that their own workers could just as easily perform.

Still, there are some factors that I do believe could push China to an outcome different from the three scenarios I laid out above. For much of this book I've drawn comparisons between China and other countries that got stuck in the middle-income trap. Of course China is different from Mexico and Brazil in many ways, and these differences may turn out to really matter. For instance, China is much more organized than most other countries. The Chinese Communist Party has generally taken a systematic approach to enforcing laws and imposing order. New technology and a commitment at the highest levels to maintaining control have already enabled China to build surveillance systems stronger than any the world has ever seen. Future technological breakthroughs and investments may make these efforts even more effective. These forces for law and order may be enough to keep China from the worst forms of entropy. Even if the economy slows and jobs disappear, the penalty for moving into organized crime might be severe enough to keep people from making that choice. China also has a prodigious propaganda machine that seeks to bolster law and order and national solidarity at many levels of society (in schools, at work, in neighborhoods). Those targeted messages may be enough to persuade large shares of the population to patiently endure hardships in ways that would be impossible in other nations, thus buying time. The rest of the economy might continue to grow, and these structurally left-out workers may be willing to wait for things to turn around. It may be that China's economy can grow far enough in that gap to avert the crisis.

Some readers may also balk at the comparisons I've drawn with the graduates—South Korea and Ireland among others. How can we look to these countries when they're so different from China in obvious ways, including being so much smaller? It's true that most of the successful countries I compare China with have smaller populations. The problem is, no other big countries have made it through the middle-income trap in recent decades. So I may be wrong about the way slowdowns and employment responses will unfold in a big country like China. On the other hand, big countries might be even more vulnerable to the middle-income trap. Mexico and Brazil might be more comparable. In some ways, the bigger the countries the more entangled they seem to become.

And of course there's always the possibility that the world economy will evolve in ways no one has anticipated. Economic history is littered with false predictions of high unemployment. In the first Industrial Revolution, when we went from agriculture to industry, people thought we were going to have huge unemployment. They were wrong. Standards of living went way up, and increased demand produced new job opportunities that absorbed large shares of those in the newly transformed labor force. In the second Industrial Revolution, the same pattern was borne out. Many people worried about rising unemployment, but in many countries the system corrected itself, and as nations grew, urbanized, and industrialized, labor from the farm was fully absorbed by the new economic sectors. It may well be that as we head into the new frontier of artificial intelligence and better technology, we will encounter yet another source of change that will allow China, and many other countries, to adapt without catastrophic unemployment.

These factors may alleviate many of the problems I believe China is facing. They may pull China through the coming decades, even with an undereducated workforce. Time will tell. For now, I'm going to focus on understanding the nation's human capital gap and making sure those inside and outside China take the risks seriously.

How probable is the catastrophic scenario? To me it doesn't seem very likely, despite the seriousness of the invisible challenge, but did anyone predict the US housing crisis and the huge costs and barely averted catastrophe that followed? As we've recently learned, even an improbable disaster is worth trying to head off. Given the scale of the potential destruction this challenge poses to China and the rest of the global economy, it seems particularly important to devote attention and resources to the problem. Even if the probability of a terrible outcome is low, wouldn't you buy insurance, just in case?

China could be facing the prospect of a world-shaking crisis. It's in that spirit, then, that I believe its leaders simply can't afford *not* to take out insurance against it. In this case, the insurance policy must be a massive effort to boost human capital as quickly as possible for all children in the country. The lower the human capital stock, the more sensitive the economy will be to any other problems that emerge. The better educated the labor force, the better able it will be to react and adapt. And if the crisis that keeps me up at night never materializes, at the very least China will have given millions of children the chance for a healthier, more prosperous life.

Acknowledgments

This book would not exist without the passion and tireless work of our many Chinese collaborators. REAP's talented and visionary principal investigators from several institutions in China—with their unmatched ability to design careful research studies and see them all the way through data collection, project implementation, analysis, and research publication—are the backbone of this organization. This group of researchers has come to feel more like family than colleagues. Hundreds of graduate students led teams of enumerators into the field, dealt with the problems that inevitably crop up in the course of a research project, helped to clean and analyze the data, and wrote excellent papers of their own. Literally tens of thousands of undergraduates volunteered their time for data collection, often spending weeks in rural villages to get to the bottom of each problem. It is this organization and all the countless hours of dedication shown by this team (more than 70 percent of them from rural China themselves) that made this book possible. This is their book too.

Six people are in a special category for whom thanks are not enough. We extend our most sincere appreciation to our friends, colleagues, frequent coauthors, and full REAP partners Matt Boswell, Prashant Loyalka, Alexis Medina, Sean Sylvia, Wang Huan, and Xueying Zhao. Without you there is no REAP and there would be no book.

We also thank all our colleagues at Stanford who have helped support the work that has gone into this book—from administrative support to coauthoring papers to friendship. I particularly thank our Stanford colleagues Chip Blacker, Belinda Byrne, Martin Carnoy, James Chu, Quitterie Collignon, Gary Darmstadt, Alberto Diaz-Cayeros, Marcel Fafchamps, Wally Falcon, Steve Felt, Tom Fingar, David Flash, Eric Hanushek, Chien Lee, Hongbin Li, Susanna Loeb, Steve Luby, Yue Ma, Beatriz Magaloni, Mike McFaul, Lori McVay, Grant Miller, Di Mo, Roz Naylor, Jean Oi, John Openshaw, Neil Penick, Rita Robinson, Gi-Wook Shin, Scott Smith, Scott Suguira, Michelle Townsend, Andrew Walder, Huan Wang, Ann Weber, Karen Yang, and more. Outside Stanford, I thank Orazio Attanasio, Nathan Congdon, James Cook, Dorien Emmers, Robert Farley, Sally Grantham McGregor, Jim Heckman, John Kennedy, Beryl Leach, Hendrick Lee, Rey Martorell, Albert Park, Johan Swinnen, Marcos Vera Hernandez, Nele Warrinnier, Howard White, Mike Wood, Mary Young, Mike Young, and Barry and Pam Zuckerman.

REAP does action research, often in the most remote parts of rural China. Funding for this research and for the implementation of our projects comes from such a large group of supporters that it's impossible to name them all here. We are fortunate to have had such a broad base of support. If you have contributed to REAP's research or helped initiate projects, large or small, we thank you. There are a few individuals and groups, however, that I should single out. They are a special group, and many of them have become my friends. Thank you to Tom and Bridget Barket and family, Rita and Vincent Chan, the Gates Foundation, Gao Guangsheng and the entire United Bank of Switzerland/Optimus China team, Give2Asia, the Haobainian Foundation, He Jin, the Jonsson family, Lawrence Kemp, Victor Koo and family, Zhou Kui and Ju Qing and family, Bowei and Christine Lee and family, Bryce Lee and Crisanta Deguzman and family, David and Joanna Li and family, Eric Li and family, Li Jianguang, Li Nan and Li Angxuan, James and Catherine Liang, Yabo and May Lin and family, Mr. and Mrs. C. K. Liu, Kingsley and Gloria Liu, Liu Xin, the Mo family, Save the Children, Josephine Shaw, Eric Shen and family, Diane and Steve Strandberg and family, David Su and family, James and Lisa Sun, Ellie and Winnie Tai, Tang Zhongyin and the Tang Foundation, Dirk Teuwen and his UCB (Union chimique belge) colleagues, Howard White and the entire team from 3ie, Eric Xu, Kersten Xu, Sha Ye and family, Yvette Yeh, Jianming Yu and Kate Li and family, and the Zeng family—especially Helen Li. The Corporate Social Responsibility (CSR) divisions and their program managers of a number of companies also deserve huge thanks, including Alibaba, Apple, Brien Holden Vision Institute, Ctrip, Caterpillar, CLSA, Dell (especially Deb Bauer, Jane Ma, and Jeremy Ford), Essilor, Global Geneva, Maitri Trust, OneSight (especially Jason Singh and Mony Iyer), San Yi, and more.

Eric Hemel gets his own paragraph. Eric found us when Scott was launching REAP from the Stanford side out of his own office and one cubicle with one research assistant. Eric came to China and visited our sites—six times. He invested in the earliest projects (saying, "Think of me as an A-round investor, providing moderate funding for the newest and/or riskiest of projects that no one else will fund"). He was the one who gave Scott advice early on—and it was not always easy advice. He pushed us to do media and to interact with Stanford alumni, to expand our website, and to do more stewardship. Eric also is the one who first suggested and supported this book. Along the way he read multiple drafts of most of the chapters and gave careful feedback that made it much stronger. We are very grateful for his unwavering persistence, support, and friendship. Thank you so very much to Eric and his wife, Barbara.

A huge thank-you to our literary agent, Jessica Papin, who has guided us through the unfamiliar world of publishing with grace and good humor from day one. Whenever we encountered a hiccup in the publishing process, Jessica went above and beyond to see us through it. We wouldn't have known what to do without Jessica, and we couldn't be luckier than to have had her by our side. Thanks for sticking by us, and ultimately finding us such a wonderful home at the University of Chicago Press.

Another big thank-you to our editor Priya Nelson for understanding and embracing this book from our first conversation and giving us such a warm welcome at the University of Chicago Press. Throughout the editorial process, her encouragement and careful eye helped us push the book to the next level. We are grateful to the entire University of Chicago Press team for their tireless efforts.

Thanks also to Wang Huan and Jenny Zhao for their hard work in spearheading the translation and editing of the Chinese version of this book so that it could reach the audience that likely has the most power and interest to avert this potential crisis.

A special thank-you to our two wonderful research assistants on the project, Laura Jonsson and Tom Kennedy. Both are rock-star graduates of the REAP internship program. They spent multiple summers doing frontline field research in rural China and show tremendous passion, dedication, and talent in all they undertake. We were very grateful for their help at a critical juncture of the writing.

Thanks also to Dan Gerstle, who provided very helpful early editorial advice.

Scott also thanks his family for all their support, including his sons and their families in West Los Angeles and Kingston, New York. To my Caabie, thank you—deeply—for supporting me always.

Natalie sincerely thanks Scott for his years of mentorship, the incredible opportunity to work on this book, and his commitment to making her a full partner in the undertaking. She also thanks the entire REAP team for their many years of guidance and friendship. She extends a special thank-you to Eric Hemel for originally suggesting her for this project. Finally, she thanks her family, her friends, and her husband, Max, who have all given her tremendous support and encouragement throughout the writing. Honorable mention goes to her dog, Dash, who came into her life just when she needed him.

Appendix: The REAP Team

This book is the culmination of decades of work by my research team, the Rural Education Action Program (REAP, http://reap.fsi .stanford.edu/).

REAP is a research organization based at Stanford University and several partner institutions in China. Founded in 2006, REAP is dedicated to discovering the causes of poverty in rural China and creating simple, effective solutions in education, health, and nutrition policy to help all children escape poverty and contribute to China's growing economy.

REAP's research focuses on four key areas:

1. Health, nutrition, and education: When children are sick or undernourished, their schoolwork suffers. REAP aims to reduce illness and improve nutrition among children so they can reach their full potential.
2. Keeping kids in school: Rural schools can be both low-quality and expensive, giving children and their parents little incentive for attendance. REAP aims to identify and solve the most serious cost and quality problems associated with rural schooling so that rural children can have access to an affordable quality education.
3. Technology and human capital: REAP is exploring the use of technology to improve schooling and health outcomes, both by providing children with extra help inside and outside of school and by educating parents in areas that are remote and hard to penetrate.

4. One thousand day initiative: The foundation of an individual's cognitive, language, and social-emotional skills is largely formed by the time a child is three years old. Believing that "brains are built, not born," REAP explores how providing the caregivers of infants and toddlers with the knowledge and resources to provide high-quality nutrition and parenting skills (or stimulation) can improve developmental outcomes and give children a chance to thrive in life.

REAP's core group consists of researchers and experts from the Freeman Spogli Institute for International Studies at Stanford University and a set of core partners in centers of academic excellence internationally and across China. In this way REAP leverages resources within this global network to increase the reach, efficiency, and impact of our work. We also have close working relationships with universities in at least ten provinces across China from which we conduct fieldwork in all these regions.

The research presented here (particularly in the second half of the book) was all amassed by this team. Gathering this data has not been an easy task. Each research project includes months of careful research design, logistical preparation, interfacing with local stakeholders, and development of research materials, including piloting all survey forms in real-world settings. We then spend hours and hours training teams of volunteers (mostly undergraduates in Chinese universities) to undertake the study under the direction of our graduate student leaders. We choose a region, obtain a list of all counties in that region, randomly select households within those counties, then pile into narrow vans and drive through mountainous areas, across rivers, over broken-down roads until we reach every family on our list. We ask standardized questions, and we don't conclude anything until we've seen the responses of the entire sample. Because poverty naturally lingers in the places that are hardest to reach, it's only through this kind of dedication that it's possible to develop a true understanding of what's happening in China today. Few organizations can match the quality of this data collection.

Pioneering Research Methodology: Focus on Impact

Another thing that makes REAP unique is its commitment to not only diagnosing problems, but also finding real, scalable, sustainable solutions. Around the world countless government entities, nonprofit organizations, research groups, and social enterprises are dedicated to improving education for vulnerable populations. Yet the problems they are committed to solving persist. Few organizations can convincingly answer a fundamental question about their programs: Do they really work?

This simple question forms the foundation of REAP's work and the basis of all its inquiries. When REAP was conceived in 2006, we realized we needed a methodology that was robust and replicable, much like research in the hard sciences, if we were to answer these questions convincingly. Our answer: *impact evaluation*.

Impact evaluation is the commitment to carefully and scientifically evaluating every project for how well it fulfills its goals. Drawing on the traditional tools of the hard sciences to evaluate the effect of projects on verifiable outcome variables, this methodology is so important because it allows for the clear delineation of causal effects and identification of causal mechanisms, key elements in the careful accumulation of scientific knowledge.

More importantly, impact evaluation is particularly well suited to bringing evidence-based change to bear on real-world problems. This is because impact evaluation assesses the aggregate effects of real interventions at scale and under realistic conditions. Impact evaluation thus allows policymakers and humanitarian institutions to target their limited resources to the projects that have been proved to do the most good.

REAP is one of few organizations conducting large numbers of large-scale impact evaluations in China today. From 2005 to 2016, REAP scholars were responsible for over half of the impact evaluation studies on education within China published in the international scholarly journals. Considering that China is home to one-fifth of the world's population (with more children than all of sub-Saharan Africa) and still struggles with serious and pervasive barriers to education, REAP is filling a critical gap.

Evidence-Based Policy Change

While REAP researchers regularly publish high-quality academic work, REAP's *primary goal* is bringing about lasting and well-targeted policy change to benefit millions of Chinese children.

Every time REAP finishes a research initiative, we write a policy brief explaining the nature of the problem and the findings of our action research and making concrete policy recommendations. This brief is then sent directly to the State Council, China's highest decision-making body. Since 2006, REAP has submitted twenty-seven policy briefs to the national government; twenty-three briefs have been "officially signed" and turned into policy. This evidence-based focus on impact and solutions has led to dramatic shifts in priority at the highest levels of government.

REAP also draws on relationships with regional and local partners to effect policy change at the provincial or county level. Often the demonstrated successes of these local efforts are the first steps that grow into larger-scale change.

This combination of scientifically robust, solution-driven research with REAP's active engagement with national, regional, and local partners has led to significant, measurable results, some of which I've detailed in the book. Among the highlights:

- From research to a US$20 billion national nutrition program: Over the course of seven large-scale research projects— including nearly 60,000 primary school students in seven provinces of rural western and central China—REAP discovered that the average rate of iron-deficiency anemia (a debilitating condition brought about by poor nutrition) among rural primary school students was above 30 percent. No one knew this was still a problem in China, but REAP was able to provide a solution through its research—that simple nutritional interventions could dramatically reduce anemia (the Chinese government was moderately interested in this finding)—and also to significantly boost students' academic performance (this caught the *full* attention of the top policymakers). Following REAP's submission of a series of policy briefs to China's top leaders, as well as countless meetings between local and provincial educational officials, China's central government launched a ten-year nationwide US$20 billion school nutrition program in 2011 that is delivering daily free school lunches to more than twenty-five million poor students.

- From research to improving young children's IQ: After our first project on early childhood (discussed above), REAP took the findings directly to policymakers. Within three months of completing the first study, REAP began a new program with the enthusiastic support and constant involvement of China's National Health and Family Planning Commission (NHFPC) as well as with the hands-on support of the Shaanxi FPC. A contingent of China's family-planning inspectors were trained in the use of the REAP parenting curriculum. We are currently building parenting centers in rural villages where children and their parents are invited to play and learn together. If this initiative can be brought to all villages, then over the next ten years this innovative partnership could change the lives of fifty million children (approximating the population of Spain or South Korea).

- Seeing is learning: Starting in 2011, REAP began a series of studies to document the veritable epidemic of uncorrected myopia that plagued rural schools in China. From grade three to grade nine, nearly one-third of students in rural China have vision poor enough to hamper their learning, yet they do not have glasses. Most don't even know they're nearsighted. Further, in a series of large-scale randomized controlled trials, REAP found that when you give nearsighted children glasses, their learning improves immediately and dramatically and learning anxiety falls. Eyeglasses can cut the achievement gap between rural and urban students in half within one academic year. A seemingly simple solution of screening vision and providing glasses is much more complex than meets the eye, owing to a multitude of factors including access, cultural norms, parental misconceptions, and cost. REAP's understanding of these issues and its ability to identify the "right" partners has led it to translate these research findings into a new social enterprise that is beginning to fill a critical gap in rural vision services: training teachers to screen children for vision problems in the classroom, fitting them for glasses where needed, and charging only as much as they can afford to pay. This four-way collaboration between the local department of education, the county hospital, the private optometry sector, and leading academic experts is known as SmartFocus. By 2020, SmartFocus's target is to have forty vision centers and to serve millions of rural students and their families. We are pleased to share that SmartFocus was a runner-up for 2016's inaugural Clearly Vision Prize, awarded to entrepreneurs and innovations judged to have the greatest potential to improve access to vision correction.

The ultimate goal of this many-faceted policy advocacy is to bring change to as many children as possible. In China the government has shown itself willing and able to accomplish miracles. We just want to help direct the charge to the issues that matter most, using solutions that have been proved to work.

Mentorship and Long-Term Sustainability

At the heart of REAP's success are long-term and mutually beneficial collaborations between a core team of researchers based at Stanford University and several institutions elsewhere in the United States, in Europe, and inside China. Much more than this, REAP is a platform that allows for new connections and dedicated partnerships between field researchers in nearly every province of China and experts at flagship universities across China, the United States, and Europe.

This collaboration benefits all sides: the world's best social scientists get the opportunity to bring their theoretical innovations out of the abstract world of academic theory and test them in the real world alongside experienced field researchers. At the same time, this platform gives young faculty within China the opportunity to work with world-renowned experts and learn the skills that will help them succeed. REAP has made a rare agreement for a team of its kind—REAP researchers from all institutions agree to share equally in the fruits of this effort: full access to the data gathered and coauthorship on all papers written using the data.

Young faculty on REAP's team are given the opportunity for incredible mentorship. Nearly every research fellow in each of REAP's China-side partners has been a visiting scholar at Stanford or its partner organizations elsewhere in the United States, where they receive weekly guidance in writing papers, the opportunity to take Stanford courses, and mentoring from other senior researchers. This partnership has helped the young researchers at REAP to become some of the most widely published scholars in their fields anywhere in the world.

In addition to mentoring young faculty who are poised to lead this movement in the coming years, REAP also prepares students to take on this critical work. REAP teaches an intensive course in impact evaluation for over a hundred graduate students from across China each year. The most promising students in the course are invited to coauthor academic papers with senior REAP researchers for publication in international academic journals. REAP has hired several dedicated writing tutors who work with graduate students year-round, helping the students improve their English academic writing and begin to write their own papers as lead authors.

The students learn not only within the classroom, but also as volunteers in the field. REAP has worked with Chinese universities to send tens of thousands of students into the field to participate in cutting-edge social science research and learn how to collect high-quality data. Students who return for multiple projects are given the opportunity to lead small teams of other students in this work, developing the leadership skills that will serve them well wherever their careers lead. And this opportunity extends to interns from places outside China. Every year REAP brings a group of high-achieving high school and university students from the world's top programs to China to conduct fieldwork. These students travel on dusty rural roads, talk to local teachers, get to know rural students, and learn to care for these communities that are often left out of modern Chinese life, even as they hone their research skills.

REAP's work enables students to enter academia at the highest levels, or to join the corporate and public sectors armed with a deep understanding of the issues in China's poor rural areas and a long-standing commitment to increasing opportunity for underserved communities. It is this next generation of impassioned, highly skilled citizens who will set the priorities for the future.

REAP is able to attract and develop this next generation of re-searchers and academic and societal leaders because REAP's own leaders, and the students they train, have a deep understanding of and empathy with the critical needs of poor rural communi-ties: they themselves are from those communities. Of REAP's cur-rent cohort of PhD and master's students, over 70 percent are from rural areas. Many of REAP's top leaders grew up in these areas. This background helps these current and future experts do better work as researchers—they intimately understand the places they are trying to help—and motivates them to work tirelessly to continue improv-ing the outcomes for these families. This is what truly sustainable change looks like.

It is this organization and all the countless hours of dedication the team has shown that have made this book possible. This is their book too.

Notes

Introduction

1. The data on college and high school attainment levels are from Hongbin Li, Prashant Loyalka, Scott Rozelle, and Binzhen Wu, "Human Capital and China's Future Growth," *Journal of Economic Perspectives* 31, no. 1 (2017): 25–48, except the China high school attainment figure, which is taken from the 2015 microcensus. For information on this census, see Lei Wang, Mengjie Li, Cody Abbey, and Scott Rozelle, "Human Capital and the Middle Income Trap: How Many of China's Youth Are Going to High School?" *Developing Economies* 56, no. 2 (2018): 82–103. As I will discuss in later chapters, the low share of the labor force with a *tertiary* education is not the fault of the Chinese leadership in recent years. Indeed, since the late 1990s, China has brought about the world's fastest-ever expansion in university enrollment. Here the problem is one of history. Before that big push, less than 10 percent of the labor force had been to college. Although today 20 to 30 percent of eighteen- to twenty-two-year-olds are in college, because of the size of the population and the low starting point, the effect of the recent increase in university education will not be fully felt for the labor force as a whole for decades. Hence it is safe to say that the low rate of university education, at least, has its roots in the time of Mao and Deng rather than in recent years.
2. "Two Paths to Prosperity," *Economist*, July 14, 1990. See chapter 2 for more on this subject.
3. High school attainment rates have been sharply divergent in rural and urban areas for decades. Now, thanks to a big push by the central government, that is finally starting to change, with more and more rural teenagers going to high school. But the fundamental inequality persists. I will talk more about this topic in chapter 4. Census data are defined by current residence status, not hukou, and so include both urban residents and rural migrants. See Li et al., "Human Capital and China's Future Growth."
4. World Bank, https://data.worldbank.org/country/china, accessed July 14, 2018.
5. Kenneth Rapoza, "A Look at China's Increasing Importance to the U.S. Econ-

196 · NOTES TO PAGES 13–24

omy," *Forbes*, September 7, 2017, www.forbes.com/sites/kenrapoza/2017/09/07/a
-look-at-chinas-increasing-importance-to-u-s-economy, accessed June 4, 2018.

6. Stephen S. Roach, "Why China Is Central to Global Growth," World Economic
Forum and Project Syndicate, September 2, 2016, https://www.weforum.org
/agenda/2016/09/why-china-is-central-to-global-growth, accessed June 4, 2018.

7. Howard W. French, *Everything under the Heavens: How the Past Helps Shape
China's Push for Global Power* (New York: Knopf, 2017).

8. Arvind Subramanian, "The Inevitable Superpower: Why China's Dominance
Is a Sure Thing," *Foreign Affairs*, September/October 2011, https://www.foreign
affairs.com/articles/china/2011-08-19/inevitable-superpower, accessed July 14,
2018.

Chapter One

1. Paul Collier, *The Bottom Billion: Why the Poorest Countries Are Failing and What
Can Be Done about It* (Oxford: Oxford University Press, 2007).

2. World Bank, International Comparison Program Database, www.worldbank
.org/en/programs/icp, accessed February 20, 2018; CIA World Factbook,
https://www.cia.gov/library/publications/the-world-factbook/rankorder/2004
rank.html, accessed May 1, 2018.

3. For more on the "chutes" that trouble the world's poorest countries, see Collier, *Bottom Billion*.

4. Income measures are reported in terms of purchasing power parity (PPP);
World Bank, International Comparison Program Database, GDP per Capita (PPP), https://data.worldbank.org/indicator/NY.GDP.PCAP.PP.CD?end=2016
&start=1990, accessed March 6, 2019.

5. Geoffrey Garrett, "Globalization's Missing Middle," *Foreign Affairs*, November/
December 2004, https://www.foreignaffairs.com/articles/2004-11-01/globaliza
tions-missing-middle, accessed November 20, 2017.

6. Note: the report does limit the countries studied in this analysis. The oil-
producing countries were not included. It also doesn't include the former
USSR countries of Eastern Europe that were more like high-income countries
before World War II, slumped during the socialist period, and then crashed.
Now many of them are bouncing back. But they are not included in this anal-
ysis because of the complications in their pathway. World Bank, *China 2030:
Building a Modern, Harmonious, and Creative High-Income Society* (Washington,
DC: World Bank, 2012).

7. Though, as I cautioned in the note above, these countries are not included on
the World Bank's middle-income trap analysis (fig. 2).

8. Over the years there has been a lot of debate in the academic world about just
how the middle-income trap functions, and what does and does not matter
for getting stuck. Some of the top hypotheses have been misguided industri-

alization and investment policies, underdeveloped banking and fiscal agencies, and insufficiently robust political institutions. Still, human capital is a crucial—and underestimated—factor at play here.

9. Yu Bai, Siqi Zhang, Ruirui Dang, Lei Wang, Cody Abbey, and Scott Rozelle, "Past Successes and Future Challenges in Rural China's Human Capital," REAP Working Paper, 2018, presented at 2017–18 CSCC Annual Conference; Hongbin Li, Prashant Loyalka, Scott Rozelle, and Binzhen Wu, "Human Capital and China's Future Growth," *Journal of Economic Perspectives* 31, no. 1 (2017): 25–48.

10. R. Barro and J. Lee, "A New Data Set of Educational Attainment in the World, 1950–2010," *Journal of Development Economics* 104 (2013): 184–98.

Chapter Two

1. Nguyen Dieu Tu Uyen and John Boudreau, "Samsung Turns Farmers into Bigger Earners Than Bankers," *Bloomberg*, October 5, 2016, https://www.bloomberg.com/news/articles/2016-10-05/samsung-turns-vietnam-s-farmers-into-bigger-earners-than-bankers, accessed September 25, 2017; Robb Young, "Made in Ethiopia: Fashion's Next Sourcing Hub," *Business of Fashion*, October 17, 2016, https://www.businessoffashion.com/articles/global-currents/made-in-ethiopia-fashions-next-sourcing-hub, accessed October 10, 2017; Finbarr Bermingham, "China's Manufacturing Exodus Set to Continue in 2020, Despite Prospect of Trade War Deal," *South China Morning Post*, January 9, 2020, https://www.scmp.com/economy/china-economy/article/3045141/chinas-manufacturing-exodus-set-continue-2020-despite, accessed February 17, 2020.

2. Yang Du, Peng Jia, and Albert Park, "Adoption of New Technology in Chinese Firms: Determinants and Impacts," conference presentation, at the Institute of Population and Labor Economics of Chinese Academy of Social Sciences, December 2017; Hong Cheng, Ruixue Jia, Dandan Li, and Hongbin Li, "The Rise of Robots in China," *Journal of Economics Perspectives* 33, no. 2 (Spring 2019): 71–88.

3. "Total Length of Public Roads in China from 2006 to 2016 (in Million Kilometers)," Statista.com, https://www.statista.com/statistics/276051/total-length-of-public-roads-in-china/, accessed February 20, 2018.

4. Girish Shetti, "One of China's Largest Steelmakers Plans to Lay Off 50,000 Workers," *China Topix*, March 11, 2016, http://www.chinatopix.com/articles/79294/20160311/china-s-major-steel-maker-lay-50-000-workers.htm, accessed September 25, 2017.

5. Tom Phillips, "The $900bn Question: What Is the Belt and Road Initiative?" *Guardian*, May 11, 2017, https://www.theguardian.com/world/2017/may/12/the-900bn-question-what-is-the-belt-and-road-initiative, accessed online December 4, 2019; "This Is Where Xi's Belt and Road Initiative Stands After Six Years,"

Bloomberg News, April 24, 2019, https://www.bloomberg.com/news/articles /2019-04-24/belt-and-road-by-the-numbers-where-xi-s-project-stands-now, accessed December 4, 2019.

6. "This Is Where Xi's Belt and Road Initiative Stands After Six Years"; "Xi Jinping's Second Belt and Road Forum: Three Key Takeaways," *Bloomberg News*, April 27, 2019, https://www.bloomberg.com/news/articles/2019-04-28/xi-jinping -s-wins-and-losses-at-his-second-belt-and-road-forum, accessed December 4, 2019.

7. Thomas Friedman was the first to make the argument that globalization has functionally "flattened" our world. Thomas L. Friedman, *The World Is Flat: A Brief History of the Twenty-First Century* (New York: Macmillan, 2005).

8. Xiaobing Wang, Jikun Huang, Linxiu Zhang, and Scott Rozelle, "The Rise of Migration and the Fall of Self Employment in Rural China's Labor Market," *China Economic Review* 22, no. 4 (2011): 573–84.

9. Fang Cai, Albert Park, and Yaohui Zhao, "The Chinese Labor Market in the Reform Era," in *China's Great Economic Transformation*, ed. Loren Brandt and Thomas Rawski (Cambridge: Cambridge University Press, 2008).

10. Note that in recent years this has started to change. There are more able-bodied workers in the villages. Thanks to globalization and automation's starting to take a share of low-wage jobs, a few men are starting to reappear in the villages. Those are the ones we worry will be left to the informal sector or might even turn to crime if they are dissatisfied with their options. Linxiu Zhang, Alan deBruaw, and Scott Rozelle, "China's Rural Labor Market Development and Its Gender Implications," *China Economic Review* 15 (2004): 230–47.

11. "Two Paths to Prosperity," *Economist*, July 14, 1990; "Making Computers for Other People May Not Be Glamorous, but It Has Shown Taiwan Its Future," *Economist*, November 7, 1998.

12. Sheryl Wudunn, "Taiwan Trying to Shift to High Tech Niches," *New York Times*, November 6, 1990.

13. Paul Blustein, "Asia's 'Dragons' Accept Trade's Pains and Gains: For Jobs Lost, New Markets Are Created," *Washington Post*, November 7, 1993.

14. In Taiwan in 1993—right in the midst of massive offshoring and the shift from manufacturing to the service sector—the jobless rate stayed at a staggeringly low 1.4 percent. Blustein, "Asia's 'Dragons' Accept Trade's Pains and Gains."

15. Kurt Badenhausen, "Ireland Heads Forbes' List of the Best Countries for Business," *Forbes*, December 4, 2013, http://www.forbes.com/sites/kurtbadenhausen /2013/12/04/ireland-heads-forbes-list-of-the-best-countries-for-business/#3a2faa 8b2f03, accessed July 22, 2018. The Human Development Index uses three major development indicators—life expectancy, education level, and per capita income—to calculate a final score for each nation. Per capita income here is reported in terms of purchasing power parity (PPP). PPP refers to a method of

standardizing values such as income or GDP across countries that use different currencies so they can be accurately compared. It is calculated by comparing the price of a standard basket of consumer goods in each economy and adjusting so that the "purchasing power" of each currency is on par. This method accounts for any differences in cost of living or inflation across countries.

16. Amusingly, much the same sentiment was expressed about Taiwan and South Korea's first forays into the high-tech economy. In 1993 an article in the *Washington Post* reported, "In Seoul, Taipei and elsewhere, many analysts wonder whether the South Koreans and Taiwanese will be able to make the leap to the next industrial stage, past the production of knock-off computers, chips and consumer electronics." See Blustein, "Asia's 'Dragons' Accept Trade's Pains and Gains."

17. "Three Kingdoms, Two Empires: China's Internet Giants," *Economist*, April 22, 2017; "WeChat's World: China's Mobile Internet," *Economist*, August 6, 2016; "Tech's Top Tier Now Includes 2 from China," *New York Times*, August 3, 2016.

18. Niall McCarthy, "The Countries with the Most STEM Graduates," *Forbes*, February 2, 2017, https://www.forbes.com/sites/niallmccarthy/2017/02/02/the-countries-with-the-most-stem-graduates-infographic/#2e8d5fc2268a, accessed October 10, 2017.

19. See, for instance, David H. Autor, Frank Levy, and Richard J. Murnane, "The Skill Content of Recent Technological Change: An Empirical Exploration," *Quarterly Journal of Economics*, November 2003.

20. "Editorial: 50 Years of Change in Education," in *Education at a Glance 2011: OECD Indicators* (Paris: OECD, 2011), https://www.oecd.org/education/skills-beyond-school/48631582.pdf, accessed February 21, 2018; Marie Clarke, "Educational Reform in the 1960s: The Introduction of Comprehensive Schools in the Republic of Ireland," *History of Education* 39, no. 3 (2010): 383–99.

21. "Editorial: 50 Years of Change in Education."

Chapter Three

1. Efforts are being made to make more room in high school for the current generation of young people, but far too many remain essentially unskilled. Any change will take time: even if every individual after 2020 goes to high school (which is the plan in China today), it will still be nearly 2040 before even half of the labor force are high school graduates. For more, see chapter 4.

2. World Bank, *World Development Report 2019: The Changing Nature of Work*, World Development Report (Washington, DC: World Bank, 2019), 81–82.

3. Stuart Auerbach, "Mexican Border Towns Boom: $1.30-an-Hour Wages Attract U.S. Companies," *Washington Post (1974–Current file)*, April 20, 1986, accessed via ProQuest Historical Newspapers, October 17, 2017; David Luhnow, "As Jobs Move East, Plants in Mexico Retool to Compete: China Takes Low-

Wage Work, So Guadalajara Targets Products Still Made in U.S," *Wall Street Journal*, eastern edition, March 5, 2004, A.1, https://www.wsj.com/articles/SB1 07844790219747253, accessed February 7, 2020.

4. Les Whittington, "Mexico Hopes to Become Industrial Tiger of 1990," *Vancouver Sun*, December 28, 1990, https://search-proquest-com.stanford.idm .oclc.org/news/docview/243495893/59F66A325FFC45F2PQ/3?accountid=14026, accessed via ProQuest, October 17, 2017.

5. Luhnow, "As Jobs Move East, Plants in Mexico Retool to Compete"; Juan Forero, "As China Gallops, Mexico Sees Factory Jobs Slip Away: China's Surge," *New York Times (1923–Current File)*, September 3, 2003, A3, accessed via ProQuest Historical Newspapers, October 31, 2017.

6. Santiago Levy and Dani Rodrik, "The Mexican Paradox," in *Project Syndicate*, August 10, 2017, https://www.project-syndicate.org/commentary/mexican -paradox-economic-orthodoxy-low-productivity-by-santiago-levy-and-dani -rodrik-2017-08?barrier=accesspaylog, accessed September 12, 2017.

7. Elisabeth Malkin, "Manufacturing Jobs Are Exiting Mexico: Business Leaders Try to Stop the Exodus of Factories to China," *New York Times (1923–Current file)*, November 5, 2002, W1, accessed via ProQuest Historical Newspapers, October 17, 2017.

8. D. Mayer-Foulkes, "Market Failures in Human Development: The Intergenerational Poverty Trap in Mexico," in *Economic Reform in Developing Countries: Reach, Range, Reason*, ed. José María Fanelli and Lyn Squire, GDN Series (Cheltenham, UK: Edward Elgar, 2008), 77–113.

9. Malkin, "Manufacturing Jobs Are Exiting Mexico."

10. "The Two Mexicos," *Economist*, September 19, 2015, https://www.economist .com/leaders/2015/09/19/the-two-mexicos, accessed November 10, 2017; Paul Imison, "How NAFTA Explains the Two Mexicos," *Atlantic*, September 23, 2017, https://www.theatlantic.com/international/archive/2017/09/nafta-mexico -trump-trade/540906/, accessed November 10, 2017.

11. Lucinda Fleeson. "Leaving Laredo," *Mother Jones* 28 (September/October 2003): 24, https://www.motherjones.com/politics/2003/09/leaving-laredo/, accessed October 17, 2017.

12. Santiago Levy and Daniel Rodrik, "The Mexican Paradox," in *Project Syndicate*, August 10, 2017 https://www.project-syndicate.org/commentary/mexican -paradox-economic-orthodoxy-low-productivity-by-santiago-levy-and-dani -rodrik-2017-08?barrier=accesspaylog, accessed September 12, 2017; Paul Imison, "How NAFTA Explains the Two Mexicos," *Atlantic*, September 23, 2017, https://www.theatlantic.com/international/archive/2017/09/nafta-mexico -trump-trade/540906/, accessed November 10, 2017.

13. Gustavo Robles, Gabriela Calderón, and Beatriz Magaloni, "The Economic Consequences of Drug Trafficking Violence in Mexico," Working Paper, Poverty and Governance Series Working Paper, Stanford University, August 2015;

Adam Popescu, "Is Mexico the Next Silicon Valley? Tech Boom Takes Root in Guadalajara," *Washington Post*, May 14, 2016, https://www.washington post.com/business/is-mexico-the-next-silicon-valley-tech-boom-takes-root -in-guadalajara/2016/05/13/61249f36-072e-11e6-bdcb-0133da18418d_story.html ?noredirect=on&utm_term=.8c1629827924, accessed February 27, 2018.

14. Lucinda Fleeson, "Leaving Laredo," *Mother Jones* 28 (September/October 2003): 24, https://www.motherjones.com/politics/2003/09/leaving-laredo/, accessed October 17, 2017; T. MacGabhann, Mexico's "Lost Generation" of Drug Addicts," *TCA Regional News*, https://search.proquest.com/docview/1772601390 ?accountid=14026, accessed November 9, 2017.

15. Robles, Calderón, and Magaloni, "Economic Consequences of Drug Trafficking Violence in Mexico."

16. Yuyu Chen, Hongbin Li, and Lingsheng Meng, "Prenatal Sex Selection and Missing Girls in China: Evidence from the Diffusion of Diagnostic Ultrasound," *Journal of Human Resources* 48, no. 1 (2013): 36–70.

17. In 2000, 90 percent of people arrested in China were men, many of them young men. Fully two-thirds of violent and property crimes were committed by men aged sixteen to twenty-five. China Law Yearbook Editorial Office, *Chinese Law Yearbook* (Beijing: Chinese Law Yearbook, 2001); Lianhe Hu, *Zhuan Xing Yu Fan Zui: Zhong Guo Zhuan Xing Qi Fan Zui Wen Ti De Shi Zheng Yan Jiu* [Transition and crime: An empirical analysis of crime during China's economic transition] (Beijing: Central Communist Party School Press, 2006).

18. The study exploited province-year level variation and concluded that male sex ratios account for one-seventh of the rise in crime from 1988 to 2004. Lena Edlund, Hongbin Li, Junjian Yi, and Junsen Zhang, "Sex Ratios and Crime: Evidence from China," *Review of Economics and Statistics* 95, no. 5 (2013): 1520–34.

19. See chapter 7 for more on this story.

20. Of course, today Spain invests heavily in high school and college. Its economy (like all economies in the world) has problems. But its human capital structure, thirty-five years after joining the European Union, is now that of a high-income country. So maybe the risk is subsiding.

21. Howard W. French, *Everything Under the Heavens: How the Past Helps Shape China's Push for Global Power* (New York: Knopf, 2017).

Chapter Four

1. This statistic is calculated based on China's 2015 microcensus, a survey of about ten million individuals that was conducted in late 2015 by the State Statistical Bureau with the utmost care to be representative of the entire nation. In our definition "dropout" refers to all citizens whose self-reported "highest level of education attained" is less than an upper secondary degree (they have

not completed a degree in either an academic or a vocational high school). The population in question is the national population aged twenty to sixty-five. Note that according to China's education policy, it is completely consistent with policy to leave before high school, after finishing nine years of compulsory education. Hongbin Li, Prashant Loyalka, Scott Rozelle, and Binzhen Wu, "Human Capital and China's Future Growth," *Journal of Economic Perspectives* 31, no. 1 (2017): 25–48.

2. China's students placed first in all three subject areas: reading, math, and science. While the performance of students in China should be considered impressive, there is a caveat. The nation's much-lauded performance on the PISA should, in fact, be taken with a grain of salt, considering that Chinese entrants were limited to students from one of China's most privileged provinces (Shanghai), while most other countries included a much more diverse (and nationally representative) cohort. In 2018 China's PISA scores were based on results from more provinces—four in total—but the question of representativeness at the national level remains. "PISA 2012 Results in Focus: What 15-Year-Olds Know and What They Can Do with What They Know," in *Program for International Student Assessment* (Paris: OECD, 2012), http://www.oecd.org/pisa/keyfindings/pisa-2012-results-overview.pdf, accessed May 1, 2018; Joshua Berlinger, "Teens from China's Wealthiest Regions Rank Top of the Class in Global Education Survey," *CNN Online*, December 3, 2019, https://www.cnn.com/2019/12/03/asia/pisa-rankings-2019-intl-hnk/index.html, accessed December 17, 2019.

3. T. E. Woronov, "Learning to Serve: Urban Youth, Vocational Schools and New Class Formations in China," *China Journal*, no. 66 (July 2011): 77–99.

4. Ai Yue, Bin Tang, Yaojiang Shi, Jingjing Tang, Guanminjia Shang, Alexis Medina, and Scott Rozelle, "Rural Education across China's 40 Years of Reform: Past Successes and Future Challenges," *China Agricultural Economic Review* 10, no. 1 (2018): 93–118.

5. While, as I said, many high schools were shut down during the Cultural Revolution, others were operating as so-called Cultural Revolution high schools. Instead of learning typical academic subjects, students in these schools were reading Mao's Red Book and doing "internships" in factories. Niny Khor, Lihua Pang, Chengfang Liu, Fang Chang, Di Mo, Prashant Loyalka, and Scott Rozelle, "China's Looming Human Capital Crisis: Upper Secondary Educational Attainment Rates and the Middle Income Trap," *China Quarterly* 228 (December 2016): 905–26; Yue et al., "Rural Education across China's 40 Years of Reform."

6. Yue et al., "Rural Education across China's 40 Years of Reform."

7. W.-J. J. Yeung, "Higher Education Expansion and Social Stratification in China," *Chinese Sociological Review* 45, no. 4 (2013): 54–80; S. Li, J. Whalley, and

C. Xing, "China's Higher Education Expansion and Unemployment of College Graduates," *China Economic Review* 37, suppl. C (2014): 567–82; Niall McCarthy, "The Countries with the Most STEM Graduates," *Forbes*, February 2, 2017, https://www.forbes.com/sites/niallmccarthy/2017/02/02/the-countries-with-the -most-stem-graduates-infographic/#690de3be268a, accessed October 10, 2017.

8. T. F. Bresnahan, E. Brynjolfsson, and L. M. Hitt, "Information Technology, Workplace Organization, and the Demand for Skilled Labor: Firm-Level Evidence," *Quarterly Journal of Economics* 117, no. 1 (2002): 339–76; L. F. Katz and A. B. Krueger, "Computing Inequality: Have Computers Changed the Labor Market?," *Quarterly Journal of Economics* 113, no. 4 (1998): 1169–213; Jakob B. Madsen and Fabrice Murtin, "British Economic Growth since 1270: The Role of Education," *Journal of Economic Growth* 22 (2017): 229–72; R. Barro and J. Lee, "A New Data Set of Educational Attainment in the World, 1950–2010," *Journal of Development Economics* 104 (2013): 184–98.

9. Lei Wang, Mengjie Li, Cody Abbey, and Scott Rozelle, "Human Capital and the Middle Income Trap: How Many of China's Youth Are Going to High School?," *Developing Economies* 56, no. 2 (2018): 82–103.

10. "Population by Age and Sex," in *China Statistical Yearbook* (Beijing: National Bureau of Statistics of China, 2015).

11. Hukou status depends upon the status of one's parents. Those with urban parents have urban hukou, those with rural parents have rural hukou. It is possible to change one's hukou, but the ways of doing so are difficult and inaccessible to the vast majority of rural people. For more, see the book's conclusion.

12. This is an issue that has a lot of variation across the country, because individual cities (and neighborhoods within cities) are free to decide their own policies toward migrant children. In most urban areas there is some access to public primary school education. In some urban areas there has even been increasing access to junior high. But even today, across China children with rural hukou have no access to urban high schools. At the level of national policy, rural students are guaranteed access to public education of any kind only in their home villages. I will discuss these negative effects of the hukou system in more detail in the conclusion. For now the point is that China's urban-rural divide is wide and largely impermeable—and hugely significant for educational outcomes.

13. This is defined by current residence status, not hukou, so it includes both urban residents and rural migrants. Li et al., "Human Capital and China's Future Growth."

14. Lei Wang, Mengjie Li, Cody Abbey, and Scott Rozelle, "Human Capital and the Middle Income Trap: How Many of China's Youth Are Going to High School?," *Developing Economies* 56, no. 2 (2018): 82–103.

15. Lei, Li, Abbey, and Rozelle, "Human Capital and the Middle Income Trap."
16. Fang Lai, Chengfang Liu, Renfu Luo, Linxiu Zhang, Xiaochen Ma, Yujie Bai, Brian Sharbono, and Scott Rozelle, "The Education of China's Migrant Children: The Missing Link in China's Education System," *International Journal of Educational Development* 37 (2014): 68–77.
17. Jikun Huang, Huayong Zhi, Zhurong Huang, Scott Rozelle, and John Giles, "The Impact of the Global Financial Crisis on Off-Farm Employment and Earning in Rural China," *World Development* 39, no. 5 (2011): 797–807.
18. In China there are two kinds of high school: academic high school and vocational high school. Note that the educational attainment rates I cited above are for any kind of high school, including both tracks. Academic high school refers to a traditional high school program, focused on general academic skills like math, reading, writing, science, and English. Vocational high schools, by contrast, focus much more time on specific professional skills. In China, academic high school is the higher prestige track, since its admission is selective (depending on scores on an entrance examination) and prepares students for the possibility of continuing on to university. Vocational high school has much lower rates of tuition and more opportunities for tuition waivers, but as I'll show in chapter 5, the quality of schooling leaves much to be desired.
19. Chengfang Liu, Linxiu Zhang, Renfu Luo, Scott Rozelle, Brian Sharbono, and Yaojiang Shi, "Development Challenges, Tuition Barriers, and High School Education in China," *Asia Pacific Journal of Education* 29 (2009): 503–20.
20. F. Lai, C. Liu, R. Luo, L. Zhang, X. Ma, Y. Bai, B. Sharbono, and S. Rozelle, "The Education of China's Migrant Children: The Missing Link in China's Education System," *International Journal of Educational Development* 37 (2014): 68–77.

Chapter Five

1. The university enrollment rate is surprisingly difficult to quantify reliably. Official figures put the number at about 30 percent, but this statistic includes many types of schooling that do not clearly fit the typical definition of university. For example, the 30 percent figure includes students enrolled in nonacademic vocational colleges as well as an approximation of the number of Chinese students enrolled in universities overseas. That's why I estimate 20 to 30 percent. As for high school, official policies have set a target for half of China's children to attend academic high schools and the other half to go to vocational high schools. In practice, the admissions targets for academic high schools are set at the level estimated to bring about this ratio.
2. Zhaohui Fo and Hui Xing, "Survey on the Implementation of the National Stipend Policy in Secondary Vocational Schools," *China Educational Development Yearbook* 3 (2011): 153–68; Małgorzata Kuczera and Simon Field, "Learn-

ing for Jobs: OECD Reviews of Vocational Education and Training; Options for China," http://www.oecd.org/china/45486493.pdf, accessed September 24, 2015.

3. To be clear, China's recent vocational education push also includes the expansion of vocational colleges. In this chapter I focus on vocational high schools, since there are more of them and therefore they are of more immediate concern for driving big shifts in the skill levels of China's labor force as a whole.

4. China National Bureau of Statistics, *China Statistical Yearbook* (Beijing: China Statistics Press, 1991); China National Bureau of Statistics, *China Statistical Yearbook* (Beijing: China Statistics Press, 2012).

5. We used a multistep procedure to construct the tests and ensure that they were valid (that they represented the types of skills students are expected to acquire in vocational high schools in China). First we used national and provincial curricular standards for vocational high schools to define the content domains for our tests. Then we collected from official textbooks a large pool of exam items that mirror these content domains. To further verify that the items were being covered in current curricula, we asked a number of vocational high school teachers to serve as content experts. We used the items selected by these content experts to create pilot tests. Finally, to ensure that our tests had good psychometric properties, we analyzed data from a pilot of more than a thousand vocational high school students. We filtered out questionable items and used the remaining items to created content-balanced tests. The final tests had a high degree of reliability (person reliability of 0.7 to 0.8). See Hongmei Yi, Guirong Li, Liyang Li, Prashant Loyalka, James Chu, Natalie Johnson, Elena Kardanova, Linxiu Zhang, and Scott Rozelle, "Are Students Thriving in Vocational Education and Training in China?" REAP Working Paper, 2015.

6. The same study found that 89 percent of kids made no progress in their vocational skills over the course of a year.

7. T. E. Woronov, "Learning to Serve: Urban Youth, Vocational Schools and New Class Formations in China," *China Journal* 66 (July 2011): 77–99.

8. These dropout rates were carefully measured and checked for accuracy by our research team. To assess dropout rates over the course of one school year, we surveyed all sample students one time in the beginning of the school year, then returned to those classrooms at the end of the year. To each class our enumerators brought a student-tracking form that included the individual information of each student who completed our baseline survey. Our enumerators marked each student on the baseline list as present, temporarily absent, transferred to another school, attending an internship, or dropped out, according to information provided by class monitors. If there was any question about the status of an individual student, we verified the information with multiple classmates and the homeroom teacher in each class.

9. In fact, my team's research has already shown that a proper regulation system can improve student outcomes. In 2015 we conducted a randomized controlled trial (RCT) of a new accountability system for China's vocational high schools. Half of the schools were enrolled in the new accountability program and given clear standards for quality: they had to ensure that their students made measurable progress in math skills and technical skills, to reduce dropout rates as much as possible, and to make sure their students were participating only in internships that were in compliance with national labor laws. Schools that did the best by these metrics would receive increased government funding and the chance at new corporate partnerships. The rest of the schools were left to continue as usual, without these new incentives. The data showed that the schools given proper incentives had made enormous progress. Students in those schools showed significant improvement in both math skills and vocational skills over the year; they reported being more satisfied with their learning, and fewer dropped out.

10. David H. Autor, Frank Levy, and Richard J. Murnane, "The Skill Content of Recent Technological Change: An Empirical Exploration," *Quarterly Journal of Economics*, November 2003.

11. E. A. Hanushek, G. Schwerdt, L. Woessmann, and L. Zhang, "General Education, Vocational Education, and Labor-Market Outcomes over the Life-Cycle," *Journal of Human Resources* 52, no. 1 (2017): 48–87. Researchers from Harvard and Stanford have shown that students' abilities in basic skills (e.g., high school math and science) are reliable predictors of long-term national growth trajectories. Policymakers ignore these skills at their peril. See Eric A. Hanushek, Paul E. Peterson, and Ludger Woessmann, *Endangering Prosperity: A Global View of the American School* (Washington, DC: Brookings Institution Press, 2013).

12. Woronov, "Learning to Serve."

Chapter Six

1. Owing teachers' salaries (*qinggongzi*, as it was known then) was common in many poor areas during the earlier period. Today the central government pays teachers' salaries for the entirety of compulsory education, defined in China to include grades one through nine.

2. The PISA (Programme for International Student Assessment) is an international test of students' learning among fifteen-year-olds. It includes reading, science, and math sections. In 2012 students from Shanghai performed the best in the world in all three subjects. In 2018 China again took the top spot, this time including students from Shanghai, Beijing, Jiangsu, and Zhejiang. For more detail see Organisation for Economic Co-operation and Development, Programme for International Student Assessment, *PISA 2012 Technical*

Report (Paris: OECD, 2013); Joshua Berlinger, "Teens from China's Wealthiest Regions Rank Top of the Class in Global Education Survey," CNN online, December 3, 2019, https://www.cnn.com/2019/12/03/asia/pisa-rankings-2019-intl -hnk/index.html, accessed December 17, 2019.

3. F. Lai, C. Liu, R. Luo, L. Zhang, X. Ma, Y. Bai, B. Sharbono, and S. Rozelle, "The Education of China's Migrant Children: The Missing Link in China's Education System," *International Journal of Educational Development* 37 (2014): 68–77.

4. J. Halterman, J. Kaczorowski, C. Aligne, P. Auinger, and P. Szilagyi, "Iron Deficiency and Cognitive Achievement among School-Aged Children and Adolescents in the United States," *Pediatrics* 107 (2001): 1381–86; R. Stoltzfus, "Defining Iron-Deficiency Anemia in Public Health Terms: A Time for Reflection," *Journal of Nutrition* 131 (2): 565S–567S; R. Stoltzfus, J. Kvalsvig, H. Chwaya, A. Montresor, M. Albonico, J. Tielsch, L. Savioli, and E. Pollitt, "Effects of Iron Supplementation and Anthelmintic Treatment on Motor and Language Development of Preschool Children in Zanzibar: Double Blind, Placebo Controlled Study," *British Medical Journal* 323, no. 7326 (2001): 1389; G. Bobonis, E. Miguel, and C. Puri-Sharma, "Anemia and School Participation," *Journal of Human Resources* 41, no. 4 (2006): 692–721; R. Luo, Y. Shi, L. Zhang, C. Liu, S. Rozelle, B. Sharbono, A. Yue, Q. Zhao, and R. Martorell, "Nutrition and Educational Performance in Rural China's Elementary Schools: Results of a Randomized Control Trial in Shaanxi Province," *Economic Development and Cultural Change* 60, no. 4 (2012): 735–72.

5. United Nations Children's Fund, World Health Organization, and United Nations University, *Iron Deficiency Anemia: Assessment, Prevention, and Control: A Guide for Programme Managers* (Geneva: World Health Organization, 2001); Renfu Luo, Xiaobing Wang, Chengfang Liu, Linxiu Zhang, Yaojiang Shi, Grant Miller, Scott Rozelle, Elaine Yu, and Reynaldo Martorell, "Alarmingly High Anemia Prevalence in Western China," *Southeast Asian Journal of Tropical Medicine and Public Health* 42, no. 5 (2011): 1204–13; Lili Li, Lei Huang, Yaojiang Shi, Renfu Luo, Meredith Yang, and Scott Rozelle, "Anemia and Students' Educational Performance in Rural Central China: Prevalence, Correlates and Impacts," *China Economic Review* 51 (2018): 283–93; Huan Wang, Wilson Liang, Laura Jonsson, Qiran Zhao, Samuel Kennedy, Gloria Breck, Jane Bai, Matthew Boswell, Scott Rozelle, and Alexis Medina, "Is China's 32 Billion Dollar Program to Fight Rural Undernutrition Working? A Mixed Methods Analysis in 100 Rural Schools in Western China," REAP Working Paper, 2017.

6. Chen-Wei Pan, Dharani Ramamurthy, and Seang-Mei Saw, "Worldwide Prevalence and Risk Factors for Myopia," *Ophthalmic and Physiological Optics* 32, no. 1 (2012): 3–16. Note that the prevalence of poor vision continues to rise with age after primary school. The rates of poor vision among students in rural middle schools and high schools range from 50 percent to more than 75 percent. Because the rate of providing glasses also increases with age, the

highest rates of uncorrected myopia are found among rural middle school students. Yue Ma, Xiaochen Ma, Yaojiang Shi, Nathan Congdon, Hongmei Yi, Sarah Kotb, Alexis Medina, Scott Rozelle, and Mony Iver, "Visual Impairment in Rural China: Prevalence, Severity, and Association with Income across Student Cohorts," REAP Working Paper, 2018.

7. See Elie Dogin, "The Myopia Boom: Short-Sightedness Is Reaching Epidemic Proportions: Some Scientists Think They Have Found a Reason Why," *Nature*, March 18, 2015, https://www.nature.com/news/the-myopia-boom-1.17120, accessed February 9, 2018.

8. Ma et al., "Visual Impairment in Rural China."

9. The result found an increase of 0.74 standard deviations in test scores under ideal conditions. This size effect from a school intervention is considered extremely high—almost double the level of learning. Xiaochen Ma, "Improving Learning by Improving Vision: Evidence from Two Randomized Controlled Trials of Providing Vision Care in China" (PhD diss., University of California, Davis, 2015).

More than ninety million students in China's school system (grades one to twelve) are suffering from poor vision, primarily myopia. Of those, approximately forty million are attending school in rural communities. Assuming that the rate of uncorrected myopia is about 50 percent (it's nearly 80 percent in elementary school and 20 percent in high school), about twenty million children don't have the glasses they need to see what's written on the blackboard. The other fifty million are attending school in urban areas, in public rural schools, and in suburban community schools (including rural areas in the eastern China provinces). We assume that all students with poor vision in these schools have access to vision care. To the extent that this is not true, our number of twenty million students with uncorrected myopia is an underestimate.

10. These results were gathered through fecal samples from elementary school students in poor rural areas. The intestinal worms discovered in this population included roundworm, hookworm, and whipworm. Xiaobing Wang, Linxiu Zhang, Renfu Luo, Guofei Wang, Yingdan Chen, Alexis Medina, Karen Eggleston, Scott Rozelle, and D. Scott Smith, "Soil-Transmitted Helminth Infections and Correlated Risk Factors in Preschool and School-Aged Children in Rural Southwest China," *PLoS One* 7, no. 9 (2012): e45939.

11. Because intestinal worm infection rates are higher in places with warmer, wetter climates, this health issue is mostly limited to China's more tropical southern provinces. Anemia and uncorrected myopia, by contrast, are widespread across the entire country. Longshan Xu, Baojun Pan, Jinxiang Lin, Liping Chen, Senhai Yu, and Jack Jones, "Creating Health-Promoting Schools in Rural China: A Project Started from Deworming," *Health Promotion International* 15, no. 3 (2000): 197–206; Peter Steinmann, Zunwei Du, Libo Wang, Xuezhong

Wang, Jinyong Jiang, Lanhua Li, Hanspeter Marti, Xiaonong Zhou, and Jürg Utzinger, "Extensive Multiparasitism in a Village of Yunnan Province, People's Republic of China, Revealed by a Suite of Diagnostic Methods," *American Journal of Tropical Medicine and Hygiene* 78, no. 5 (2008): 760–69; Huan Zhou, Chiho Watanabe, and Ryutaro Ohtsuka, "Impacts of Dietary Intake and Helminth Infection on Diversity in Growth among School Children in Rural South China: A Four-Year Longitudinal Study," *American Journal of Human Biology* 19, no. 1 (2007): 96–106.

12. Chengfang Liu, Louise Lu, Linxiu Zhang, Renfu Luo, Sean Sylvia, Alexis Medina, Scott Rozelle, Darvin Scott Smith, Yingdan Chen, and Tingjun Zhu, "Effect of Deworming on Indices of Health, Cognition, and Education among Schoolchildren in Rural China: A Cluster-Randomized Controlled Trial," *American Journal of Tropical Medicine and Hygiene* 96, no. 6 (2017): 1478–89.

13. M. He, J. Zeng, Y. Liu, J. Xu, G. P. Pokharel, and L. B. Ellwein, "Refractive Error and Visual Impairment in Urban Children in Southern China," *Investigative Ophthalmology and Visual Science* 45, no. 3 (2004): 793–99.

14. Ai Yue, Lauren Marsh, Huan Zhou, Alexis Medina, Renfu Luo, Yaojiang Shi, Linxiu Zhang, Kaleigh Kenny, and Scott Rozelle, "Nutritional Deficiencies, the Absence of Information and Caregiver Shortcomings: A Qualitative Analysis of Infant Feeding Practices in Rural China," *PLoS One* 11, no. 4 (2016): e0153385.

15. Louise Lu, Chengfang Liu, Linxiu Zhang, Alexis Medina, Scott Smith, and Scott Rozelle, "Gut Instincts: Knowledge, Attitudes, and Practices Regarding Soil-Transmitted Helminths in Rural China," *PLoS Neglected Tropical Diseases* 9, no. 3 (2015): e0003643.

16. "What About Eye Exercises?," Freeman Spogli Institute, Stanford University, http://reap.fsi.stanford.edu/research/what-about-eye-exercises.

17. Lu, Liu, Zhang, Medina, Smith, and Rozelle, "Gut Instincts."

18. S. Sylvia, T. Shi, H. Xue, X. Tian, H. Wang, Q. Liu, A. Medina, and S. Rozelle, "Survey Using Incognito Standardized Patients Shows Poor Quality Care in China's Rural Clinics," *Health Policy and Planning* 30, no. 3 (2015): 322–33.

19. Data from United Nations World Food Program. See Scott Rozelle, Jikun Huang, and Xiaobing Wang, "The Food Security Roots of the Middle-Income Trap," in *The Evolving Sphere of Food Security*, ed. Rosamond L. Naylor (New York: Oxford University Press, 2014), 72.

20. Eugenio Maul, Silviana Barroso, Sergio R. Munoz, Robert D. Sperduto, and Leon B. Ellwein, "Refractive Error Study in Children: Results from La Florida, Chile," *American Journal of Ophthalmology* 129, no. 4 (2000): 445–54.

21. In fact, research suggests that poor and middle-income countries are about equally likely to face high rates of intestinal worm infection: there is no clear income effect for reduced infection below the per capita GDP threshold of about US$20,000. It should be noted that, unlike anemia and poor vision, the prevalence of intestinal worms also depends critically on climate—worms can

survive and reproduce only in places with warm, wet conditions. This is therefore another factor that makes worm infection more likely in poorer areas, given that the tropical global south is an area of higher poverty overall. Still, intestinal worm infection rates are very low in high-income countries within this climate region. Jeffrey Bethony, Simon Brooker, Marco Albonico, Stefan M. Geiger, Alex Loukas, David Diemert, and Peter J. Hotez, "Soil-Transmitted Helminth Infections: Ascariasis, Trichuriasis, and Hookworm," *Lancet* 367, no. 9521 (2006): 1521–32; Rachel L. Pullan and Simon J. Brooker, "The Global Limits and Population at Risk of Soil-Transmitted Helminth Infections in 2010," *Parasites and Vectors* 5, no. 1 (2012): 81; Frédérique Chammartin, Ronaldo G. C. Scholte, Luiz H. Guimarães, Marcel Tanner, Jürg Utzinger, and Penelope Vounatsou, "Soil-Transmitted Helminth Infection in South America: A Systematic Review and Geostatistical Meta-analysis," *Lancet Infectious Diseases* 13, no. 6 (2013): 507–18.

22. Many middle-income countries (including such diverse countries as Brazil, China, Costa Rica, Malaysia, Russia, and Tunisia) have Gini ratios (the standard measure of inequality) above 40, and some are even in the high 50s. Simon Kuznets established this relation in a well-known paper in 1955. The Kuznets curve charts the relation between economic growth and income inequality, showing that income inequality tends to increase as countries move from low to middle income and tends to fall once countries reach high income. S. Kuznets, "Economic Growth and Income Inequality," *American Economic Review* 45 (1955): 1–28; Scott Rozelle, Jikun Huang, and Xiaobing Wang, "The Food Security Roots of the Middle-Income Trap," in *The Evolving Sphere of Food Security*, ed. Rosamond L. Naylor (New York: Oxford University Press, 2014), 64–86.

23. Of course, as we saw in the previous chapter, many of those building blocks do still seem to be lacking in many vocational high schools. P. W. Glewwe, E. A. Hanushek, S. D. Humpage et al., *School Resources and Educational Outcomes in Developing Countries: A Review of the Literature from 1990 to 2010*, NBER Working Papers (Cambridge, MA: National Bureau of Economic Research, 2014).

24. The size of the effect was about 0.2 standard deviations. R. Luo et al., "Nutrition and Educational Performance in Rural China's Elementary Schools." For example, the Tennessee Student/Teacher Achievement Ratio program reduced class size from twenty-two to fifteen, and test scores improved by 0.21 standard deviations. See Alan B. Krueger and Diane M. Whitmore, "The Effect of Attending a Small Class in Early Grades on College-Test Taking and Middle School Test Results: Evidence from Project STAR," *Economic Journal* 111 (2001): 1–28.

Our research also proved that anemia could be eliminated at very low cost. The multivitamin we administered to students costs only ten cents per student per day. If every child in poor areas of rural China in grades one to nine (all twenty-six million of them) were given a vitamin each day for a year, the cost of eliminating anemia and raising school performance would be only about US$600 million. This is a trivial amount, less than 0.05 percent of the national education budget. If the government could put a tiny portion of its vast investment in rural education into eradicating this unnecessary disease, students in rural areas might finally catch up to their urban peers. A full description of our work on anemia can be found online at https://reap.fsi.stan ford.edu/publications/reap_brief_118_are_we_there_yet_the_long_road_to _eliminating_undernutrition_in_rural_chinas_schools.

25. Xiaochen Ma, "Improving Learning by Improving Vision: Evidence from Two Randomized Controlled Trials of Providing Vision Care in China" (PhD diss., University of California Davis, 2015).

26. To learn more about this work or get involved, read about the social enterprise Smart Focus Vision: http://reap.fsi.stanford.edu/docs/learning-focus.

Chapter Seven

1. Sharon Bradley-Johnson, "Cognitive Assessment for the Youngest Children: A Critical Review of Tests," *Journal of Psychoeducational Assessment* 19 (2001): 19–44.

2. The research on anemia in schoolchildren is reported in chapter 6.

3. Further confirmation of the basic result that rural babies are beset with high rates of delayed development came from a research group at Peking University. Using parental questionnaires rather than direct testing of children, they found that 40 percent of children one to thirty-five months old in Shaanxi and Guizhou Provinces showed signs of developmental delays. Ethnic groups: China officially recognizes fifty-six ethnic groups. Most of the national population belongs to the Han ethnicity, making up over 90 percent of all people in the country.

4. I estimate that approximately six million of China's infants and toddlers are currently living in migrant communities, which accounts for 13 percent of all rural babies. Wang Lei, Wilson Liang, Sun Yonglei, Li Mengjie, Cody Abbey, and Scott Rozelle, "Are Infant/Toddler Developmental Delays a Problem across Rural China?" *Journal of Comparative Economics*, 2019.

5. In almost all the studies using the Bayley Scales of Infant and Toddler Development (BSID), urban infants and toddlers were tested as part of hospital-based cohort studies. In these studies the investigation teams recruited respondents—who were all urban residents—during routine pre- or postnatal visits to large urban hospitals (e.g., in Guangzhou, Xi'an, and Wuhan). By examining the share of the populations that scored less than 1.3 standard deviations (< -1.3 SDs), the nature of ECD cognitive outcomes of China's urban populations was consistent with the nature of healthy populations worldwide.

The share of infants and toddlers (aged two to thirty-six months) who could achieve cognition (or BSID Mental Development Index—MDI) scores only < 80 (or ≅ < -1.3 standard deviations—SD) was 9.1 percent (in Guangzhou, n = 297), 7.9 percent (in Xian, n = 206), and 4.9 percent (in Wuhan, n = 122).

See Q. Gu, M. Gao, Y. Li, and X. Wei, "The Survey Search of the Parenting Behavior in Migration Workers," *Journal of Child Health Care* 3 (2009): 365–66; S. Shi, J. Shi, X. Guan, J. Zhang, and M. Hu, "Analysis of Influential Factors of Infant Development," *Maternal and Child Health Care of China* 16 (2001): 635–37; X. Sun, Y. Ren, and Z. Su, "Study on Bayley Scales of Infant Development," *Maternal and Child Health Care of China* 11 (1996): 51–53; S. Xie, X. Wang, and Y. Yao, "The Application of Bayley Scales of Infant Development in Infant Nursing," *Journal of Nursing (China)* 13 (2006): 76–77; S. Xu, H. Huang, J. Zhang, X. Bian, N. Lv, Y. Lv, and Y. Chen, "Research on the Applicability of Bayley Scales of Infant and Toddler Development, Third Edition, to Assess the Development of Infants and Toddlers in Shanghai," *Chinese Journal of Child Health Care* 19 (2011): 30–32.

6. C. Bereiter and S. Engelmann, *Teaching Disadvantaged Children in the Preschool* (Englewood Cliffs, NJ: Prentice Hall, 1966).

7. "Give Me a Child," *Economist*, October 29, 2016, http://www.economist.com /news/international/21709292-boosting-health-toddlers-bodies-and-brains -brings-multiple-benefits-too-often.

8. Students were evaluated using the WISC questionnaire as well as the Raven IQ test. For more detail see REAP Working Paper 315.

9. Susan P. Walker, Theodore D. Wachs, Julie Meeks Gardner, Betsy Lozoff, Gail A. Wasserman, Ernesto Pollitt, Julie A. Carter, and International Child Development Steering Group, "Child Development: Risk Factors for Adverse Outcomes in Developing Countries," *Lancet* 369, no. 9556 (2007): 145–57; Qian-Qian Xin, Bo-Wen Chen, De-Lu Yin, Feng Xiao, Rui-Li Li, Tao Yin, Hui-Min Yang, Xiao-Guo Zheng, and Li-Hong Wang, "Prevalence of Anemia and Its Risk Factors among Children under 36 Months Old in China," *Journal of Tropical Pediatrics* 63, no. 1 (2016): 36–42; Renfu Luo, Yaojiang Shi, Huan Zhou, Ai Yue, Linxiu Zhang, Sean Sylvia, Alexis Medina, and Scott Rozelle, "Micronutrient Deficiencies and Developmental Delays among Infants: Evidence from a Cross-Sectional Survey in Rural China," *BMJ Open* 5, no. 10 (2015): e008400.

10. We conducted a careful RCT study. We divided a randomly selected group of babies into two groups: one group was given a daily dose of multivitamins for six months; the other group was left to continue as before. The results showed that giving babies daily multivitamins in their cereal did raise cognition levels slightly, but it was not enough to bring cognition rates into the normal range across the population.

11. Note that research has shown that the negative effects of iron deficiency at

early ages are difficult to reverse. These studies suggest that whatever portion of slowed development is due to low iron levels may be correctable only through preventive efforts that target prenatal iron levels. If iron deficiency is allowed to continue through early childhood, the cognitive damage may be irreversible even after iron levels improve. This may suggest that China's children could be further helped through programs that seek to improve maternal nutrition before and during pregnancy. This is a more difficult policy to undertake for China's rural population, since many mothers remain living in harder-to-reach migrant communities right up to the last few months of their pregnancy. Note, however, that addressing anemia does still have positive effects on learning outcomes for schoolchildren (as we saw in the previous chapter). See B. Lozoff, E. Jiminez, J. Hagen, E. Mollen, and A. W. Wolf, "Poorer Behavioral and Developmental Outcome More Than 10 Years after Treatment for Iron Deficiency in Infancy," *Pediatrics* 105, no. 4 (2000): e51.

12. A World Bank policy guide defined "early childhood stimulation" as "providing young children with constant opportunities to interact with caring people and to learn about their environment from the earliest age," adding, "In practice, stimulation is about parents and other family members and caregivers being responsive to the emotional and physical needs of children from birth onward, playing and talking with them (even before children can respond verbally) and exposing them to words, numbers, and simple concepts while engaging in daily routines." Sophie Naudeau, *Investing in Young Children: An Early Childhood Development Guide for Policy Dialogue and Project Preparation* (Washington, DC: World Bank, 2011), 32.

13. Bruce D. Perry, "Childhood Experience and the Expression of Genetic Potential: What Childhood Neglect Tells Us about Nature and Nurture," *Brain and Mind* 3, no. 1 (2002): 79–100; W. Dennis, *Children of the Creche* (New York: Appleton-Century-Crofts, 1973). Like most things babies need, mental stimulation is most important before the age of about two or three years. In the study of Lebanese orphans, the children who were not taken out of the negligent orphanage before two years of age were left for the rest of their lives with IQs far below normal and with serious behavior problems. Children who were adopted into loving homes before age two, by contrast, eventually grew into adults with normal IQs and normal social skills. M. Winick, K. Meyer, and R. Harris, "Malnutrition and Environmental Enrichment by Early Adoption," *Science* 190 (1975): 1173–76; N. Lien, K. Meyer, and M. Winick, "Early Malnutrition and 'Late' Adoption: A Study of Their Effects on the Development of Korean Orphans Adopted into American Families," *American Journal of Clinical Nutrition* 30 (1977): 1734–39; Michael Rutter, "Developmental Catch-up, and Deficit, Following Adoption After Severe Global Early Privation," *Journal of Child Psychology and Psychiatry* 39, no. 4 (1998): 465–76.

14. Bruce D. Perry, "Childhood Experience and the Expression of Genetic Potential: What Childhood Neglect Tells Us about Nature and Nurture," *Brain and Mind* 3, no. 1 (2002): 79–100.

15. Anne Fernald, Virginia A. Marchman, and Adriana Weisleder, "SES Differences in Language Processing Skill and Vocabulary Are Evident at 18 Months," *Developmental Science* 16, no. 2 (2013): 234–48; B. Hart and T. Risley, *Meaningful Differences in the Everyday Experience of Young American Children* (Baltimore: Brookes, 1995), Subsequent research has confirmed these findings, even drawing direct causal relations between parents' speech patterns and children's vocabulary. See, for example, Erika Hoff, "The Specificity of Environmental Influence: Socioeconomic Status Affects Early Vocabulary Development via Maternal Speech," *Child Development* 74, no. 5 (2003): 1368–78; D. Walker, C. Greenwood, B. Hart, and J. Carta, "Prediction of School Outcomes Based on Early Language Production and Socioeconomic Factors," *Child Development* 65 (1994): 606–21.

16. Ai Yue, Yaojiang Shi, Renfu Luo, Jamie Chen, James Garth, Jimmy Zhang, Alexis Medina, Sarah Kotb, and Scott Rozelle, "China's Invisible Crisis: Cognitive Delays among Rural Toddlers and the Absence of Modern Parenting," *China Journal* 78 (2017): 50–81.

17. Renfu Luo, Fang Jia, Ai Yue, Linxiu Zhang, Qijia Lyu, Yaojiang Shi, Meredith Yang, Alexis Medina, Sarah Kotb, and Scott Rozelle, "Passive Parenting and Its Association with Early Childhood Development," *Early Child Development and Care*, DOI: 1080/03004430.2017.1407318.

18. Cai Fang, *China's Economic Growth Prospects: From Demographic Dividend to Reform Dividend* (Cheltenham, UK: Edward Elgar, 2016).

19. Maureen M. Black, Susan P. Walker, Lia C. H. Fernald, Christopher T. Andersen, Ann M. DiGirolamo, Chunling Lu, Dana C. McCoy, Gunther Fink, Yusra R. Shawar, Jeremy Shiffman, Amanda E. Devercelli, Quentin T. Wodon, Emily Vargas-Baron, and Sally Grantham-McGregor, "Early Childhood Development Coming of Age: Science through the Life Course," *Lancet* 389 (2017): 77–90; Susan P. Walker, Theodore D. Wachs, Julie Meeks Gardner, Betsy Lozoff, Gail A. Wasserman, Ernesto Pollitt, Julie A. Carter, and International Child Development Steering Group, "Child Development: Risk Factors for Adverse Outcomes in Developing Countries," *Lancet* 369, no. 9556 (2007): 145–57.

20. The Colombia study had separate interventions testing the effects of parenting training (as mentioned above) and micronutrient supplementation. Consistent with the findings from my team, parenting training seemed to be more effective. In particular, their study results showed significant positive effects on child cognition from the parenting training, whereas the micronutrient supplementation had no significant effects. Orazio P. Attanasio, Camila Fernández, Emla O. A. Fitzsimons, Sally M. Grantham-McGregor, Costas Meghir, and Marta Rubio-Codina, "Using the Infrastructure of a Conditional

Cash Transfer Program to Deliver a Scalable Integrated Early Child Development Program in Colombia: Cluster Randomized Controlled Trial," *BMJ* 349 (2014): g5785.

21. "Marcela Temer Presents Happy Child Programme to Foreigners," Presidency of the Republic of Brazil website, May 9, 2017, http://www.brazil.gov.br/about -brazil/news/2017/05/marcela-temer-presents-happy-child-programme-to -foreigners, accessed November 24, 2019.

22. Samuel Berlinski and Norbert Schady, *The Early Years: Child Well-Being and the Role of Public Policy* (Washington, DC: Inter-American Development Bank, 2015).

23. The curriculum targets four areas of child development: motor, language, cognitive, and social-emotional. In total, our six-month curriculum included 144 activities for children eighteen to forty-two months of age. The REAP team also assembled sets of toys and books to accompany each week's activities, including balloons, play doctor kits, building blocks, and miniature basketball hoops.

24. James J. Heckman, *Giving Kids a Fair Chance* (Cambridge, MA: MIT Press, 2013).

25. Patrice L. Engle, Maureen M. Black, Jere R. Behrman, Meena Cabral De Mello, Paul J. Gertler, Lydia Kapiriri, Reynaldo Martorell, Mary Eming Young, and International Child Development Steering Group, "Strategies to Avoid the Loss of Developmental Potential in More than 200 Million Children in the Developing World," *Lancet* 369, no. 9557 (2007): 229–42.

26. The results showed effect sizes within the range of 0.5 to 1 standard deviations, a huge improvement. Save the Children, *Early Childhood Care and Development: A Positive Impact* (Myanmar: Save the Children Myanmar Field Office, 2004); C. Kagitcibasi, D. Sunar, and S. Bekman, "Long-Term Effects of Early Intervention: Turkish Low-Income Mothers and Children," *Journal of Applied Developmental Psychology* 22 (2001): 333–61; O. P. Attanasio, C. Fernández, E. O. A. Fitzsimons, S. M. Grantham-McGregor, C. Meghir, and M. Rubio-Codina, "Using the Infrastructure of a Conditional Cash Transfer Program to Deliver a Scalable Integrated Early Child Development Program in Colombia: Cluster Randomized Controlled Trial," *BMJ* 349 (2014): g5785; Susan P. Walker, Theodore D. Wachs, Julie Meeks Gardner, Betsy Lozoff, Gail A. Wasserman, Ernesto Pollitt, Julie A. Carter, and International Child Development Steering Group, "Child Development: Risk Factors for Adverse Outcomes in Developing Countries," *Lancet* 369, no. 9556 (2007): 145–57; S. P. Walker, S. M. Chang, C. A. Powell, and S. Grantham-McGregor, "Effects of Early Childhood Psychosocial Stimulation and Nutritional Supplementation on Cognition and Education in Growth-Stunted Jamaican Children: Prospective Cohort Study," *Lancet*, no. 366 (2005): 1804–7.

27. See, for example, Sophie Naudeau, Naoko Kataoka, Alexandria Valerio,

Michelle J. Neuman, and Leslie Kennedy Elder, *Investing in Young Children: An Early Childhood Development Guide for Policy Dialogue and Project Preparation*, Africa Regional Educational Publications, Directions in Development, Human Development (Washington, DC: World Bank, 2011); Sally Grantham-McGregor, Yin Bun Cheung, Santiago Cueto, Paul Glewwe, Linda Richter, Barbara Strupp, and International Child Development Steering Group, "Developmental Potential in the First 5 Years for Children in Developing Countries," *Lancet* 369, no. 9555 (2007): 60–70.

28. Heckman, *Giving Kids a Fair Chance*; J. J. Heckman, "Skill Formation and the Economics of Investing in Disadvantaged Children," *Science* 312 (July 2006): 1900–1902.

29. S. Sylvia, N. Warrinnier, R. Luo, Y. Shi, O. Attanasio, and S. Rozelle, "From Quantity to Quality: Delivering a Home-Based Parenting Intervention through China's Family Planning Workers," REAP Working Paper, 2016.

Conclusion

1. Of course the forces that brought about stagnation in Japan, and collapse in the Soviet Union for that matter, were very different from those China is up against today. The point of these examples is that very often countries do not bear out our expectations for limitless growth. Economic slowdowns can be hard to see coming.

2. Generally one's hukou can be changed only through routes that are not open to most rural people, such as going to university in a big city or working at a large urban firm.

3. This issue has a lot of variation across the country, because individual cities (and neighborhoods within cities) are free to set their own policies toward migrant children. In most urban areas there is some access to public primary school education. In some, there has even been increasing access to junior high. But even today, across China children with rural hukou have no access to urban high schools. And national policy only guarantees rural students access to public education in their home villages.

4. My team's research has shown that these children—those living in rural areas with their parents—are doing worse on a number of outcomes than the left-behind children (LBCs) who attract attention in the press. For instance, children living with their parents in poor rural areas were found to have higher rates of infection with intestinal worms and of uncorrected myopia and worse schooling outcomes than children who had been left behind by one or both parents. Chengchao Zhou, Sean Sylvia, Linxiu Zhang, Renfu Luo, Hongmei Yi, Chengfang Liu, Yaojiang Shi, Prashant Loyalka, James Chu, Alexis Medina, and Scott Rozelle, "China's Left-Behind Children: Impact of Parental Migra-

tion on Health, Nutrition, and Educational Outcomes," *Health Affairs* 34, no. 11 (2015): 1964–71.

5. In recent years the Chinese public has been roiled by a series of tragedies affecting LBCs. In 2015 a group of four left-behind siblings decided to commit suicide. They were found dead days later by the neighbors, their little bellies full of pesticides. In the winter of 2013, a group of five left-behind children climbed into a large trash bin and lit a fire to try to keep warm; they were asphyxiated within hours. These and numerous other incidents have led to widespread horror and increasingly outraged public calls to find some way to help these children. The government is beginning to take notice too. In response to the suicide in 2015, Premier Li Keqiang publicly stated, "Such a tragedy cannot be allowed to happen again" and made calls to improve government supervision of left-behind kids. Nicola Davison, "The Story of China's Left Behind Children," *Telegraph*, August 25, 2015, https://www.telegraph.co .uk/news/worldnews/asia/china/11824563/The-story-of-Chinas-left-behind -children.html, accessed July 19, 2018. Statistics from the Sixth Population Census—China National Bureau of Statistics, 2011. Yu Bai, Michael Neubauer, Tong Ru, Yaojiang Shi, Kaleigh Kenny, and Scott Rozelle, "Order Matters: The Effect of Second-Wave Migration on Student Academic Performance in Northwest China," REAP Working Paper, 2016; John Sudworth, "Counting the Cost of China's Left-Behind Children," *BBC News, Beijing*, April 12, 2016, http://www .bbc.com/news/world-asia-china-35994481, accessed November 25, 2016.

6. In our most innovative study, we compared the quality of private migrant schools with that of rural public schools—thus assessing the two choices available to most rural families. That study was our most rigorous because it compared students from the same hometowns who were enrolled in each type of school. The results showed that learning outcomes were much better in rural public schools than private migrant schools. Fang Lai, Chengfang Liu, Renfu Luo, Linxiu Zhang, Xiaochen Ma, Yujie Bai, Brian Sharbono, and Scott Rozelle, "The Education of China's Migrant Children: The Missing Link in China's Education System," *International Journal of Educational Development* 37 (2014): 68–77; Xiaobing Wang, Renfu Luo, Linxiu Zhang, and Scott Rozelle, "The Education Gap of China's Migrant Children and Rural Counterparts," *Journal of Development Studies* 53, no. 11 (2017): 1865–81. Josh Chin, "Will School Closures Prompt Migrants to Flee?," *Wall Street Journal*, April 19, 2011, https://blogs.wsj.com/chinarealtime/2011/08/19/will-school-closures-prompt -migrants-to-flee/, accessed May 31, 2018.

7. My team conducted a survey of twenty-five- to thirty-year-olds living in a large number of provinces. The results make the incentive problem clear. According to our data, only a small minority of rural students who make it to high school in poor rural counties end up staying in their home counties. More

than seven out of ten rural children (in many cases the share is even higher) who get a high school education in their rural counties leave for college or for work, and very few ever come back to work and live.

8. So what do local leaders spend their precious fiscal resources on? A trip to the county seat of almost any poor rural county, the heart of any county, clearly shows the priorities of local governments. Today almost all have downtown shopping malls with gleaming statues, urban gardens, and wide sidewalks. There are brand-new, expansive central plazas for evening events and weekend markets and festivals. Streetlights, riverside parks, and imposing pagodas dot the landscape in even the poorest counties. Renovated government buildings have modern facades and landscaping. An analysis of fiscal transfers from above down to rural counties tells the story: for every 100 yuan transferred from above, 130 yuan is spent on urban infrastructure (mixing transfers from above with local funds); in contrast, for every 100 yuan of transfers from above, less than 50 yuan goes to education or health. The result is widespread underinvestment in these much-needed areas.

9. "Population by Age and Sex," in *China Statistical Yearbook* (Beijing: National Bureau of Statistics of China, 2015).

10. Income is reported in purchasing power parity (PPP) terms.

11. India does not officially report this number, so this is an estimate based on the statistics that 40 percent of youth attended high school in 2015 and 30 percent attended in 2008. If the numbers were about 20 percent in the 1990s and 15 percent in the 1970s and 1980s, this would amount to 29 percent of the total labor force. Pawan Agarwal, *Higher Education and the Labor Market in India*, Indian Council for Research on International Economic Relations (ICRIER) (Washington, DC: World Bank, 2006); "Education in India," September 20, 2011, World Bank, http://www.worldbank.org/en/news/feature/2011/09/20/education-in-india, accessed April 29, 2018.

12. Note that other groups are working on this issue too: Save the Children, China Development Research Foundation, and UNICEF, among others. There are many ways to address this issue; we need all these efforts and more.

13. This is a partnership with immense potential. The NHFPC has a vast cohort of former inspectors who are already posted in every town in China, no matter how poor or remote. They have information and birth records for all the children in each village. They are also much better educated than most people in these villages—most are high school- or college-trained professionals who are members of China's civil service, and many are doctors. Perhaps most important, by making use of the vast resources of this government agency, China has the chance to bring the parenting program to millions of families in a very short time. And there is the political will to make this happen. In the fall and winter of 2017/18, the national government formally recognized the need for policy and investment support in early childhood (birth to three years old).

This is a big breakthrough, given that in the past most of the responsibility for early childhood education in China has been fully ceded to parents and the family. To be sure, parents (and grandparents) are at the heart of the solution. But as shown in the previous chapter, there is a role for the government in this unique period of rapid transition—as families adjust from raising future peasants (as they have done for the past five thousand years) to raising children who can go to high school and college and thrive in China's future high-skilled, innovation-based economy. The entire economy depends on getting this right.

14. My team has found a workable solution to the myopia problem through a program that enlists teachers to do a preliminary vision screening, then refers the kids who fail that test to the local county hospital for proper vision testing and fitting glasses at low cost. We have shown that when the children of rural China have quality vision care, get glasses, and wear them, no other intervention improves school performance, student confidence, and ultimately educational achievement so dramatically at so little cost.

Fortunately the government has already shown a willingness to make nutrition a priority in schools. In 2011 it launched a nationwide Nutritious School Lunch program that is now bringing meals to rural children across the country. While this is a good first step, research suggests that the quality of the lunches has so far not been high enough to alleviate the nutrition problems, and anemia rates remain high. This program should be enhanced with more dollars per student, augmented by a program to provide nutritional supplements and vitamins that are sure to address the most critical nutritional gaps keeping kids from learning.

In fact, the limited effectiveness of the school lunch program to date is an example of how fiscal decentralization hampers the state's ability to address educational barriers in rural areas. In the initial design of the policy, the national government committed to providing four renminbi (RMB) per day per student, while the local governments were tasked with contributing matching funds of three RMB per day per student. This budget would have been about right—my team's calculations suggest that seven RMB is just about the minimum needed (eight to nine yuan would be better) to provide a nutritious school lunch up to international standards in rural areas (WHO suggests that a nutritious lunch needs to contribute 40 percent of each student's daily nutritional needs). Unfortunately, the skewed incentives of decentralization have ensured that not all of that money is finding its way into the program.

Our research shows that although the four RMB from the national government is in fact making it to the school level and being used as planned, in many rural schools the mandated contribution of the local government is missing. As a result, decentralization has left many rural schools without the money they need to provide good lunches, and thus a funding shortage in some areas has turned the Nutritious School Lunch into a free non-nutritious lunch. The lesson here is that not only are programs needed, but they must be implemented in a way that can solve the underlying problem—even in poor rural areas. I believe that for this particular policy to work as intended, the national government will need to take on responsibility for fully funding the program and ensuring proper implementation at the local level. Huan Wang, Wilson Liang, Laura Jonsson, Qiran Zhao, Samuel Kennedy, Gloria Breck, Jane Bai, Matthew Boswell, Scott Rozelle, and Alexis Medina, "Is China's 32 Billion Dollar Program to Fight Rural Undernutrition Working? A Mixed Methods Analysis in 100 Rural Schools in Western China," REAP Working Paper, 2017.

15. There will be a lot of pressure for some youth to not attend high school. It has to be recognized that there is a high opportunity cost for a seventeen-year-old to be attending school, even with no tuition or fees. Even if tuition is eliminated, poor families may find it difficult to forgo the wages their teenage children could be earning in the labor market. Further, the serious barriers to learning and cognition that my team has unearthed in rural children's infancy and early school years may make it much more difficult for them to succeed in China's current model of academically rigorous, highly competitive academic high school. Policymakers should begin to discuss how to deal with these hurdles. Otherwise no amount of expansion in enrollments will truly deliver on the promise of universal high school education.

16. Making high school free might seem like a big outlay, but the total cost of providing high school education for all rural children would be US$7.2 billion per year, less than 2 percent of the China's total education budget for 2015. In comparison, in 2014 alone China invested a full US$141 billion in infrastructure. It's high time for China's government to place less emphasis on building up the physical capital needed in a poor country and start giving priority to the *human* capital that will have a much higher rate of return as China moves into this new economic phase. And there are other places in China's budget where there is room for reshuffling. In the past few years, China has made headlines by dramatically increasing the foreign aid it's providing to Africa. That's a worthy goal, and certainly that money can do a lot of good in Africa as well. But China needs to address the issues at home first. If it were to continue giving the same amount of aid to Africa for eleven months of the year but keep one month's aid money at home, that would be enough to build and run 200,000 parenting centers across rural China. China has recently announced dramatic plans to build a high-speed rail system from Xi'an to Urumqi. That's a showy investment, but it's unlikely to pay off nearly as well as investing in education. So instead of that one railroad (let people fly from Xi'an to Urumqi), China could fund preschools in rural areas for five years. This is a crisis of potentially catastrophic proportions, and it must be treated as such. Tuition for an average rural high school student is about US$300, and a single year of high

school would need to provide for about twenty-four million rural students (the size of three birth cohorts). Hongbin Li, Prashant Loyalka, Scott Rozelle, and Binzhen Wu, "Human Capital and China's Future Growth," *Journal of Economic Perspectives* 31, no. 1 (2017): 25–48.

17. CIA, *World Factbook*, https://www.cia.gov/library/publications/the-world-factbook/rankorder/2004rank.html, accessed May 1, 2018.

Index